MW01258446

Sibley's
New Mexico
Campaign

Sibley's New Mexico Campaign

Martin Hardwick Hall

Foreword by Jerry Thompson

UNIVERSITY OF NEW MEXICO PRESS
ALBUQUERQUE

Library of Congress
Cataloging-in-Publication Data

Hall, Martin Hardwick.
 Sibley's New Mexico campaign / Martin Hardwick Hall ;
foreword by Jerry Thompson. — University of New Mexico
Press paperback ed.
     p.   cm.
 Originally published: Austin : University of Texas Press,
1960. With corrections.
 Includes bibliographical references and index.
 ISBN 0-8263-2277-8 (alk. paper)
 1. New Mexico — History — Civil War, 1861–1865 —
Campaigns. 2. Sibley, Henry Hopkins, 1816–1886. 3. United
States — History — Civil War, 1861–1865 — Campaigns. I. Title.
E470.9.H3 2000
972´.07—dc21   00-028625

First published 1960 by University of Texas Press.
First University of New Mexico Press edition, 2000.
Introduction © 2000 by the University of New Mexico Press

*For T. Harry Williams and
the late Frank L. Owsley*

Contents

Acknowledgments

I AM DEEPLY GRATEFUL TO THE LATE FRANK L. OWSLEY OF THE UNIVERSITY OF ALABAMA, who first directed my study of this phase of the war, and to Dr. T. Harry Williams of Louisiana State University, who provided encouragement, guidance, and assistance in completing this work for publication. Dr. Edwin A. Davis, head of the Department of History at Louisiana State University, indicated the location of a number of valuable primary materials, read the entire manuscript, and made many helpful suggestions as to content and style.

I wish to thank the following individuals and staffs of the various institutions who generously allowed me access to their manuscript collections, or provided me with microfilm, photographs, and photostatic copies: the National Archives and Records Service; the Archives Division of the Texas State Library, especially Mrs. B. Brandt; the University of Texas Library; Mrs. Eleanor B. Sloan and her efficient staff of the Arizona Pioneers' Historical Society; the State Historical Society of Colorado; Dr. George P. Hammond, Director of the Bancroft Library of the University of California; the Henry E. Huntington Library; the New York Public Library; the New York Historical Society; the Library of Congress; Miss Helen P. Caffey of the Thomas Branigan Memorial Library of Las Cruces, New Mexico; the El Paso Public Library; Mr. Josiah P. Rowe III of Fredericksburg, Virginia; Mrs. C. M. Newman of El Paso, Texas; and Mr. Frederick Hill Meserve of New York City.

A number of individuals were especially helpful in aiding my research: Mrs. Anne J. Dyson, Reference Division, and Mr. George J. Guidry, Jr., Microfilm Department, of the Louisiana State University Library; Mrs. R. B. Durrill of Van Horn, Texas; Mrs. Minnie Tevis Davenport of Tucson, Arizona; Miss Ruth E. Rambo and Mrs. Elma A. Medearis of the Library of the Museum of New Mexico; Mr. George W. Baylor of Tucson, Arizona; Mrs. T. J. Holbrook of Austin, Texas; Mr. John B. Ashe of the University of Texas; Miss Winnie Allen of the Eugene C. Barker Texas History Center; Mrs. T. W. Lanier, Mr. M. H. Thomlinson, and Mr. H. Y. Ellis, all of El Paso, Texas; Dr. Jack D. L. Holmes of McNeese State College.

Because of the generosity of the United Daughters of the Confederacy, which bestowed the Mrs. Simon Baruch University Award, I was enabled to travel to a number of research centers to collect much "new" material. The result was a wholesale revision of my original dissertation, for which the prize was awarded.

Dr. Robert H. Fuson, Professor of Geography at Louisiana State University in New Orleans, merits special recognition for the outstanding cartography. The five maps are based on the New Mexico Surveyor General's map of 1861, the pertinent maps found in the *Atlas to Accompany the Official Records,* and various contemporary maps published by the United States Geological Survey.

Thanks are due Mrs. Betty Groh of New Orleans for accomplishing the onerous task of typing the manuscript, and to Mr. Adlai Stevenson Turner of New Orleans and to Messrs. Frank Baldanza and Michael J. Ardoin, both of Louisiana State University, for critically reading the text.

M. H. H.

Foreword

It was not until the approach of the centennial of the Civil War that any serious scholarship appeared on the war in New Mexico Territory. Yet in the mountains and deserts of the Southwest in 1861 and 1862, eighteen hundred miles west of Washington and Richmond, the war raged. From the cactus-studded summit of St. Augustine Pass at the north end of the majestic Organ Mountains to the conifer-lined heights of Glorieta Pass at the southern end of the snow-crowned Sangre de Cristos, Americans killed Americans as they struggled for territory and the soul of a nation.

Many historians, who concentrated their efforts on the war in the East, failed to realize that despite the relatively small number of men involved, Brigadier General Henry Hopkins Sibley's New Mexico campaign was one of the most important of the war. Although General Sibley never clearly articulated operational objectives and a few of his men even thought they were headed to Missouri "through the back door," it is evident, as one of the general's artillery commanders, Captain Trevanion T. Teel, later revealed, that California was the real objective of the Confederate offensive. "On to San Francisco," was to be the Texan battle cry.

Had the overall objectives of the expedition been fully realized, the history of the Southern Confederacy conceivably could have been radically altered. Rebel control of the Territories of New Mexico, Utah, and Colorado, as well as the acquisition of California, would have more than doubled the size of the struggling Confederacy. A trans-continental Southern nation stretching from Richmond to San Francisco, from the Atlantic to the Pacific, would certainly have nudged the English and French towards diplomatic recognition of the infant Confederacy, a vital necessity for eventual independence. West-coast harbors, as well as the golden slopes of California's Sierra Nevada and Colorado's gold- and silver-laden Rockies, would have helped fill Rebel coffers and make the Confederate States of America a reality. Moreover, General Sibley's negotiations with the governors of Chihuahua and Sonora might have set in motion the acquisition of those areas, either by diplomacy or conquest.

Military success in the desert Southwest was certain to have had a far-reaching psychological impact on both the North and South. In fact, the Battle of Valverde, the largest Civil War battle in the Rocky Mountain West, was fought only days after the Confederate loss of Fort Henry and Fort Donelson. The Battle of Glorieta was contested less than two weeks prior to the Battle of Shiloh. The Stars and Bars floating over Santa Fe and Tucson and a Rebel army moving into Colorado would undoubtedly have softened the impact of the depressing defeat of the Rebel army at Shiloh and the death of General Albert Sidney Johnston.

It is easy to argue in retrospect that Sibley's grandiose expedition was doomed to failure long before the determined Rebels under Colonel William "Dirty Shirt" Scurry reached the heights of Glorieta Pass. His operation was plagued by poor logistics, partly as a result of the inability of Confederate sympathizers Simeon Hart and James W. Magoffin to stockpile badly needed supplies at El Paso. Nonetheless, the doomed Bowie knife-wielding Texans continued to advance into a hostile and rugged land in the dead of winter. Weakened and demoralized by hunger and disease amidst an increasingly hostile Hispanic population, it is doubtful that the Texans could have held New Mexico even if Fort Union and the entire territory had been secured.

In the final analysis, the Confederate victory at Glorieta Pass was indeed the "Gettysburg of the West." The dark billowing smoke that poured forth from the burning Rebel quartermaster stores, camp and garrison equipage, and ordnance supplies in the rocky depths of Apache Canyon, forced a grim Confederate retreat from Santa Fe, Albuquerque, and, eventually, the verdant Mesilla Valley. With the Rebel withdrawal to San Antonio went General Sibley's hopes of conquering New Mexico Territory and Richmond's dreams of a western empire and the actualization of a Confederate Manifest Destiny.

One of the first scholars to realize the importance of Sibley's New Mexico Campaign was Martin Hardwick Hall. Hall, who devoted his academic life to the study of the war in New Mexico, was born at Calexico, California, on August 30, 1925. He graduated from Canoga Park High School in 1943 and went on to earn history degrees from the University of New Mexico (B.A., 1950), the University of Alabama (M.A., 1951), and Louisiana State University (Ph.D., 1957), where he studied and wrote his dissertation, "The Army of New Mexico: Sibley's Campaign of 1862," under the Pulitzer Prize-winning historian, T. Harry Williams. Hall lectured on Civil War and Southern history at Arkansas State College, McNeese State University, and the University of Texas at Arlington, where he taught for seventeen years. Besides being a popular lecturer, Dr. Hall authored or edited four books and fifteen articles on the war in New Mexico. He was murdered by an unknown assailant at his home in Arlington, Texas, on January 20, 1981.

Prior to his tragic death, Martin was kind enough to read and comment on my draft of a biography of General Henry H. Sibley. By this time Hall was completing his meticulously researched *Confederate Army of New Mexico*. He also solicited my personal copy of his classic *Sibley's New Mexico Campaign* so as to correct several minor and relatively insignificant errors that included wrong middle initials for a few of the men of the Sibley Brigade. He also corrected several of the counties where many of the men had been recruited and mustered. Hall had confused Thomas Jefferson Green, the North Carolina-born veteran of the Texas Revolution and the Mier Expedition, with Thomas "Tom" Green, who commanded the Fifth Texas Cavalry in Sibley's Army of New Mexico and was decapitated in an attack on Union gunboats at Blair's Landing, Louisiana, on April 12, 1864. All of Hall's mistakes have been corrected in this new edition by the University of New Mexico Press. General readers, genealogists, and scholars are certain to welcome a second edition of Hall's trail-blazing *Sibley's New Mexico Campaign,* a valuable and critically acclaimed study from which all future scholarship would be soundly based. In the final analysis, Hall substantiates the war in New Mexico as a vital part of a much larger tragedy that was the American Civil War.

Jerry Thompson
Texas A&M International University
December 28, 1999

Introduction

WHEN MOST PEOPLE THINK OF THE MILITARY ASPECTS OF THE WAR FOR SOUTHERN Independence today they automatically picture the bloody battles and campaigns east of the Mississippi, giving, perhaps, only an occasional thought to the events which transpired west of the River. To those possessing such stereotypes it may seem startling indeed to discover that in 1861 and 1862 the Territory of New Mexico (comprising the present-day states of Arizona, New Mexico, and part of Nevada) — a largely arid, cactus-studded, thinly populated wilderness abounding with hostile Indians — witnessed a part of that sanguinary conflict. For example, two hard-fought battles and a number of minor engagements took place in what is now the state of New Mexico, a skirmish ensued between Union and Confederate detachments some forty miles west of Tucson, Arizona, and Southern scouts ventured to within at least eighty miles of California.

In 1861 the southern region of the present-day states of Arizona and New Mexico was avowedly pro-Southern, and conventions held in Mesilla and Tucson in March voted for secession from the Union and annexation to the Confederacy — an action taken one month or more *later* by Virginia, Arkansas, North Carolina, and Tennessee. The South responded by creating from New Mexico the Territory of Arizona, which, at least on paper, stretched from the Texas border to the Colorado River. The Confederacy also dispatched a military expedition to occupy and hold the vast remainder of the Territory of New Mexico. Most contemporaries believed this to be but a stepping stone toward a far more important goal — the occupation of California and the securing of a port on the Pacific.

Relatively few accurate accounts have been written about this, the westernmost, phase of the war. Even while the campaign was in progress scant attention was paid it, with the exception of the Texans, by most of the Southern and Northern peoples. Late 1861 and early 1862 saw great armies clashing in the eastern theaters of war. The focus of attention on these momentous events, close at home for most Americans, naturally relegated to obscurity a campaign in a sparsely settled region in which only a few thousand troops were involved. The purpose of this work is to describe and to evaluate the Confederacy's major military attempt to control the West in an effort to broaden the military perspective of the South's bid for freedom and independence.

Although to most Southerners the campaign in New Mexico passed virtually unnoticed, to Texans it loomed large in importance. It was relatively "close to home," and it was concerned with Texas' western ambitions; in addition, the Army of New Mexico (as the Confederate force was called) was composed almost entirely of Texans, the only exceptions being the commanding general, several other officers, and some members of companies recruited in Arizona. Practically all areas of the state, as well as all walks of life in the state, were represented in its ranks. A number who had achieved prominence during the Texas Revolution, the period of the Republic, or the War with Mexico set the example for their countrymen by readily joining the Confederate army to defend their state and their new nation. Lieutenant Colonel William R. Scurry, Captains William P. Hardeman and Charles M. Lesueur, and Major Richard T. Brownrigg had been members of the Secession Convention, the latter acting as secretary. Many won fame during this campaign, in subsequent ones, or in the postwar period. Lieutenant Colonel Scurry and Colonel William Steele were promoted to brigadier general, while Colonel Thomas Green and Major Arthur P. Bagby rose to the rank of major general. Both Scurry and Green were martyred on the field of battle in 1864. Lieutenant Joseph D. Sayers, adjutant of the Fifth Regiment, was elected governor of Texas in 1898 and 1900.

The Confederate venture into New Mexico ultimately ended in failure, but Texas did not forget what her sons had done there. Today three counties bear the names of men who played prominent roles in that campaign — Tom Green, Scurry, and Sutton — while one, Val Verde, commemorates the major victory. The Texans who took part in this campaign never received greater praise, however, than that accorded them by their commanding general, who wrote after the battle of Valverde (Val Verde): "Nobly have they emulated the fame of their San Jacinto ancestors."

Martin Hardwick Hall
Louisiana State University
in New Orleans, 1959

Sibley's
New Mexico
Campaign

1

New Mexico on the Eve of the War

IN 1861 THE NEWLY-BORN CONFEDERATE STATES OF AMERICA STRETCHED FROM THE
Atlantic Ocean to the western limits of Texas. Though this was a relatively large
area, many Southern leaders were hardly content, for they envisioned their country running from sea to sea. This dream of "manifest destiny" certainly was not
outside the realm of possibility. The Confederates believed that a majority of the
people of southern California were pro-slavery in sympathy, and would gladly
join them if given the opportunity. Southerners naturally expected that the western territories, having been held in common by all the states, would be divided
equitably between the two nations which had formerly composed the old Union.
Because of geographical proximity, it was logical that those territories seized
from Mexico — Utah and New Mexico — would be assigned to the South. In addition, the Confederates believed that their claim to these lands was greater
because the South had from the first favored the War with Mexico and had sent
her sons to do most of the fighting.

Southerners were particularly interested in New Mexico. For nearly a decade
they had been promoting a southern Pacific railroad, the Gadsden Purchase
having been negotiated solely with that aim in mind. Obviously, any southern
railroad running to the Pacific would have to pass through New Mexico. Southern influence was especially marked in the area, as evidenced by the territory's
enacting a slave code. Though conceivably a region for future slave expansion,
the geographical position of the territory outweighed all other considerations:
New Mexico was the key to Pacific expansion.

Of those who pointed out the importance of New Mexico to the Confederacy,
none was more convincing than the editor of the Houston *Telegraph*. Without
New Mexico, he warned:

> . . . the Federals have us surrounded and utterly shut in by their territory,
> with the privilege of fighting us off from commerce with the Pacific as well
> as with Northern Mexico. They confine slave territory within a boundary

that will shut us out of ¾ of the underdeveloped territory of the continent adapted to slavery. They also render it utterly out of the question in future years to take advantage of the changes in our neighboring Republic and add to our Confederacy those rich States of Mexico, so necessary to our future development. They destroy all prospect of a railroad to the Pacific for us, and thus make our commerce forever tributary to them. We must have and keep . . . [New Mexico] at all hazards.. . . [1]

With so much at stake in the Far West, it is not surprising that when war broke out, the Confederacy determined to seize New Mexico by force.

At the onset of the secession crisis, the Territory of New Mexico consisted of the present-day states of Arizona, New Mexico, and part of Nevada. Though this was a vast region, only a very small part of it was inhabited by white men. To most travelers the country seemed to be hardly more than a great wasteland of mountains, and plains, and desert. Its apparently worthless nature had prompted Charles M. Conrad, while Secretary of War (1850–1853), to recommend that the citizens of New Mexico be paid for their property, and that the country be turned over to the Indians. A United States attorney from Pennsylvania who had made the circuit in New Mexico described the territory in this manner:

> Compared with the rest of the Union, New Mexico may be called a desert land, and a large portion of it is almost as unfitted for agricultural purposes as the plains of Arabia. In appearance it is the most ancient country I have ever seen, and looks as though it might have been worn out long before the rest of our earth was made. The mountains are mostly barren, barring a stunted growth of pine-trees; the plains are almost as sterile, as the small fertile valleys are like angels' visits, "few and far between."[2]

In addition to geographical factors, the hostility of large numbers of Indians had played a significant part in restricting the settlement of the territory.

The census of 1860 listed the population, exclusive of Indians, as approximately eighty-six thousand. The great bulk of the citizenry were Mexicans (viz., natives of Mexican descent) whose minds, according to the Pennsylvania attorney, "are as barren as the land, with as little hope of being better cultivated."[3] According to the census, approximately 90 per cent of the people lived north of Fort Craig in the small farming villages and towns which dotted the Río Grande and its northern tributaries. Santa Fé, the capital and principal city, boasted a population of 4,635. The next in size were Albuquerque and Las Vegas, each with a few more than 1,000 inhabitants.

As the terminus of the Santa Fé Trail, the capital enjoyed a prosperous trade with the East. The overwhelming majority of the people of the territory, however, were engaged in agricultural and pastoral pursuits. A few native families, estimated at 500 to 700, controlled the economic wealth. This landed aristocracy had inherited their estates from ancestors who had received them originally as grants awarded by the king of Spain. Long isolated from the rest of the world, even the elite of the native class manifested but slight interest in external matters. [4] Since they had become American citizens by the terms of the treaty of Guadalupe-Hidalgo only a little over a decade before, it is not surprising that they were interested only in their own domestic problems. National issues seemed too alien and too remote to concern them.

Prior to the cession of the territory to the United States, a few American merchants and traders had settled in New Mexico. Some had gained prominence and influence by marrying into the more important native families. Even after 1848 the American (viz., "Anglo-Saxon") population increased slowly, for, compared with other territories, New Mexico offered few inducements to immigrants. By 1861 several thousand Americans, in addition to military personnel, were residing in the territory. Most of these were governmental officials, professional men, merchants, traders, and miners. Though small in number, they tended to dominate the political affairs of the territory through their influence over the native politicians. During the decade of the 1850s New Mexico had come to be identified progressively with the interests of the slave-holding states. Important reasons for this were New Mexico's commercial relationship with the slave state of Missouri, and the preponderance of Southerners in the territory. Many army officers serving in the region were from the South, as were the majority of the appointed territorial officials.

Southern influence was enhanced after the election of Miguel A. Otero as territorial delegate in 1855. When New Mexico became American territory, Otero was one native determined to adjust to the change. Educated in New York and St. Louis, he had become thoroughly familiar with American life and politics. At first he, like the great mass of his people, cared neither one way nor the other about the slavery issue. During his first term in Washington, however, he began to adopt a pro-Southern viewpoint. His sentiments in this respect became especially pronounced after his marriage to a native South Carolinian. Since he was New Mexico's representative to Washington and was the most influential native politician in New Mexico, his acceptance of the pro-Southern viewpoint greatly bolstered the South's hope of eventually bringing New Mexico into the Union as a slave state. [5]

The importance of Southern influence in territorial politics was particularly evident in 1857. In that year the legislature passed an act stipulating that no free

Negro could remain longer than thirty days in the territory, while those already in residence were to post bond as a guarantee of good behavior. The climax came in 1859 when, under the influence of Otero's supporters, the legislature enacted a stringent slave code. The census of 1860 listed eighty-five free Negroes in New Mexico. The number of slaves, most of whom were domestics belonging to army officers and governmental officials, was estimated at twenty to thirty. Obviously there was little need for a slave code, but passage of one served the political purpose of announcing that New Mexico was aligning herself with the South.

Though Negro slavery was virtually nonexistent, two other forms of involuntary servitude were widespread. For generations the New Mexicans had enslaved captured hostile Indians. Though there were no laws governing this practice, the citizenry nevertheless considered it a just custom. The system of domestic servitude called peonage, though not classed as slavery, actually amounted to it in fact. One writer noted that the only practical difference between it and Negro slavery was that the peons were not bought and sold in the market as chattels. Peonage was recognized by law and, in essence, was a contract between master and servant. For his services the peon was paid a wage of about five dollars a month, out of which he was to support himself and his family. The master usually operated a general store, where the peon had to buy every article he needed. By charging high prices, and by the advancement of loans, it was an easy matter for the master to keep the servant chronically in debt. By law the peon had to work for the master until all his debts were paid. Since it was almost impossible for a servant to become solvent, he was forced to work for his master for life. Parents heavily in debt even had the right to bind their children out as peons. An Eastern observer noted that one of the most objectionable features in the system was that the master was not obliged to maintain the peon in sickness or old age. When he became too old to work any longer, the peon was cast adrift to provide for himself. In short, peonage gave the master all the advantages of slavery without any of its responsibilities.

In 1853 the United States negotiated the Gadsden Purchase with Mexico. As previously noted, the purpose in acquiring this 45,535-mile tract, which included the southern part of present-day Arizona and New Mexico, was to obtain a suitable route for a southern Pacific railroad. Added to the Territory of New Mexico, the area encompassed in the purchase came to be known generally as Arizona. In addition to the possibility of New Mexico's entering the Union as a slave state, the territory, now expanded to include Arizona, became even more important to Southerners because of the increased strategical value of its geographical location.

The Mesilla Valley of the Río Grande, which formed the eastern extreme of that part of southern New Mexico called Arizona, was about forty miles long, averaged two miles in width, and contained approximately two-thirds of Arizona's population. It was isolated from the more populous upper country—New Mexico proper—by a stretch of desert called the Jornada del Muerto. Mesilla, with her population of almost twenty-five hundred, was the largest town in the valley, and the second largest in the entire territory. As the center of trade and commerce, the town enjoyed greatly enhanced prosperity with the establishment of the Overland Mail in 1858. Clustered along the Río Grande were a number of small villages such as Amoles, Santo Tomás, Las Cruces, Picacho, Doña Ana, and Robledo. Fort Fillmore, located on the eastern side of the Río Grande below Las Cruces, afforded the valley partial protection against the hostile Apaches.

The Mexicans constituted the bulk of the population, with agriculture and grazing as their principal occupations. The American minority in the Mesilla Valley was far more active and aggressive in dominating the political affairs of the area than was the case in New Mexico proper. Most of the Americans were originally from Texas, and apparently carried with them their disdain of Mexicans in general. In October, 1860, the Mesilla *Times* appeared as the valley's first newspaper.[6] Staunchly pro-Southern from the first, this weekly mirrored the sentiments of the overwhelming majority of the American residents.

Because of the proximity of Texas, the Americans in the Mesilla Valley were closely associated with the Texans living in and around the town of El Paso,[7] located in the El Paso del Norte Valley of the Río Grande. The three most important and influential citizens of this westernmost extremity of the "Lone Star State" were Josiah F. Crosby, Simeon Hart, and James W. Magoffin.

Crosby first came to the El Paso area from the interior of Texas in 1852. Two years later he was elected to represent El Paso County in the state legislature. Since his election in 1857 he had been serving as district judge for the entire region west of the Pecos.

About a mile or so above El Paso, near the point where the Río Grande emerges from the mountains into the valley, Simeon Hart had constructed a large home and flour mill in 1851. Though born in New York, he had spent much of his life in Missouri. During the Mexican War he had served with distinction in the Doniphan Expedition. His mill, having a capacity of one hundred barrels a day, supplied the flour needs of a large region extending east to San Antonio, west to Tucson, and south to Rosales, Chihuahua. His home, mill, and adjacent buildings were called "El Molino," or simply "Hart's Mill."

Below El Paso, and nearly opposite the Mexican city of El Paso del Norte (present-day Ciudad Juárez), James W. Magoffin established a trading post in 1849. Magoffin was a Missourian and had engaged in the Santa Fé trade prior to his serving as United States consul in Chihuahua. During the Mexican War he had acted as a special agent, and was largely responsible for the peaceful occupation of New Mexico by United States forces. "Magoffinsville," as his spacious Spanish-style home, stores, warehouses, and other buildings on his property were collectively called, was the center of the social and commercial life of the community. Since 1854 Fort Bliss had been located at "Magoffinsville," on a lease basis, with Magoffin serving as post sutler.

Through their great wealth and by marriage into aristocratic Mexican families, Magoffin and Hart exerted considerable influence over the Mexican population on both sides of the Río Grande. The fact that Magoffin, Hart, and Crosby were vociferously pro-Southern in their sentiments was to contribute greatly to the early successes of the Confederacy in far western Texas and Arizona.

When the United States acquired the Gadsden Purchase, the territory west of the Mesilla Valley was nearly deserted because of the ravages of the Apaches. Americans drifting into the area shortly afterwards found that it abounded in mineral wealth. Heedless of the Indian menace, the lure of riches soon attracted large numbers of miners and adventurers. Within a relatively short time, Arizona gained a reputation as a silver district.

One of the liveliest centers was Pinos Altos (also referred to in the singular, i.e., Pino Alto), a gold mining town located near the continental divide northwest of Mesilla. By 1860 its population was estimated to be around eight hundred, of whom five hundred were Americans. Not far distant were other mines rich in copper ore. To the west, in what is now the state of Arizona, Tubac and Tucson were the two most important towns to reap the effects of the silver boom.

Tubac, located in the Santa Cruz Valley, had been completely abandoned before the United States acquired the Gadsden Purchase. The operation of several large silver mines within a radius of twenty miles of the town, however, gave it a new lease on life. Though it had only about 350 people in 1860, it was the business center of the silver district, and the home of Arizona's first newspaper, the Tubac *Weekly Arizonian*.

Tucson lay on the main road from the Río Grande to California, and on the major route to Sonora, Mexico, and the seaport of Guaymas. Her favorable location near the mineral discoveries and the coming of the Overland Mail transformed this sleepy little village into a roaring boom town of over nine hundred. Most of the American newcomers, both floating and settled, came from Southern states, either directly, or by way of California.

If ever an area epitomized the lawless, wild frontier, it was western Arizona on the eve of secession. Tucson was a place of resort for traders, speculators, gamblers, horse thieves, murderers, and vagrant politicians, and the center of vice, dissipation, and crime. One critic caustically observed that those who were no longer permitted to live in California found the climate of Tucson congenial to their health. In fact, he opined that the Vigilance Committee of San Francisco did more to populate the new territory than the silver mines. Sylvester Mowry, a prominent mine owner, laid the blame for this deplorable condition squarely on the shoulders of the Federal government for its failure to extend law and protection. With western Arizona in a state of virtual anarchy, every man went armed to the teeth, and scenes of bloodshed were an everyday occurrence.

As early as 1854 the Americans south and west of the Jornada had been agitating for separate territorial status. One reason for this sentiment was Arizona's geographical isolation from the more populous upper country. But of far greater significance was the determination of the native politicians of New Mexico proper to retain control of the territorial government. Without an equitable representation in the legislature, Arizona's needs and demands, in large measure, were consistently ignored. Even the Americans in New Mexico proper, including the appointed officials, acquiesced in this matter, lest they antagonize the natives and lose their support. Aggravating the problem was the inadequate system of military protection. Most Arizonans believed that if they were organized as a separate territory, the Federal government would take a greater interest in protecting them from the forays of the merciless Apaches.

To achieve their aim the Arizonans, from 1854 on, drew up petitions, called conventions, and sent delegates to Washington to plead their cause—all to no avail. Primarily responsible for these national rebuffs was the mounting, bitter sectional animosity. Northern congressmen feared that if Arizona were organized as a territory, she would later try to enter the Union as a slave state. Stymied in their efforts on the national level, the Arizonans finally took matters in their own hands. In April, 1860, thirty-one delegates met in Tucson to draw up a constitution establishing a provisional government for Arizona, or that part of New Mexico lying south of 33° 40' . Selected as governor was Lewis S. Owings of Mesilla, who in turn appointed most of the important territorial officials. The provisional government was to function until Congress extended territorial recognition. Sylvester Mowry, who previously had served as Arizona's special representative, was reappointed delegate to Washington. Though he did his utmost to secure Congressional approval, his efforts again ended in failure.

With the formation of the Confederacy, Southerners were certain that New Mexico was destined to become a part of their nation. An abundance of evidence appeared to support this contention. The passage of the slave code seemed to indicate beyond a shadow of a doubt where the sympathies of the people lay. Miguel Otero's continued reelection as delegate offered further testimony of the natives' proslavery proclivities. Two newspapers (Santa Fé *Gazette* and Mesilla *Times*) disseminated the Southern viewpoint. In the economic realm, northern New Mexico was closely associated with the slave state of Missouri, while southern New Mexico

(Arizona) was within the orbit of Texas. Not to be overlooked was the fact that both the territorial governor, Abraham Rencher, and the departmental military commander[8] were North Carolinians, while the territorial secretary was a Mississippian. Few Southerners doubted that New Mexico would shortly cast her lot with the Confederate States.

Unfortunately for the South, the situation in New Mexico was not so favorable. As early as February, 1861, Territorial Secretary Alexander M. Jackson, in replying to a Mississippi political acquaintance, painted a grimmer, more realistic picture of the territory's internal affairs. Some Southerners apparently entertained the hope that the New Mexicans would call a constitutional convention and then petition the Confederacy for admission as a state. Jackson pointed out that, with the exception of the Americans in Arizona, the natives, primarily because of their fear that statehood would bring increased taxation, would never take such action. The only factor which had reconciled the Mexicans to American rule, he observed, was the abolition of the onerous exactions suffered during the Spanish and Mexican periods. During the legislative session just concluded the month before, a bill calling for a constitutional convention had been introduced, only to go down to defeat.

As long as the New Mexicans manifested pro-Southern sympathies, the Confederacy's title to the territory would be secure. But Jackson emphatically made it clear that Southern sentiment among the natives was superficial and ephemeral. Since territorial politics was but a reflection of Federal power, he warned that Northern influence and patronage could easily reverse the present climate of opinion. He therefore urged the recently formed Confederate government to demand New Mexico at once before the Lincoln administration could appoint territorial officials, and particularly before the next session of the legislature, scheduled to convene the first Monday in December, 1861. This was important, for if the natives knew their territory would be assigned to the Confederacy, they would maintain their pro-Southern sympathies. Just the news of Lincoln's election had been sufficient to influence several delegates to the last legislative session to adopt a pro-Republican viewpoint. Jackson was convinced that had it not been for strenuous efforts on his part, the assembly would have repealed the slave code. The governor, of course, would have vetoed the bill, but the damage from the propaganda standpoint would have been irreparable. Jackson feared that if the South did not act at once, Republican influence would surely bring about repeal of the slave code in the next session. Such action would serve notice that New Mexico now sided with the North. This would naturally be a serious, if not insuperable, impediment to the cession of the territory to the South.

An additional factor which increased Jackson's anxiety was the great number of miners, the majority of whom were from free states, who were drifting from Colorado into northern New Mexico. The secretary felt that these "Pike's

Peakers" would constitute the only sizable group vehemently opposed to joining the Confederacy. But one of them, he believed, would make more noise than a hundred Mexicans, and before the year was out this "lawless and contentious clamor" would be considered the voice of New Mexico. "Before this class succeed in obtaining by fraud and violence the influence they got in Kansas by the same means, the future destiny of New Mexico should be determined—otherwise it is determined already."[9]

Of prime importance concerning the ultimate position of New Mexico was the fact that she was commercially dependent upon Missouri. Jackson prophesied that the action Missouri took in the secession crisis would have more effect upon the native population than all other considerations combined. Others familiar with territorial affairs also agreed that "as goes Missouri, so goes New Mexico." If such were to be the case, the obvious danger to Southern claims was the possibility that Missouri, though a slave state, might remain in the Union.

In conclusion, Jackson stressed the point that New Mexico's natural resources had been grossly underrated. Her stock-raising capacity was "unsurpassed" and her untapped mineral wealth "inexhaustible." All that the territory needed to reach her potential was protection against the hostile Indians. Again he warned that "Southern Statesmen must realize the fact at once that if New Mexico is to be acquired for the South, it must be done," assuming war did not break out, "by the South in her settlement with the balance of the late firm. Reliance on these people further than their goodwill, notwithstanding their present proclivities, will be misplaced."[10]

On January 28, 1861, the Texas secession convention met in Austin. After the secession ordinance was ratified by the people, Texas became the seventh state to leave the old Union. Since the convention's course of action was a foregone conclusion, Simeon Hart addressed a letter to Delegate William R. Scurry suggesting that commissioners be appointed to invite Arizona and New Mexico to join the South. Scurry's subsequent resolution was approved, and the convention appointed Hart commissioner to New Mexico proper, while Philemon T. Herbert, an attorney and delegate from El Paso County, was to treat with the citizens of Arizona. In the hope of stimulating the New Mexicans to initiate action on their own, the convention addressed the following resolution:

Resolved that this Convention recommends to the citizens of the Territory of Santa Fe or New Mexico the propriety of immediately proceeding to form a State constitution recognizing the institution of slavery, and that they be requested to apply to the Southern convention at Montgomery for admission into the confederacy of Southern States.[11]

When notified of his appointment, Hart immediately entered into correspondence with the principal citizens of New Mexico with whom he had been associated for many years, both socially and in business. For some reason—possibly because his outspoken Southern sentiments might entail his arrest by the military—Hart's civilian and army friends warned against his appearing in person. Heeding their advice, he remained in El Paso while several New Mexicans whom he had employed as secret agents gathered information and endeavored to propagate the Southern cause. After a few weeks matters appeared to be progressing so favorably that he selected Captain Henry Clay Cook, a former army officer, to journey to Santa Fé as his representative.

Cook arrived at the capital on May 18 armed with letters of introduction. After several days of informal talks with the leading civilian and military figures, Cook was delighted to report that all were unanimous in their support of the South. He maintained that he did not come into contact with a single individual of importance who held an opinion to the contrary, or even hear of such a person. He noted, however, that the presence of the Federal army would deter the citizens from taking any overt action unless the Confederacy made it known that she wanted New Mexico and would send aid to secure it.

The Arizonans lost no time in declaring their support of secession. On February 23, 1861, the Mesilla *Times* published a petition calling for delegates to attend a general convention to be held in Mesilla on March 16 to determine whether or not to join the South. Three days later Philemon T. Herbert informed Provisional Governor Owings that the state of Texas had appointed him to confer with the citizens of Arizona and to invite them to join the confederacy which the slave states were establishing. Herbert received a very cordial welcome from the delegates of the "Convention of the People of Arizona," which met in Mesilla as scheduled. He was delighted to report that the citizens of the Mesilla Valley and those at Pinos Altos were overwhelmingly in favor of the South. The convention voted unanimously to repudiate the authority of the old Union government, and to seek annexation to the Confederacy as a territory.

One week later, on March 23, the citizens of faraway Tucson held a similar meeting, which ratified a resolution proclaiming "That under any and all circumstances our sympathies are with the Southern Confederacy, and in the event that it shall be composed of a majority of the Southern States, we earnestly desire that she will extend to us the protection necessary to the proper development and advancement of the Territory."[12] In a special election the people of both eastern and western Arizona overwhelmingly ratified the actions of their conventions.

Since the earliest days of Spanish colonization, New Mexico had suffered from the attacks of hostile Indians. Shortly after the United States acquired the territory, the War Department set about constructing a chain of forts designed to protect the inhabitants as much as possible from this perennial menace. In early 1861 the more important ones were Forts Defiance and Fauntleroy in the northcentral region near the approaches to the Navajo country, Fort Union to the northeast on the Santa Fé Trail, Fort Marcy at Santa Fé, Fort Craig on the Río Grande about 30 miles south of Socorro, Fort Stanton in the Sacramento Mountains some 140 miles northeast of Mesilla, Fort Fillmore in the Mesilla Valley, Fort McLane southwest of Pinos Altos, Fort Breckinridge about forty-five miles northeast of Tucson, and Fort Buchanan in the Sonoita Valley, approximately forty-five miles southeast of Tucson. Santa Fé was the seat of departmental headquarters, while the depot of supply was in Albuquerque.[13] The military forces consisted of two regiments and one battalion of infantry, one regiment of mounted riflemen, and four companies of dragoons (the mounted rifles and dragoons were shortly designated as cavalry).

The defense of New Mexico was highly inadequate, regardless of the army's efforts. Not only were most of the posts insufficiently garrisoned, but many of the troops, being infantry, were virtually useless in the pursuit of Indians on horseback. What few mounted soldiers there were proved invaluable. Under these circumstances, the Indians continued their depredations relatively unrestrained. Arizona, being within the domain of the fierce Apaches, suffered the greatest, although New Mexico proper was subjected to the incursions of Navajos, Utes, and Comanches. Early in 1860 the territorial legislature petitioned Congress to establish seven additional permanent posts,[14] but the sectional conflict in Washington prevented any action.

The election of Lincoln and resultant secession found the army officers in New Mexico, as elsewhere, divided in their sympathies. In every post the chief topic of conversation was secession, and bitter were the many arguments that ensued. As an example, several officers and their wives were dining with Captain and Mrs. Dabney H. Maury in Santa Fé on Christmas day, 1860. "The possibility of war between the North and South was freely discussed at the table, with considerable excitement, and so hotly at times the ladies were embarrassed considerably. There were advocates for both sides, while others were reticent as to their sentiments."[15] As the earliest states seceded, tension rose to a fever pitch. At Fort Union a young lieutenant noted that zealous Southerners were exerting "tremendous efforts" to coax their brother officers to resign in order to join the Confederate army. Though thoroughly devoted to the Union himself, this lieutenant felt that "Very few officers would not prefer to serve the south, who have always treated us well, to the north who have always abused us."[16]

News of the firing on Fort Sumter on April 12 reached New Mexico early in May. With the outbreak of war now a reality, most Southern officers resigned their commissions and left New Mexico to offer their services to the Confederacy. Among those who took this course were Colonel Thomas T. Fauntleroy, former departmental commander, Lieutenant Colonels John B. Grayson and

George B. Crittenden, Majors Henry H. Sibley, James Longstreet, and R. B. Reynolds, Captains Dabney H. Maury, Andrew J. Lindsay, John Stevenson, Richard S. Ewell, and Cadmus M. Wilcox, and Lieutenants Joseph Wheeler and Lawrence S. Baker, and Assistant Surgeon E. N. Covey. The enlisted men did not have the privilege of resigning as did the officers. If a soldier left before his term of enlistment expired (five years), he was guilty of desertion. It appears that the great majority of the enlisted personnel in New Mexico remained loyal to the Union, or were at least indifferent to the great issue at hand. Some, however, did leave to join the Confederate army.

In command of the department during this exodus of Southern officers was Colonel William W. Loring, a North Carolinian, who had assumed the position only a short time before on March 22, 1861. True to the dictates of his native state, on May 13, he, too, forwarded his resignation to Washington. Unlike his brother officers, he elected to remain at his post until formally relieved. After several weeks, he apparently became restless, for on June 11, he left Santa Fé for Fort Fillmore, there to await word from Washington regarding his resignation. Fort Fillmore, though in New Mexico, was only forty miles from El Paso, Texas, where semiweekly stage facilities were available for transportation to the East. Before leaving Santa Fé, Loring, though still officially in command, placed Colonel Edward R. S. Canby in general charge of departmental affairs.

When Texas withdrew from the Union, General David E. Twiggs, the departmental commander, surrendered all military property to the commissioners of the state of Texas. All Union troops were subsequently ordered to withdraw to the coast, preparatory to leaving the state. In compliance with these instructions, Lieutenant Colonel I. V. D. Reeve, commandant of Fort Bliss, set out on March 31 with his forces. Before abandoning his post, he turned over all military property (estimated to be a twelve-months' supply of subsistence and ammunition for approximately two companies) to James W. Magoffin and all public funds to Simeon Hart, they being the authorized state agents for that area.

Since Fort Fillmore was only a short distance away, Magoffin, Hart, and Crosby feared that the Union troops there might descend upon Fort Bliss to reclaim the abandoned military property. A few days after Loring's departure from Santa Fé, a letter from a resigned major at El Paso reached headquarters. This former officer, Henry H. Sibley, implored Loring to remain at his post a little longer, at least until a Confederate force could arrive to take charge of the public property at Fort Bliss. Sibley urged him, if he had already left, and was consequently unable to prevent his successor from attempting to capture the supplies, to send word to Hart immediately. "Your seat in the stage," he added, "may at the same time be engaged."[17] Canby read this communication and jumped to the conclusion that Loring was involved in treasonable activities with the Texas authorities in El Paso. Even though Loring was still at Fort Fillmore and officially head of the department, Canby immediately assumed full command "without reference to him." As he put it, "I have not hesitated, since this information was communicated to me, to exercise the command and to give any orders or to take any measures that I considered necessary to protect the honor or the interests of the Government."[18] There can be no doubt of Loring's sympathies, but there is no evidence to indicate that he deliberately attempted to utilize his position as departmental commander to the advantage of the Confederacy, as Canby believed.

Edward Richard Sprigg Canby, who shortly was confirmed as the new departmental commander, was born in Kentucky in 1819. After graduation from West Point in 1839, he served first in the Seminole War, and then in escorting the Cherokee, Creeks, and Choctaws to Indian Territory. During the Mexican War he took part in the siege of Vera Cruz and the battles of Cerro Gordo, Contreras, and Churubusco. For gallant and meritorious conduct in the latter two battles, he was awarded a brevet majorcy. As a result of his bravery at Belén Gate, he was elevated to the rank of brevet lieutenant colonel. In 1855 he was promoted to major and assigned to frontier service in western Wisconsin and Minnesota. After a tour of duty at Fort Bridger, Utah, he led an expedition against the Navajos in New Mexico. The breakup of the Union found him in command of Fort Defiance where, on May 14, 1861, he received the rank of colonel of the Nineteenth Infantry.

On assuming command at Santa Fé on June 11, Canby found his department in serious straits. The troops had gone unpaid for many months. Even if the money the paymaster had on hand were distributed, many soldiers would still have been left unpaid for several months' service. The Texans in El Paso sought to take advantage of this situation by encouraging the enlisted men, particularly those at Fort Fillmore, to desert with their horses, arms, and other equipment, to join the Confederate army. A major inducement was the promise to pay all arrearages due them. The resignation of many Southerners had not only resulted in widespread demoralization, but had left a serious shortage of officers. To partially alleviate this situation, Canby later appointed a number of enlisted men to serve in the capacity of acting commissioned officers.

During the preceding two years, near-droughts had produced a scarcity of water, crops, and grass. Many horses and mules had died, leaving the military forces seriously short of riding and draft animals. Hostile Indians continued their depredations, thereby placing a severe strain upon the territory's weakened defenses. The civilian population, too, was a cause of concern. Canby believed the natives north of the Jornada, with perhaps a few exceptions, to be loyal. But he noted that they were so apathetic in disposition it would be difficult to get them to take measures to defend their territory. In Arizona, of course, the people had already proclaimed their allegiance to the Confederacy. As a consequence, Canby found himself in command of a department divided within itself.

On June 14, just three days after Canby had taken charge of the department, orders arrived in Santa Fé directing that all the regular infantry be marched to Fort Leavenworth, Kansas, as soon as practicable. To replace these troops, the army stipulated that two regiments of volunteers should be raised from the New Mexican citizenry. Aware that the immediate removal of the regular infantry would seriously weaken the territory's defenses, the New War Department instructed the departmental commander to distribute the remaining regulars, and any available volunteers, at such points as would best protect the interests of the United States government. Canby complied immediately by ordering in the infantry from the interior and most distant posts. He informed Washington, though, that because of the scarcity of horses and mules throughout the territory, the departure of the troops would be unavoidably delayed for some time. Until transportation could be procured for their march, he planned to concentrate the various companies of the Fifth Infantry at Albuquerque and Fort Union, and those of the Seventh at Fort Fillmore. One of the unfortunate consequences of the calling in of the infantry was the abandonment of Forts Buchanan and Breckinridge. Inadequate as the military protection might have been, the withdrawal of the soldiers now left the people of western Arizona completely at the mercy of the Apaches.

In addition to requesting Governor Rencher to issue a call for recruits to fill the ranks of the two volunteer regiments, Canby also asked Governor William Gilpin of Colorado to raise several companies to garrison Fort Garland—a post which, though within Canby's jurisdiction, was located within the Territory of Colorado. The recruitment of the volunteer regiments proceeded slowly, and the Colonel observed that the calibre of the recruits was very poor. In addition to the continuing Indian raids and the hostile attitude of the Arizonans, rumors were rampant that an invasion from Texas was imminent. In view of these pressing problems, Canby asked the adjutant general for permission to retain at least one of the infantry regiments until the volunteers could attain some degree of instruction and discipline. But on July 12 he was chagrined to learn that the War Department had ordered the withdrawal of all remaining regulars from the territory. Certain that Washington was unaware of New Mexico's critical condition, Canby dispatched Captain Robert A. Wainwright to the capital to present an accurate picture. The Captain was to make it clear that if all the regulars were pulled out, it would inevitably result in the abandonment of the country and the absolute loss of the immense amount of public property in or en route to the territory.

Fort Fillmore, the southernmost post in the territory, was located in the midst of a people hostile to the Union. The news of the fall of Fort Sumter was received in Mesilla with enthusiastic cheers. The Mesilla *Times* had reflected this display of Confederate patriotism by printing a sketch of the "Stars and Bars" under which was a poem entitled "Our Flag," and the lyrics to "Dixie Land." A strong pro-Union resident of El Paso observed that a Confederate flag was flying in Mesilla and that the valley was "as much in the possession of the enemy as Charleston is."[19]

Canby learned from reliable sources that the Texans in El Paso, in cooperation with citizens of the Mesilla Valley, might attempt to seize Fort Fillmore. To prevent such a possibility, he instructed Major Isaac Lynde, commanding Fort McLane, to abandon his post and move his men and equipment to Fort Fillmore. With a garrison to be composed eventually of seven companies of infantry and two of mounted rifles, Canby hoped that Lynde would not only overawe the local population, but march southward to capture the government property at abandoned Fort Bliss.

Major Lynde arrived at his new post on July 4. Three days later he reported that Fort Fillmore was poorly situated for defense. Built in a basin, it was commanded, and half-way surrounded, by sand hills densely covered with chaparral. He surmised that a force of one thousand could come within five hundred yards of the post under perfect cover. If an enemy mounted artillery on the hills, the fort would be rendered helpless. The post's defenseless nature, as well as the attitude of the local population, prompted Lynde to advise that neither the post nor the valley was worth the "exertion" of holding. In case of a Texan effort to invade Arizona, he deemed it far wiser to withdraw beyond the Jornada del Muerto to Fort Craig.

Canby apparently agreed with Lynde's observations. On July 15 he notified the major that as soon as the troops from Forts Buchanan and Breckinridge arrived from western Arizona, he was to abandon Fort Fillmore. Forts Craig and Stanton would then be the southernmost bastions of defense. But even at these strategic points the regulars were to be withdrawn just as rapidly as Canby could replace them with volunteers. As the departmental commander was engaged in making the best of his difficult situation, the Confederates at El Paso took the offensive.

Although the Federal garrison had abandoned Fort Bliss on March 31, and Arizona had declared her allegiance to the South shortly thereafter, the Confederacy was slow to dispatch military forces to the area. As the weeks passed, the American residents grew progressively more alarmed. Not only were they endangered by the presence of Union soldiers, but they also were exposed to the ever increasingly frequent inroads of the Apaches. In the belief that perhaps the Texas and Confederate authorities might be unaware of their critical condition, or of the value of annexing Arizona, a number of citizens addressed urgent appeals to both governments calling for immediate military aid.

With the withdrawal of the Federal army, Texas' frontier was left unguarded. The secession convention had endeavored to provide some protection by authorizing the raising of two volunteer regiments. But when the state joined the Confederacy, the duty of frontier security then devolved upon the national government. On May 24 Brigadier General Earl Van Dorn, Confederate commander of the Department of Texas, ordered the regarrisoning of the abandoned posts. Four companies, plus a battery of artillery, were assigned to Fort Bliss. Not until the latter part of June and early July, however, did these detachments of the Second Regiment Texas Mounted Rifles reach their destination.

In regard to Fort Bliss, Van Dorn had more in mind for the garrison than mere defense. He knew that Union troops were stationed at Fort Fillmore. He believed that if the Texans launched a surprise attack they could easily capture the Federals. But he feared that if the enemy there suspected such a move they would get out of reach by falling back to the safety of Fort Craig or Fort Stanton. Entrusted to the command of the troops reoccupying Fort Bliss was Lieutenant Colonel John R. Baylor, an intrepid frontiersman, and the regiment's second in command.

Baylor interpreted the concentration of troops at Fort Fillmore—only forty miles to the north—as evidence that the Federals were planning an offensive. Rather than wait complacently for the enemy to attack, he determined to strike first as Van Dorn had suggested. With a force of about three hundred men, he set out. Moving cautiously northward, he succeeded in reaching, without detection, on the night of the 24th a point on the river near Fort Fillmore. He planned to entrench his force between the post and the Río Grande and cut off the enemy's animals as they went to water early that morning. He then hoped that the Federals would sally from their fortress to attack him in his strong position. Obviously he was unaware of the defenseless nature of Fort Fillmore and how easily it could have been invested. Even so, his strategy might have succeeded had it not been for a deserter from his ranks who warned the garrison. Thwarted by this unforeseen development, Baylor withdrew to Mesilla, six miles distant. The townspeople received the Confederates with a tremendous ovation, and "Vivas and hurrahs rang them welcome from every point."[20]

On learning that the Texans had entered Mesilla, Lynde decided to take the offensive. Baylor received ample warning of his approach, however, because of the large clouds of dust kicked up by the Union command as it moved along. By the time the Federals had drawn up in battle formation before the town, the Confederates had had sufficient time to take defensive positions on house tops, and behind corrals and other protective cover. When Baylor refused a formal demand to surrender, Lynde launched a rather half-hearted assault, which was quickly repulsed with a Union loss of three killed and six wounded. Rather than continue the attack, the Federal commander ordered his troops to retire to Fort Fillmore. He was now more firmly convinced than ever that his position in the Mesilla Valley was untenable.

On July 27, the Union troops set fire to their post, and started out on the long road through the mountains to Fort Stanton. All proceeded well at first. But as the sun rose higher in the heavens, the heat became unbearable, while the dust was nearly stifling. As the trail ascended the grade to San Agustín Springs, scores of exhausted, thirst-suffering infantrymen began dropping by the wayside.

The columns of smoke rising from the direction of Fort Fillmore, and the clouds of dust moving eastward, enabled Baylor to quickly discern Lynde's intent. Immediately he ordered his mounted force in pursuit. Later in the day as the Confederates moved swiftly along the road, they began encountering, and disarming, large numbers of Federals who were too weak from heat exhaustion to resist. Lynde sounded the call to arms, but when he saw that only about one hundred infantrymen were able to respond, he considered it useless to resist. He himself was so overcome from the heat that he could not ride his horse. As he viewed the situation, "honor did not demand the sacrifice of blood after the terrible suffering"[21] his troops had already undergone. Without the firing of a shot, the Union commander surrendered his demoralized army of about five hundred men—seven companies of the Seventh Infantry, and three[22] of mounted rifles—to a Confederate force numbering less than three hundred.[23] In addition to prisoners, Baylor captured all their transportation, arms, ammunition, commissary and quartermaster stores (including 200 cavalry mounts, and 270 head of beef cattle), and four pieces of artillery. Since he was in no position to guard, or even to feed, such a large number of captives, Baylor released the entire command on parole, and allowed them to proceed northward into New Mexico proper.

On August 1, with the area south of the Jornada cleared of the enemy, Baylor formally took possession of Arizona in the name of the Confederate States of America. Until such time as Congress took action, he proclaimed a provisional government for the Territory of Arizona, and appointed officials to office. Baylor, assuming the position of military governor, decreed that Confederate Arizona included all that part of New Mexico lying south of the parallel of 34°.[24]

In reporting his activities to General Van Dorn, Baylor pointed out that the vast mineral resources of Arizona, in addition to its position affording an outlet to the Pacific, made its acquisition a matter of considerable importance to the Confederacy. Now that he had taken possession of the territory, he trusted a force sufficient to occupy and hold it would be sent by the government under some competent man. Even before Baylor had arrived at Fort Bliss, the Confederacy had already planned to send an army to New Mexico under the command of a "competent" man.

2

The "Sibley Brigade" Marches to New Mexico

SHORTLY BEFORE BAYLOR ARRIVED AT FORT BLISS, HENRY HOPKINS SIBLEY WAS COMMISSIONED a brigadier general in the army of the Confederacy with instructions to raise a brigade to drive the Federal forces from New Mexico. Distinguished in appearance, this veteran soldier was born in Natchitoches, Louisiana, in 1816. From 1838, the date of his graduation from the United States Military Academy (ranking 31 in a class of 45), until his resignation, he had served with distinction in the United States army. As a young lieutenant of the Second Dragoons, he had seen service in the Seminole wars in Florida. Attaining the rank of captain in 1847, he fought in the War with Mexico, taking part in the siege of Vera Cruz, the skirmish of Medelín, the battles of Cerro Gordo, Contreras, Churubusco, and Molino del Rey, and in the capture of Mexico City. For gallant and meritorious conduct at Medelín, he received a brevet majorcy. After the war he was on frontier duty at various posts in Texas. He was stationed in Kansas during the antislavery conflict, and he later took part in the Utah expedition against the Mormons. In 1860 he marched to New Mexico to engage in a campaign against the Navajo Indians. Aside from his military exploits, he had also achieved success as an inventor. In 1856 he patented the Sibley tent, patterned after the plains Indians' teepees, which was adopted by the United States army.

With the outbreak of the War for Southern Independence, Sibley was stationed at Taos, New Mexico, as captain of the Second Dragoons. Though elevated to the rank of major on May 13, 1861, he resigned his commission the same day in order to offer his services to the South. June 12 found him and several other resigned officers at Hart's Mill preparing to take the stage for San Antonio, and from there to the capital of the Confederacy.

"We are at last," he wrote, "under the glorious banner of the Confederate States of America . . . [which is] indeed a glorious sensation of protection, hope, and pride."[1] He commented that when he had passed into Texas from New Mexico the "Southern verdure and familiar foliage" filled him with "enthusiasm and home feeling." To say that the area of extreme western Texas—though certainly part of the Confederacy—exhibited the scenery of the South, especially Sibley's home state of Louisiana, attests to what extent this romantic soldier was overwhelmed by his emotions.

Believing that the best of the rank and file of the army in New Mexico were pro-Southern, Sibley regretted the "sickly sentimentality" which had overruled his desire to bring his whole command with him. By leaving without his men, he felt he had betrayed and deserted them. In this respect, he summed up his feelings by saying, "I wish I had my part to play over again; no such peace scruples should deter me from doing what I considered a bounden duty to my friends and my cause. I do not advocate the meeting of duplicity and dishonesty by the like weapons, but if I capture the treasury buildings I shall certainly not send back to my enemy the golden bricks."[2]

Arriving in San Antonio on the morning of June 20, six days after boarding the stage at Hart's Mill, Sibley took passage on another to Berwick's Bay, Louisiana. From there he rode the railroad to New Orleans, where he received the welcoming acclaim of his fellow citizens. During his brief stay in the Crescent City Sibley was offered the command of a Louisiana volunteer regiment. This honor he politely declined, for he had far greater plans for the future. Shortly afterward, he set out for Richmond, Virginia, where he talked with President Jefferson Davis and unfolded his plan for securing Arizona and New Mexico. Several individuals,[3] including some resigned officers, accompanied him to the capital. They were presumably present when he spoke with the President, and served to support his statements concerning affairs in the territory and the feasibility of his plan.

It was not necessary for Sibley to convince Davis of the importance of these territories. His problem was to point out to the President how easy it would be for an army under his command to drive the enemy from the region. Many factors made Sibley confident of success. During his tour of duty in New Mexico he naturally had acquired a great deal of information concerning the resources of the country, the condition of the Federal army, the amount of military supplies, the attitude of the population, and other pertinent information. He was convinced that the Federal army there was so small and so inefficient that it would be no match against a Confederate force. Capitulation would quickly follow once he entered the territory, and the large quantities of war matériel at the various posts and depots would fall into his hands. He believed that virtually all the American population was pro-Southern, and that the native Mexicans would either come to his aid, or at least not hinder his efforts. Sibley counted upon the agricultural resources of the Mesilla and El Paso del Norte valleys for commissary supplies and, as a safeguard, he planned to purchase additional supplies from the neighboring Mexican states.

A cardinal feature of his strategy was that the proposed New Mexican campaign would be primarily self-sustaining—there would not even be a need for a supply line. After being initially equipped and supplied in Texas, his army would get all other necessary war matériel from the defeated enemy and thus would literally live off the land. The possibility of gaining this vast strategic area with such apparent ease, and at a minimum of expense, was undoubtedly the major factor which convinced the President of the soundness of Sibley's plan. After all, there was little to lose, yet much to be gained, if successful.

Trevanion T. Teel, one of Sibley's officers in the subsequent campaign, stated in a postwar account that just before Sibley assumed command of his army he revealed in a private conversation his grandiose plans for the West. According to Teel, Sibley's ultimate goal was the conquest of California and the annexation of northern Mexico. After New Mexico had been occupied, the army, swelled by recruits, would move on to take California. Once that was accomplished, negotiations would be opened with Mexico to secure Chihuahua, Sonora, and Lower California either by purchase or by conquest.

Possibly the Confederate government ultimately intended Sibley to move into California if successful in New Mexico. But if that was the case, there is no record of it. Perhaps Richmond preferred to wait until New Mexico was safely occupied before planning the next move. As to the annexation of parts of Mexico, the Confederacy was definitely not interested—for international reasons—during the period of war. Only when foreign recognition of Confederate independence was achieved could any such plans against Mexico be formulated. There is no reason to doubt the validity of Teel's account of Sibley's ambitions. Undoubtedly the general, highly visionary as he was, simply had let his imagination run away with him.

Sibley was commissioned a brigadier general on July 5, 1861. Three days later he received his orders:

SIR: In view of your recent service in New Mexico and knowledge of that country and the people, the President has intrusted you with the important duty of driving the Federal troops from that department, at the same time securing all the arms, supplies, and materials of war.[4]

He was instructed to proceed immediately to Texas, where, in cooperation with General Earl Van Dorn, he was to organize as quickly as possible two full regiments of cavalry, one battery of howitzers, and such other forces as he might deem necessary. Realizing later that two regiments would not be enough, he increased the number to three. Sibley's orders were of a general nature, for he was to be guided by circumstances and his own good judgment. In short, he was given practically a free hand in the conduct of his New Mexican campaign. With such an active and distinctive background in the regular army, this newly commissioned general gave the Confederacy every reason to believe great things could be expected of him.

Sibley arrived in New Orleans from Richmond on July 15. Those who had accompanied him to the Confederate capital had also received commissions and they now composed his provisional staff. At least one member, Lieutenant Colonel Henry C. McNeill, went directly to Texas to act as Sibley's mustering officer. After a stay of slightly over two weeks in New Orleans, the general, accompanied by his family, set out for Texas. On August 12 he reached San Antonio, where he set up his headquarters. Local newspapers not only announced his arrival, but also publicized his aim of organizing a brigade for "frontier service." Volunteer companies were called upon to "rendezvous at the earliest day possible at San Antonio armed and fully equipped for a Winter campaign."[5] Filled with enthusiasm, Sibley was fully confident that he would be able to raise and organize his brigade in a short time. News of Baylor's success in Arizona convinced him even more of the ease with which the remainder of New Mexico could be taken, thus further stirring his eagerness to get underway for the West.

Unexpected difficulties soon arose to shatter Sibley's plans for rapidly getting his command into the field. Though Governor Edward Clark ordered the proper number of companies to report to Sibley for duty, most proved to be entirely disbanded, or so reduced in size as not to meet the minimum set for Confederate service. Since it was a popular misconception that the brigade would be filled only by units ordered out by the governor, other companies not so organized consequently did not offer their services. To overcome this false impression Sibley was compelled to appeal directly to the public, particularly through the medium of the patriotic press, for recruits. Even so it required some time to counteract the effects of this "misplaced reliance" upon the state system. A cause of further delay was the competition for men which grew out of the calls from those regiments required for service east of the Mississippi. Apparently a good many Texans preferred glory in the eastern theater rather than in the desolate and barren waste lands of Arizona and New Mexico.

Van Dorn was to have supplied Sibley with as much ordnance equipment as he could spare from the depots under his command. Not long after Sibley's arrival in San Antonio, Van Dorn was relieved from duty, and his key subordinates proceeded to Galveston to meet General P. O. Hébert, the new departmental commander. For several weeks Sibley was unable to locate any officer authorized to issue supplies. Complicating the picture was the reluctance of state authorities to allow war matériel to leave the department, believing as they did that a Federal attack on the Texan gulf coast was imminent. Sibley seized the bull by

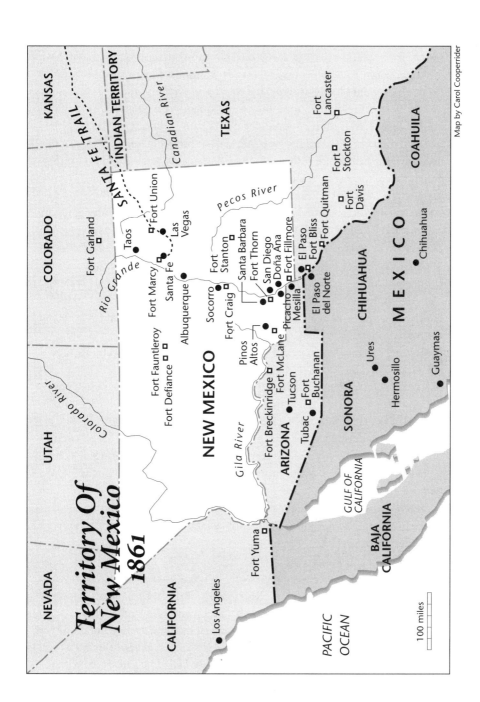

Territory Of
New Mexico
1861

NEVADA

UTAH

CALIFORNIA

COLORADO

KANSAS

INDIAN TERRITORY

SANTA FE TRAIL

Colorado River

Canadian River

TEXAS

Fort
Lancaster

Fort Garland

Fort Union

Taos

Fort Marcy
Santa Fe

Las
Vegas

Pecos River

Fort
Stockton

Rio Grande

Fort Fauntleroy

Albuquerque

Socorro

Fort
Stanton

Fort
Davis

Fort Defiance

Fort Craig

Santa Barbara
Fort Thorn

San Diego
Doña Ana
Fort Fillmore

El Paso
Fort Bliss

Fort Quitman

NEW MEXICO

Pinos
Altos

Mesilla
Picacho

El Paso
del Norte

CHIHUAHUA

Chihuahua

Gila River

Fort Breckinridge

Fort McLane

Fort
Buchanan

MEXICO

Tucson

ARIZONA

Tubac

Ures

SONORA

Hermosillo

Guaymas

COAHUILA

GULF OF
CALIFORNIA

BAJA
CALIFORNIA

Fort Yuma

Los Angeles

PACIFIC
OCEAN

100 miles

Map by Carol Cooperrider

the horns in taking to his brigade those ordnance supplies which he deemed indispensable and which could be spared by the department. He obviously had overstepped his authority, but he justified his action on the grounds that to have awaited the return of a responsible officer would have incurred an indefinite delay which would have paralyzed his command for the winter.

The first company to join Sibley, subsequently designated Company A, Fourth Texas Cavalry, was commanded by William P. Hardeman and was composed of men from Guadalupe and Caldwell counties. On August 27, 1861, this unit, as was to be the case with all others of the brigade, was sworn into Confederate service "for the war." The following day Captain A. J. Scarborough's company — styled the "Davis Rifles" — was mustered in as Company B. By September 20 the Fourth Regiment had attained its full complement of ten companies. Its commander, Colonel James Reily, was originally from Ohio, but had moved to Texas in 1836 or 1837 and had become a prominent citizen. He was described as the beau ideal of a gentleman and officer, and in looks and actions the very counterpart of Robert E. Lee. Shortly after its organization the Fourth moved from the camp first established by Captain Hardeman on León Creek to Camp Sibley, which was situated on the west bank of Salado Creek six miles from San Antonio on the Austin road.

Colonel Thomas Green began organizing the Fifth Texas Cavalry Regiment at Camp Manassas on Salado Creek two miles above the Fourth. The first unit to join him was Captain John S. Shropshire's company from Colorado County. "Daddy" Green, as the Colonel was affectionately called, was born in Virginia in 1814. He graduated from the University of Tennessee and from Princeton College, and was admitted to the bar in 1835. The next year, at the age of twenty-one, he joined the Texan revolutionary army to fight his first battle at San Jacinto. In 1841 he became clerk of the Supreme Court of Texas. As a captain in the War with Mexico, his daring aggressiveness during the battle of Monterey won him commendation as a soldier and a leader. When the War for Southern Independence broke out, he resigned his position as Supreme Court clerk to join the Confederate army.

On October 4, 1861, Captain Powhatan Jordan's company from Bexar County was mustered in as Company A of the Seventh Texas Cavalry, then under Colonel William Steele. Four days later Captain Gustav Hoffmann's company of Germans from New Braunfels was sworn in. Finally, on October 26, the tenth company of the Seventh was mustered in, thus completing the ranks of the Sibley Brigade. Colonel Steele was born in Albany, New York, and had graduated from the United States Military Academy in 1840. Like Sibley, he had served with the Second Dragoons. During the Mexican War he earned the brevet of captain for bravery in the battles of Contreras and Churubusco. Later he was stationed in

New Mexico, Kansas, Dakota, and Nebraska. He resigned his commission in the United States army on May 30, 1861, at Fort Scott, Kansas, in order to join the Confederacy. Steele set up Camp Pickett, several miles above the Fifth, on Salado Creek for the training of his regiment.

The Fourth, Fifth, and Seventh Regiments, Texas Cavalry (or Mounted Volunteers) were generally referred to by the men as the First, Second, and Third Regiments, respectively, of the Sibley Brigade. In this account, however, the regiments will be designated by their official numbers to avoid confusion. Each regiment consisted of approximately nine hundred men, thus making a total of some twenty-seven hundred for the whole brigade. Although classed as cavalry, the three regiments were really mounted infantry (dragoons). Sibley appointed all the field officers, but the men themselves elected their own company officers. Each company had one captain and, in general, one first lieutenant, two second lieutenants, four sergeants, and four corporals. A number of companies had additional personnel such as buglers, blacksmiths, and farriers. At the time of the first muster the average size of the companies was about 80 officers and men, though the range ran from as low as 56 to as high as 112. After this first muster and before the regiments left for the West, a considerable number of new recruits were added to the various companies. Each soldier was expected to furnish his own horse, horse equipment, and weapons. Those who were unable to do so were supplied by "public and private subscriptions."

The rolling country northeast of San Antonio echoed with shouts and commands as the eager recruits received instruction in the art of war. The training program called for drilling as infantry in the morning and as cavalry in the afternoon. There were "'roll calls' by morning and by night, as also 'tattoo' and 'reveille' according to the forms prescribed on page 2299 of the revised edition of the military statutes."[6] In addition, a stringent guard duty was maintained night and day. Winfield Scott's *Infantry-Tactics* and W. J. Hardee's *Rifle and Light Infantry Tactics* were "consulted on all occasions, as well as was the country's good, in disciplining the 'Saplings' who by reasons of their zeal were easily 'bended.'"[7] Within a short time, Sibley's raw recruits began to be transformed into reliable soldiers.

Although the men were to have supplied their own weapons, practically every company reported a shortage. In an effort to solve this problem, Sibley utilized the credit of the Confederate government to buy firearms on the open market. As a result, the brigade came to be armed with practically every type of small arm in existence: squirrel guns, bear guns, sportsman's guns, single and double-barreled shotguns, navy revolvers, six-shooters, Minié muskets, common rifles, and many others. Few armies have ever had a more motley collection of weapons. In addition to the small arms, there was a battery of four mountain howitzers, attached to the Fourth Regiment under the command of Lieutenant John Reily (Colonel Reily's son), which was serviced by a detachment of men drawn from the different companies of the regiment. A battery of four others was attached to the Fifth Regiment under Lieutenant William S. Wood and manned in the same manner as Reily's. Green's regiment had two companies (B and G), captained by Willis L. Lang and Jerome B. McCown respectively, which were armed with lances and six-shooters. The picturesque lancers, who were Sibley's pride and joy, bore weapons that consisted of three-by-twelve-inch blades mounted on nine-foot shafts that also boasted eight-by-seventeen-inch red pennants.

The soldiers' "uniforms," particularly those of the enlisted men, were of a nondescript nature. Most wore only the civilian clothes they had brought with them. With winter weather approaching, Sibley and his regimental officers addressed pleas to the citizens of Texas to contribute warm clothing and blankets for the brigade's needy. In San Antonio the Ladies' Southern Aid Society was instrumental in collecting a large amount of blankets, comforters, quilts, flannel shirts, socks, drawers, and other items, as well as some cash. Several planters of the area donated one to two bales of cotton, from which the sales proceeds were used to purchase needed goods. The quartermaster apparently issued some equipment, for a member of the Fifth Regiment related that he was given a full military uniform, which included a haversack, pants, drawers, pantaloon boots, and a broadcloth coat with brass buttons. It is quite probable that these were goods which the state of Texas had acquired from the Federal quartermaster depots when General Twiggs surrendered the department.

On October 21, 1861, a grand brigade review was held, with Sibley's daughter presenting a battle flag to a company of lancers. Though the Seventh Regiment had not quite reached its quota, it would do so shortly. The first two regiments had completed their training—brief as it was—and Sibley now felt it was time to begin the march to Fort Bliss.

"A finer brigade of men and horses I do not believe can be found in the Confederate army," boasted a correspondent of the Houston *Telegraph*. "Most of the men . . . have entered the service for the war, not for pay, but for love of country."[8] Another later observed that the brigade "is composed of what is probably the best material for an army that the world affords. That distinct type of mankind, the south-western frontiersman, inured to all hardships, of indomitable energy, familliar [sic] with the use of fire-arms, at home on horseback, and fired with the love of country and for the redress of wrongs. There is no conflict which they would not undertake, and none can occur on these lines in which they will not be perfectly successful."[9]

Early on the morning of October 22, 1861, "boots and saddles," followed in fifteen minutes by "assembly," broke forth loud and clear upon the crisp, cool air of Camp Sibley. In a matter of moments the Fourth Regiment was saddled and formed in a solid square. At the command "Attention!" silence reigned supreme, and Colonel Reily commenced addressing some thought-provoking remarks to his troops. They were on the eve of leaving a land that many might never see again, he observed, for on this day they were bidding farewell to family and friends to try their fortunes on the field of battle in defense of their country's honor. The people of Texas and the nation expected much from them, and he expressed confidence that their valor would not prove disappointing.

At the close of his remarks, Reily removed his hat, requesting all to do likewise. He then read an inspirational prayer written by Alexander Gregg, Episcopal bishop of Texas. So eloquent was the delivery that "everyone was moved to tears and solemn thoughts."[10] The San Antonio *Herald* boasted, "This is the spirit with which to go into battle, and we are glad to witness it among our troops."[11] In a few seconds the meditative mood was shattered by the command, "By fours from the right, march!"

For the first few miles everyone was silent. Many were thinking of home and loved ones, while others were inspired by the martial display their lines made as they mounted and descended the hills on the road leading to San Antonio. The regiment had no band to enliven the occasion, but as the troops drew near the city, they started singing the stirring strains of *The Texas Ranger.* "Such music . . .," recalled a participant, "will ne'er be heard again, as was heard by the rocks and rills in the environs of San Antonio that morning."[12]

At one o'clock the Fourth rode into the main plaza of the city and again formed a solid column. At this time the Nacogdoches company presented Colonel Reily with a handsome battle flag as a compliment from his old friends of that county. Reily made another short, vigorous speech, but the cheering of those in front prevented the rear ranks from hearing much more than, "Fellow Soldiers!" General Sibley came forward afterward and, in a few unguarded remarks, convinced all that he was no orator. Even so, his brief address displayed much originality and determination. One soldier suggested that had his horse stopped prancing, the general would have had a much better opportunity to display his oratorical abilities. Proudly Sibley told his men that though they were still green saplings bending to discipline, they would make the best soldiers in the world. On bidding the regiment "adieu," he received three rousing cheers. With drums beating and flags flying, the gallant force filed from the plaza—"every man, from the General downwards, confident of victory."[13]

After leaving San Antonio, the Fourth marched about seven miles before encamping near León Creek. While the men remained idle the next day, the regimental staff completed final arrangements for the long march ahead. Since water at many of the springs along the way was inadequate for large groups at a time, it was deemed necessary to divide the regiment into three sections which would march a day apart. Captain Hardeman set out with the first squadron (Companies A, F, and Reily's battery), followed the next day by Lieutenant Colonel William R. Scurry's (B, D, G, and H), and finally by the third section (C, E, I, K) led by Colonel Reily himself.

The main road to Fort Bliss, consisting of almost seven hundred miles of hardly more than wagon ruts, passed through vast, rolling plains, bleak and inhospitable deserts, and rugged mountains. Most of the route lay within the realm of hostile Indians. In addition to the long wagon train,[14] the regiment carried along its own beef herd. Daily travel, of course, would be limited by how far the beeves could be driven, and by the distances between water holes.

Meanwhile Colonel Baylor wrote Sibley on October 25 that Canby was preparing to launch an offensive into the Mesilla Valley with an army of twenty-five hundred men. His force being too small to offer effective resistance, Baylor warned that unless Sibley's regiments arrived soon, he would be compelled to evacuate. In fact he had already completed arrangements for shipping his supplies and equipment to the safety of Fort Quitman. He also ordered large quantities of corn sent to Fort Davis, not only for the use of Sibley's troops when they passed by, but for his own men should they fall back that far.

Baylor reported, in addition to this impending threat from the north, that a Federal army commanded by General Edwin V. Sumner had landed at Guaymas, Sonora, and was now en route across northern Mexico to join Canby at Mesilla. To verify this report, he had sent spies out along the road over which such a force would have to travel. He also dispelled any false notions Sibley might have entertained in regard to the cooperation or, at least, the passiveness of the natives. The Mexicans, he pointed out, were decidedly Northern in sentiment, and would "avail themselves of the first opportunity to rob us or join the enemy. Nothing but a strong force will keep them quiet."[15]

Colonel Reily was encamped at Fort Clark when the express arrived with news of Baylor's plight and his plea for reinforcements. Anxiously the Colonel ordered his three sections to set out on "double quick time." Sibley received Baylor's communication in San Antonio the same day his Fifth Regiment left Camp Manassas for the West. The General was pleased to learn of Canby's intended advance, for earlier he had advised Baylor to make a threatening demonstration against Fort Craig to entice the Federals to pursue him. With the enemy lured from the safety of his fortress, and with the timely arrival of his brigade, Sibley planned to destroy or capture the bulk of the Union army with one stroke. The plan sounded feasible, but could his regiments reach the Mesilla Valley before Canby?

At eleven o'clock on the morning of November 7, Green's Fifth Regiment filed from Camp Manassas. As the troops passed through San Antonio, the ladies of the city waved their white handkerchiefs as if to say, "Brave boys, victory awaits you."[16] Early on the morning of November 10, after having encamped for two days on León Creek, the regiment started for Fort Bliss. From his carriage on a hill a short distance away, Sibley reviewed the troops. "The whole regiment shouldered arms and marched by in regular order," whereupon "The old Gen. pulled off his hat and gave them a general salute."[17]

It seems incredible that during this romantic age—particularly in horse-conscious Texas—that a general would review his soldiers from a carriage and not from a horse. This, as well as other evidence, indicates that Sibley was suffering from ill health. Such being the case, a shadow was already cast over the future operations of the New Mexican campaign. Certainly an ailing general cannot make decisions as accurately or inspire confidence in his men as surely as can one who is healthy and robust.

That night the Fifth stopped about five miles east of Castroville at a place where the men could obtain water from a pond. The following morning the regiment passed through Castroville, and encamped that evening near an "old Dutchman's" who had a good well of water. As the troops marched through D'Hanis the next day, old Mexican women ran to the road with butter, eggs, chickens, watermelons, and other items, but no one bought anything. On reaching the Frío River—six miles east of Uvalde—on November 14, the ammunition guards received orders to load their guns. This was the beginning of hostile Indian country and would continue to be, almost to the very limits of Fort Bliss.

As is the case with virtually all military units, the Fifth had its share of disciplinary problems. It was particularly difficult for Texans—products of the frontier as they were—to yield completely to military regimentation. Nevertheless, discipline must be maintained if an army is to function at its best, and examples must be made of offenders. While the regiment remained in camp, several days after passing by Uvalde, a private who had struck Captain Ira G. Killough was court-martialed and sentenced to wear heavy irons for one month. While on the march he was to be tied to the end of a baggage wagon and forced to walk. This was a humiliating and severe punishment, for the horse-riding Texans seldom walked any great distance. A few days later another general court-martial was held for three men who had been found sleeping on sentry duty. Each was condemned to close confinement on bread and water for ten days, but the sentences were later remitted.

As the Fifth passed by Fort Clark, a large number of the regimental sick were left at the post hospital. One day later Green arrived at San Felipe Springs, near present-day Del Río. While resting at the springs, some of the soldiers went hunting or fishing, others went to visit Mexico (the Río Grande was only four miles from camp), while others washed their dirty clothes, or just relaxed. Up to this time Green's men had marched in a body, but from San Felipe Springs on, the regiment would move in three squadrons just as had the Fourth. Major Lockridge set out with the first group on November 22, to be followed in one and two days by the others.

With two regiments on the road and the other preparing to leave shortly, Sibley decided that the time had come for him and his staff to set out for Fort Bliss. Leaving San Antonio on November 18, they could make the journey in a fraction of the time the regiments could, encumbered as the latter were by large numbers and slow-moving baggage wagons and herds. The General passed by the three sections of the Fifth at San Felipe Springs and beyond. As he approached Fort Lancaster on November 28 the lieutenant commanding that post had his company appear in dress uniform to pay him full military honors. Sibley was so impressed that he personally took charge of the company to see how well it was drilled. The sergeant "was on the right, marching by two's; the command was given by the Gen'l, 'file left,' which was . . . unheard, and on they went at a brisk trot," ascending a nearby mountain. As they disappeared Sibley turned around muttering, "Gone to Hell!" In the evening the company returned to find that the "General had gone on his way rejoicing to New Mexico."[18]

On December 14, 1861, General Sibley, having established his temporary headquarters at Fort Bliss, assumed command of all Confederate forces in Texas at and above Fort Quitman and in the Territories of Arizona and New Mexico. This included his own brigade of three regiments and Baylor's command (now under the immediate command of Major Charles L. Pyron) which included the following units (and possibly one or two others): four companies (A, B, D, E) of the Second Regiment Texas Mounted Rifles, Captain Trevanion T. Teel's Light Company B, First Regiment Texas Artillery, and five companies of locally recruited volunteers (Captain Bethel Coopwood's "San Elizario Spy Company," Captain George M. Frazer's "Arizona Rangers," Captain John Phillips' "Brigands," Captain Thomas Helm's "Arizona Guards," and Captain Sherod Hunter's company of Arizona volunteers. Sibley designated the troops under his command the "Army of New Mexico."

Although the General declared martial law throughout his jurisdiction, he did not intend to supersede the authority of Colonel Baylor. To be sure, Sibley had taken charge of all troops, but Baylor was to continue exercising the functions of civil and military governor of Arizona.

On December 20 Sibley issued a proclamation designed to acquaint the people of New Mexico with his aims, as well as with the benefits to be derived by becoming a part of the Confederacy. He declared that his army was entering New Mexico to take possession of the territory for the Confederacy. This was but just, since by geographical position, by similarity of institutions, and by commercial interest, New Mexico's destiny lay with the South. He pointed out that the present war waged by the North to subjugate and oppress the Southern people had already failed. As evidence he cited the battles of Manassas, Springfield, Lexington, Leesburg, and the capture of the Mesilla Valley.

The General informed the natives that he and his army were coming as friends to throw off the yoke of Northern military despotism. Indeed, as soon as he had secured the territory, he promised to establish a new government composed of the country's leading men — a government devoted to reestablishing and preserving the people's religious, civil, and political liberties. In a further effort to insure native support, Sibley formally abolished the United States law levying taxes upon the citizens of New Mexico.

Sibley made it clear that he was making war only upon the Union army and, as such, he expected the people to continue their peaceful pursuits. He personally guaranteed life and property and promised to pay fair prices for all forage and supplies his army might need while in New Mexico. Realizing that many natives had been forced into the Union army, Sibley exhorted them to throw down their arms on his approach. He warned that those who refused to do so, or those who destroyed supplies to prevent his use of them, would feel the wrath of his army.

Sibley implored his old comrades in arms still in Federal service to renounce their allegiance and join the "colors of justice and freedom!" They could do this without loss of honor, he reasoned, for they had never entered the service of one part of the old Union to fight against another. To those who accepted, he promised (officers as well as enlisted men) equivalent ranks in his army. "In the sight of God and man," the General pleaded, "you are justified in renouncing a service iniquitous in itself and in which you never engaged."[19]

Confederate agents distributed copies of the proclamation, printed in both Spanish and English, throughout the villages of New Mexico. According to the governor of the territory, however, Unionist citizens gathered them up and delivered them to the military commander before they could be disseminated. The governor scoffingly averred that, even if circulated, Sibley's proclamation would have no effect.

It seems appropriate at this point to complete the description of the march Sibley's men made to Fort Bliss. Typical of all were the experiences of the second squadron of the Fifth Regiment. This unit left San Felipe Springs on November 23 and by noon had reached the Devils River. "This is a most revolting name," observed one soldier, "to call a stream of the best water on the route between"[20] San Antonio and El Paso. The road from this point northward to Beaver Lake followed the course of the river closely. The extremely rugged, rocky, and hilly terrain came down almost to the water's edge, making it necessary to cross and recross the river as many as six times in one day. Though the road may have been close to water, the dust kicked up by the horses, wagons, and herd was stifling. From Camp Hudson the squadron moved on to encamp near Beaver Lake, a body of water formed by the Devils River.

After preparing a two-days' ration of bread and beef, the men set out in a northwesterly direction. The command did not reach a spring that night, so it was necessary to make a dry camp (i.e., one without water). At daylight the next day, the squadron set out briskly and thirstily, and by one o'clock had reached Howard Spring. Since the spring was about twelve feet deep, the water had to be brought to the surface in buckets. Being such a slow and tedious operation, only the soldiers and their horses received water — the draft and beef animals had to do without. From Howard Spring the squadron traveled over more rugged hills and rocky terrain. Though they had to make another dry camp, they were rewarded the following day on reaching the refreshing waters of Live Oak Creek. After a day's layover near Fort Lancaster, the men continued on to the Pecos River and, for two days, followed its course upstream. The horses were very fond of the salty water of the Pecos, but as far as the soldiers were concerned, it was fit only for making coffee. Wood was scarce, the weather was cold, the road was rocky and dusty, and by now the squadron's food consisted solely of beef and wormy crackers. Could life be more miserable? No doubt the men echoed the feelings of a member of the Fourth Regiment who had commented earlier: "When I go to another war, I'm goin' to it a way I can get to it quicker than I can this 'ere one."[21]

The road at last turned westward from the Pecos, along Escondido Creek, and the squadron reached Escondido Springs, where wood and good water were plentiful. The following day, December 7, the men arrived at Fort Stockton. It was now exactly a month since the Fifth Regiment had moved from Camp Manassas. Fort Stockton was about 399 miles from San Antonio, and in the neighborhood of 300 more to Fort Bliss. Since the next day was Sunday, the command, as was customary, remained in camp while many attended the "preaching."

The squadron's provisions were now all but exhausted, and the supply train was seventy or so miles ahead at or near Fort Davis. Leaving Fort Stockton, the command marched due west to León Holes, and then southwesterly until reaching water again at Barrilla Springs. The country had become mountainous, for the road was entering the Davis Range. On December 12 the men camped on Límpia Creek and were met by provision wagons sent to their relief. Wood and water abounded here, and the soldiers got "'sop & biscuit' which eats 'tremendous well.'"[22] The trail followed Límpia Creek through Wild Rose Canyon — some of the most beautiful country of Texas. On December 15 the squadron arrived at Fort Davis, a post established in 1854 and named in honor of the then secretary of war, Jefferson Davis. There was a sutler at the post, and many of the soldiers got "tight" and bought new suits of clothes. Since the fort was situated in a mountain fastness, it was deemed necessary to break the squadron up into companies to facilitate moving through the passes. From the Davis Mountains the companies marched through scenic foothills, passing by Barrel Springs and Dead Man's Hole. Instead of continuing on the regular stage road leading to Van Horn's Wells, the troops followed a new trail—probably because the grass was better—from Dead Man's Hole to the Río Grande. The principal water holes along this route were named Brigade Springs (where the squadron was reunited), which was eight miles from Dead Man's Hole, and Sibley Springs, which was about forty-five miles beyond Brigade Springs (the new trail and the two springs are only approximated on the accompanying map). Although this new trail proved to be exceedingly rough, the wonders of nature abounded, and many were thrilled by the sight of mustangs and other wild animals grazing in the meadows.

Christmas day proved no different from any other. After eating a breakfast of biscuits, coffee, and poor beef, the men marched a distance of fifteen miles. Two days later they arrived at Fort Quitman, located several hundred yards from the Río Grande.[23] The worst of the march was over, for Fort Bliss was only about eighty miles up the valley. Since Mexico was so near, the officers read their men the articles of war and constantly maintained a strong guard.

As the squadron moved northward toward Fort Bliss, the men noted that the unhealthy river water was giving their horses "scours." On New Year's day the breakfast was not much of an improvement over that of Christmas: beef, biscuits, curshaw, and coffee without sugar. Two days later the three sections of the Fifth Regiment were reunited at last at Fort Bliss. The arduous march from San Antonio had taken slightly less than two months.

The Fourth Regiment had arrived about two weeks in advance of the Fifth and was now encamped twenty-five miles north of Fort Bliss at Willow Bar in Arizona. On Christmas morning Colonel Reily temporarily turned over command of his regiment to Captain A. J. Scarborough, since of the officers present he was the next in rank. Reily then called his troops into line to bid them "adieu," for Sibley had selected him for a special diplomatic mission. The republic of Mexico at this time was torn by internal disorders complicated by the intervention of England, Spain, and France. The authority of the national government had consequently declined appreciably, allowing many state governors to rule virtually autonomously. Realizing this, Sibley dispatched Colonel Reily as his personal representative to the neighboring border states of Chihuahua and Sonora. Reily's instructions specifically embodied the following: (1) He was to learn if the national government of Mexico had signed an agreement allowing United States troops to cross her northern frontier to attack the Confederacy. If this was true, the Colonel was to inquire as to what actions the two governors would take should the North take advantage of the agreement. (2) Since hostile Apaches after raiding in one country generally took refuge in the other to avoid capture, Reily was to suggest an accord allowing the forces of each nation to cross the international border while in "hot pursuit" of such Indians. (3) He was to ask the governors to confirm the right of Southern agents to buy supplies in their respective states. (4) From the governor of Sonora he was to request the additional privilege of establishing a Confederate depot at the port of Guaymas with the right of transit through Sonoran territory to Arizona.

Reily received a cordial welcome in Chihuahua, but in Sonora — dangerously close to Unionist-held California — he was accepted with far less enthusiasm. Both Mexican executives appear to have been skilled in the art of diplomacy. While appearing to be friends of the Southern cause, neither made any actual concessions. Although Reily boasted that he had achieved complete success, the only thing he received from the governors was confirmation of the right of Confederate agents to buy supplies in their respective states.

Two of Sibley's regiments had now safely made the march from San Antonio. With a battalion of the Seventh only ten days behind, he issued the following congratulatory proclamation to his men:

GENERAL ORDER——No. 2
Head-quarters Army of N. M.
Ft. Bliss, Tex., Jan. 9th, 1862.

The General Commanding expresses to the Troops under his command, his high appreciation of the patience, fortitude, and good conduct, with which, in spite of great deficences [sic] in their supplies, they have made a successful and rapid march of seven hundred miles in mid winter, and through a country entirely devoid of resources.

The General congratulates his troops upon the prospect of early and important services, for the successful accomplishment of which, their past conduct is an ample guarantee; and he is assured that he will never be disappointed in his early boast, that "We could go any where, and do any thing."

By order of
Brig. Gen. H. H. Sibley.
Tom. P. Ochiltree, A. de C. & A. A. At. Gen., A. N. M.[24]

A correspondent of the New Orleans *Picayune,* after describing the great difficulties encountered on the long march, pointedly asked, "Is not this enough in itself to make veterans of men?"[25]

SIBLEY'S NEW MEXICO CAMPAIGN

Sibley now ordered the units of the Army of New Mexico to rendezvous at old Fort Thorn, preparatory to launching the offensive. This post, located on the Río Grande about forty miles north of Mesilla and about ninety south of Fort Craig, had been abandoned in 1859 because of the prevalence of sickness there. The shortest route to Fort Craig from the Mesilla Valley was by way of the ninety-mile stretch of desert, the Jornada del Muerto. But with so many animals accompanying his army, Sibley deemed it far wiser to take the longer river road where water would always be available.

The Fourth Regiment, already in the Mesilla Valley, arrived first at Fort Thorn and set up camp above the post on the east side of the Río Grande. After about a week's rest and recuperation at Fort Bliss, the Fifth set out. As Green's men passed through Las Cruces, Colonel Baylor reviewed them to the accompaniment of martial music supplied by the Second Regiment's brass band. The Fifth reached Fort Thorn on January 17 and encamped nearly opposite the post about two and a half miles below the Fourth. Four days later Sibley and his staff arrived.

While awaiting the remaining units of the invasion force, Sibley and his staff checked last-minute strategic details concerning the movement against Fort Craig. Sibley confidently believed this post would easily fall before the might of his Texans. Once the impediment was removed, he felt certain the rest of New Mexico could be occupied without serious opposition. To determine the best method of attack, he dispatched a spy company of fifty men to reconnoiter the area about the fort.

After a stay of twelve days, the Fifth received orders to move farther up the river, presumably in preparation for leading the advance, as well as to find better grazing for the livestock. Though it was bitterly cold, the morning of January 29 dawned beautifully over the Confederate encampments. The distant mountains, whitened by snow, presented a picturesque scene which most of the cold-ridden troops failed to appreciate. After leaving behind one company heavily afflicted with pneumonia, the Fifth marched up river about twenty miles and encamped. Many took advantage of the subsequent lull in activity to wash their clothes in the frigid river, or to take their horses out to graze. Others were "complaining, some sick, some cooking, some cursing the army, some cursing the Confederacy, some playing cards, some hunting, while others . . . [were] reading their Bibles."[26] Green enforced a strict routine; roll call was at four o'clock in the morning, retreat came at sundown, followed by another roll call at eight o'clock at night.

On February 4 the first five companies of the Seventh Regiment, commanded by Lieutenant Colonel John S. Sutton, arrived at Fort Thorn. The other three were reported to be some three hundred miles behind.[27] Accompanying the battalion was a sutler's train. Sibley allowed the merchants to display their goods within the confines of Fort Thorn. Their stock consisted of a large variety of liquors, many kinds of preserved fruits, candy, tobacco, pipes, and on an average of one pair of pants to every ten men in the Fourth Regiment, for which unit alone they were appointed.

From Fort Thorn Sibley ordered Captain Sherod Hunter's independent company, which was attached to Pyron's (formerly Baylor's) command, to take post at Tucson. The General was anxious to protect western Arizona, not only because its citizens were pro-Southern, but also because that region was important in mineral deposits. From Tucson the Confederates could open communications with southern California, the bulk of whose citizens Sibley believed to be in sympathy with the Confederacy. Hunter made the 280-mile march as rapidly as possible, reaching Tucson on February 28. His timely arrival was hailed by a majority of the citizens, if not the entire population of the town.

Sibley was now ready to move up the Río Grande to launch his long-awaited New Mexican campaign.

By now some of Sibley's weaknesses as a general and as a strategist had begun to manifest themselves. The task of commanding such a large number of men and the problems arising from conducting a campaign hundreds of miles from a base of supply demanded a man of greater talent and foresight. Even by romantic standards, the General appears to have been a dreamer— "too prone to let the morrow take care of itself,"[28] as one of his officers wrote in later years. Not only did Sibley apparently suffer from poor health, but he was also a heavy drinker. There are indications that his efficiency as a commander was hindered both by a lack of physical strength and by overindulgence.

Sibley had hoped to reach New Mexico early in the fall, but the first week of February found him at Fort Thorn with only two and a half regiments of poorly armed, badly clothed, and ill fed men. As one soldier described it, "Forage, there was none; commissary supplies were getting scarce; the cold season was coming; clothing was being needed; all of which the country afforded none."[29]

The weakest point in Sibley's strategy was in regard to logistics. That the New Mexican campaign would be self-sustaining was, of course, a prime feature of his plan. So certain was he that adequate supplies would be obtained in the West that he purposely dispatched his regiments from San Antonio with only enough provisions to subsist them en route.

Several factors accounted for Sibley's overconfidence. While his brigade was being formed, he had contracted with Judge Crosby[30] and Simeon Hart to purchase commissary items from Mexico. These foodstuffs, he thought, plus what the Mesilla and Río Grande valleys produced, would surely prove adequate until he moved into New Mexico proper.

When Sibley reached Fort Bliss he learned to his dismay that Baylor's men had consumed practically all available goods in the immediate area. But worst of all, Hart and Crosby had failed to amass adequate supplies from Mexico. Though foodstuffs and other items were plentiful, particularly in Sonora, the Mexicans refused to sell anything for Confederate scrip. Since Sibley did not have a dollar of specie in his quartermaster, he was unable to buy. Even the natives on this side of the Río Grande were reluctant to accept anything but hard money. The credit of the Confederate government in the Far West, at least, was almost nonexistent. It seems surprising, indeed, that Sibley was not aware of this situation before departing from San Antonio.

If supplies were scarce in the south, Sibley undoubtedly felt that New Mexico proper would provide all his needs. This was particularly true in regard to war matériel. Though he had tried to arm his brigade better, he was not overly concerned by his failure to do so. Greatly underrating the Union army in New Mexico, Sibley confidently expected to move into the territory and, with little or no resistance, take possession of all its garrisons, forts, and supply depots. The General had failed to realize that perhaps before the arrival of his Confederate forces a vigorous Union commander might have called up additional troops and greatly strengthened his position. A more able general would have paid far more attention to any changes in the military setup of his enemy. But of such matters, Sibley was apparently not unduly worried. Viewed from today's perspective, the New Mexican campaign was at best a romantic gamble—victory or disaster lay uneasily in the hands of fate.

Of more practical concern to Sibley was the fact that smallpox and pneumonia were daily thinning the ranks of his army. Smallpox had broken out among Baylor's troops several weeks before the arrival of Sibley's regiments, and hasty efforts were made to vaccinate all who had not yet contracted the disease.[31] Winter weather and lack of warm clothing and blankets accounted for the large number of pneumonia cases. Before leaving for Fort Thorn, Sibley was compelled to establish a general hospital at Doña Ana.

Lack of discipline was another source of worry for the commander of the Army of New Mexico. The individualism that had always characterized the frontier made it difficult for Sibley's troops to submit completely to authority. This was particularly evident when units of the brigade were in the Mesilla Valley. While it was Sibley's policy to treat the natives with kindness and justice, many soldiers acted otherwise. Although the men had orders not to graze their horses in the green Mexican wheat fields, hundreds did so anyway. The excuse generally was "My horse got loose and I could not find him."[32] A reprimand would follow, often with a day or two extra duty, but this did not compensate the Mexicans whose fields had been damaged. To protect themselves against the bitingly cold weather, many soldiers forcibly moved into the Mexicans' adobe homes, crowding the family into one room or driving them out altogether. Since the Texans were short of supplies, they stole practically everything they could lay their hands on. According to one Union correspondent, females, either in or out of their homes, were not safe. A Confederate soldier maintained in later years, however, that the women were "appropriated" only with their consent. At any rate, the behavior of the troops enraged the whole native population and caused intense feelings of hostility. Had the brigade been adequately supplied and better disciplined such a situation would never have come about. Needless to say, a poorly disciplined army is not as effective in battle.

While the Texans were concentrating at Fort Thorn, hostile Apaches came to be a real menace. Heavy escorts were necessary for grazing livestock lest the Indians drive the animals off. Small detachments were often attacked with the resultant loss of invaluable supplies. One band of Indians only about three miles from Fort Thorn set fires which burned the grass down to the river opposite the post. "The mountains here are full of Indians," wrote one soldier, "and we dread them worse than we do the Lincolnites, by odds."[33]

The Indians committing these acts were in no way in league with the Union forces. The Apaches were at war with all white men, whether they were Union, Confederate, or civilian. Indeed, the Federals were also feeling the ravages of Indians, particularly the Navajos. Later on, Sibley, in an effort to reduce the menace, encouraged private forays against them, and legalized the enslavement of captives.

While the Confederates might be having troubles, spies brought news that the Federals were, also. One report told of a mutiny of a New Mexican volunteer company, and the subsequent desertion of several others. Miguel Otero reportedly had declared for the South, and large numbers of New Mexicans were flocking to his banner. A Federal lieutenant who had deserted his company at Fort Craig related that the 1,400 New Mexican volunteers Canby had at that post were highly demoralized and did not want to fight. Though many of the stories which came to Confederate ears were exaggerated, or even false, it was reassuring, cheering news.

When the Confederate rank and file learned that Canby was filling his army with natives, the old Texan enmity of Mexicans became manifest. Here was perhaps another, though latent, motive for the New Mexican campaign — retaliation for the treatment received by the members of the Texan Santa Fé Expedition of 1841. One soldier bitterly observed that "We did not care to fight the New Mexicans, but they have dared to raise their arms against us, and far off we can hear the wailing cry of anguish from the dungeons of Perote. It comes from the Texan prisoners placed there by the treachery and wiles of these New Mexicans. Even on our march we can see the 'footprints of blood' left upon this long and weary road by the Santa Fé prisoners. Those who have read the stirring history of these wrongs by the able pen of Kendall, can easily appreciate the feelings of Texans who find the same men in arms against us. They will call upon their patron saints in piteous tones to save them from the just indignation and vengeance of the 'Tejanos.'"[34] Lieutenant Colonel Sutton of the Seventh Regiment had been a captain on that ill-fated adventure, and within him, no doubt, burned the fire of retribution.

Regardless of the suffering caused by lack of adequate food supplies, morale appeared to be high among Sibley's men. If a correspondent's glowing account is reliable, the General had captured the imagination of his men: "Gen. Sibley manages this army of Texans as if they were his old '2d Dragoons.' They all love him, and have every confidence in his bravery, prudence and capability. Wherever he wills they should go, even into 'The mouth of Hell or the jaws of Death,' would they go willingly, merrily singing, 'Ours not to reason why, Ours but to do or die.'"[35] From this description it appeared a certainty that the Army of New Mexico would prove invincible.

3

General Canby Prepares
To Meet the Confederate Threat

Major Lynde's surrender of July 27, 1861, resulting in the loss of the southern part of the Territory of New Mexico as well as a large number of regulars, was a severe blow which made Colonel Canby's position more difficult than ever. Even at this late date, in July, the departmental commander did not know for certain whether the Union government intended to hold, or to abandon New Mexico. But until he was informed definitely, he acted on the assumption that the high command did plan to retain the territory, and so exerted even greater efforts to overcome the damage wrought by Lynde's action. Fort Union, located in the northeastern part of the territory, was moved from its old position under a mesa and rebuilt as a strong fortification with bomb-proof quarters about a mile out in the valley. Fort Craig, situated on the Río Grande about 100 miles south of Albuquerque and some 117 north of Mesilla (by way of the Jornada), was greatly strengthened by the throwing up of earthworks. Because of the strategic locations of these two posts, Canby considered them to be the keys for any contemplated future defensive or offensive operations within his department.[1]

One of Canby's chief problems was that of securing adequate quantities of vital war matériel. The department's annual supply of ordnance had not arrived, nor had he heard from the government in regard to its disposition. On August 16 he wrote the general in chief again about this matter, for there was not enough artillery to arm a single post properly and, except for small arms, ammunition was exceedingly limited. Canby's quartermaster had been unsuccessful in obtaining cavalry remounts or even draft animals for supply wagons. The situation was critical. "If it is the intention of the Government to retain this department," the Colonel concluded, "I urgently recommend that the supplies necessary for the efficiency of the troops . . . should be furnished as soon as practicable."[2]

The attitude of the natives north of the Jornada del Muerto continued to be a source of grave concern. Canby still believed that their apathetic disposition would make it virtually impossible to raise an adequate volunteer force from among them. Even if such were accomplished, he contended that no reliance could be placed on such troops unless they were strongly supported by regulars.

The most that could be expected from them, in Canby's opinion, was the garrisoning of two or three fortified points until the government's policy in regard to New Mexico could be "settled and expressed."

The departmental commander was not alone in his skepticism concerning the abilities of the native volunteers. The chief of the Fort Union ordnance depot wrote Canby a letter, copies of which were sent to General John C. Fremont, commander of the Western Department, and the Secretary of War in which he pointed out that "A residence of twelve years among these people enables me to know, and it is the opinion of every well-informed, candid person resident among them, that without the support and protection of the Regular Army of the United States they are entirely unable to protect the ... Territory ... no matter how many there may be or how well armed the New Mexican volunteers are."[3] Ceran St. Vrain, colonel of the First Regiment New Mexico Volunteers, and his second in command, Lieutenant Colonel Christopher "Kit" Carson, not only endorsed this statement, but earlier had written Fremont essentially the same thing. It was their fervent hope that, in the light of reality, the order for the removal of the regular forces from New Mexico would be rescinded.

The War Department had already altered its previous stand several days before the above letter was written. Apparently Captain Wainwright, whom Canby had sent to Washington to explain the situation in New Mexico, had succeeded. In an order dated August 13, the general in chief notified the departmental commander that the regulars were still to be withdrawn from New Mexico, but "at such time and in such manner as will not expose the Territory to conquest or invasion from Texas before the volunteer forces of New Mexico are properly organized, armed, and posted."[4] At last the government's policy in regard to New Mexico had been "settled and expressed."

While Canby was combating problems in New Mexico, not all was well from the Union standpoint in the newly created neighboring Territory of Colorado. Governor William Gilpin wrote Canby that though the results of a recent election showed an overwhelming Union majority, there was nevertheless a strong secession element present. Colorado, like New Mexico, was dependent upon supplies coming from the east over an eight-hundred-mile route — a lifeline now constantly threatened by hostile Indians. For these reasons Gilpin deemed it absolutely essential to raise and maintain an adequate volunteer force for home defense. For the arming of such a body, he asked Canby for all necessary guns and equipment. It was impossible, of course, for Canby to meet this request, as he barely had enough ordnance matériel to equip those volunteer units which had been authorized for his department. He did assure the governor, however, that in the event of a revolt in Colorado, he would dispatch enough guns and equipment to enable the Colorado volunteers to suppress it.

Meanwhile the War Department raised New Mexico's quota of volunteers by two regiments. Canby was greatly chagrined for he did not believe the original quota could be raised, let alone this additional levy. He consequently wrote Governor Gilpin that because of New Mexico's inability to raise sufficient numbers it might become necessary to call upon him to organize four or six companies in Colorado.

The volunteer forces that the War Department stipulated should be raised in New Mexico for terms of three years were to consist of two regiments of infantry and two of cavalry. Canby realized quite early that the cavalry could not be secured for that length of time; so he authorized the mustering in of mounted companies for six months only. As anticipated, the recruiting and organization of the volunteers proceeded slowly. By early September St. Vrain's infantry regiment had been organized, but was still lacking about two hundred men to bring its various companies up to par. Eight companies had been mustered in for the Second Regiment and some four hundred enlistees were still needed. The organization of the two cavalry regiments had just begun, only one company having been sworn in so far. In the hope of meeting the volunteer quota, the governor of New Mexico planned, as a last resort, to call out the militia and "force the people to do what they seem indisposed to do voluntarily."[5]

In mid-November Canby informed the paymaster general again that military operations in New Mexico for several months had been greatly embarrassed, and were now almost entirely paralyzed by the lack of funds. Many of the regulars had not been paid for more than twelve months, and the volunteers not at all. This situation had caused much suffering and some dissatisfaction among both classes of troops. But more important, it had almost effectually put an end to the raising of volunteers—few New Mexicans desiring to serve in the army without pay. Although one attempt to borrow money for the government had failed, Canby reported that a new effort to secure a loan gave hope of being at least partially successful. To insure its success, the chief quartermaster, the chief commissary, and the departmental commander had to promise that the money would be repaid in treasury notes bearing 7.3 per cent interest. Canby requested the paymaster general to make arrangements to redeem this pledge, for in the event of his failure to do so, the Colonel had made himself personally liable for the interest.

Hostile Indians had now increased the frequency of their raids. The Navajos and Mescalero Apaches were the principal offenders, but the Kiowas and Comanches also contributed their share of death and destruction. Because the Navajos were the largest tribe in the northern part of the territory, they were the chief menace. Not all members of this tribe were hostile, and many bands followed a policy of peace. Nevertheless, when retaliatory forays were sent against marauding groups, oftentimes the peaceful members suffered the consequences of the white man's wrath. Canby feared that such indiscriminate treatment would cause even the peaceful Indians to rob and plunder.

Some of the raids, if they were not caused by an unscrupulous group of Mexicans who profited from buying the Indians' plunder, were at least encouraged by these opportunists. Of major importance was the fact that these individuals were not restrained by the moral pressure of the population in general. As long as the marauders found a ready sale for their plunder and captives, Canby believed, it would be impossible to prevent their depredations. He informed the governor of New Mexico that the army's duty of protection involved a reciprocal obligation upon the people, and unless the citizenry denounced the illegal acts of a few vicious individuals and supported the enforcement of the laws, any military action would be futile. Meanwhile the Colonel, assuring the people he would use all means at his disposal to protect them, posted troops at key approaches in the Navajo country in a double effort to restrain hostile Indian bands, as well as to give ample warning of the coming of a raiding party.

In spite of tremendous difficulties, by early December Canby had accomplished near-miracles in the strengthening of New Mexico's military position. In the logistical sphere, his operations continued to be greatly hampered, but supply trains from the east were now nearing Fort Union. In general, his quartermaster and commissary stores were in good condition and, combined with the supplies due to arrive shortly, would be sufficient to meet his needs until new shipments came in the spring. Foodstuffs such as beef, flour, beans, and salt were purchased locally. Most of the horses were too light for cavalry or draft purposes, but fortunately some animals had arrived from the east, and more were expected soon. Ordnance stores were still inadequate, since the annual consignment had been detained at Fort Leavenworth. Canby hoped to alleviate this situation somewhat by buying up as much ammunition as he could from local civilian sources. Scarcity of money to meet the needs of his disbursing officers was still vexing. To alleviate this problem somewhat, Canby suggested that the War Department send small amounts of money at frequent intervals rather than one annual lump sum as was the customary practice.

The regular troops were in excellent condition — well instructed and disciplined, zealous and loyal. The only drawback lay in the lack of officers and recruits to maintain company quotas. In some instances Canby found it necessary to appoint enlisted men as acting commissioned officers. The regulars had the best arms obtainable, the infantry having the Springfield rifled musket, and the cavalry the Harper's Ferry rifle, Colt's navy pistol, Sharp's and Maynard's carbines, and a few Colt revolving rifles for experimental use. The regulars had good uniforms in adequate supply, but the men were ill-equipped in regard to all types of accouterments.

The volunteers, on the other hand, were improving so slowly in discipline and instruction that Canby did not believe they could achieve efficiency "in any reasonable period." As the Colonel put it, "They are deficient in self-reliance and military spirit, and their ignorance of the English language and want of capacity for instruction are serious obstacles to a rapid improvement."[6] Only for Indian or partisan warfare, or for use in conjunction with regulars or volunteers of American origin, did he believe that they might make valuable auxiliaries. Still doubting that New Mexico's quota could be met, Canby suggested that one or two regiments of volunteers from the east be sent to replace the regulars when they were withdrawn. He reiterated that the New Mexican volunteers, without the support of regular troops or of volunteers drawn from some other section of the country, could not be relied upon to resist an invasion of the country, if one was attempted. The volunteers were equipped with older model firearms. Uniforms of an inferior quality had already been distributed to two regiments, while the clothing for the other two was scheduled to arrive shortly on the train from the east.

Canby believed that he was now strong enough to launch an offensive against Baylor's Confederates to reclaim the southern part of his department. In late December he arrived at Fort Craig to assume command and to take care of last-minute details. The regulars were to form the bulk of his army, but some picked volunteers would be taken along. As everything approached a state of readiness, Canby was stunned to learn on December 26, that the Confederates in the Mesilla Valley had been reinforced by fourteen hundred men, and that another army of two thousand was moving by way of the Pecos to attack central and northern New Mexico.[7] Marching against Baylor was now out of the question, as the departmental commander was faced squarely with the grave task of defending his far-flung territory from invasion.

Although the reported Confederate reinforcements were much larger than he had anticipated, Canby's greatest anxiety lay in keeping open his line of communication with the east. If this vital artery were cut, his command would be completely isolated from any aid coming from that quarter. The necessity of concentrating his forces to challenge the impending invasion from the south prevented the dispatch of sufficient numbers to garrison Forts Wise and Garland — important posts protecting the eastern road. As a consequence, on January 1, 1862, Canby asked Governor Gilpin, as he had done several times previously, to send as many companies of Colorado volunteers to those forts as was possible. The life line to the east had to be kept open at all costs.

Canby had received what he believed to be reliable information that the main Confederate invasion would come by way of the Pecos, supported by a cooperating movement from the Canadian River. According to his sources, the Texans had not raised as many troops as planned, so the Pecos-Canadian plan, or at least the Canadián part of it, had been suspended temporarily. On January 2 Colonel Baylor had appeared before Alamosa with a raiding party, only to discover that the Union detachments had fallen back to the safety of Fort Craig. Canby reasoned that Baylor's raid might have been a feint designed to trick him into thinking that the main Confederate force was coming by way of the Río Grande when in reality it was marching from the Pecos. To guard against being caught unaware, the departmental commander devised a plan of defense which would be effective against an invasion from either route.

Fort Craig, the key fortress defending New Mexico on the Río Grande road, was reinforced. If the Confederates came up the Pecos, to reach the Río Grande Valley, they would have to come by way of Galisteo or the Carnuel or Abó passes. Canby's strategy called for the establishment of an intermediary base at Belén, located just above Abó Pass on the Río Grande about thirty miles south of Albuquerque and around seventy above Fort Craig. Here he would station a force of regulars which would serve as a nucleus for the concentration of troops recalled from all points not immediately threatened by the enemy. This large force at Belén, kept constantly on the alert and ready to move at a moment's notice, could be quickly dispatched to meet the enemy coming from the Pecos by either of the three routes, or speedily marched to Fort Craig's support if the Texans came up the Río Grande.

Canby set out from Fort Craig for Belén on January 6. Accompanying him were three companies of regular cavalry, three of infantry, a light battery, and four companies of volunteer infantry. With the regulars as the nucleus, Canby established his reserve base at Belén. The volunteers which had come up with him were used to escort wagon trains going to Fort Craig. Canby left Fort Craig in charge of Lieutenant Colonel Benjamin S. Roberts and a garrison of 1,400 men, consisting of six companies of regulars, ten of volunteers, one of spies and guides, and two of militia. In addition, he had subject to his call six companies of volunteers which could join him within twenty-four hours. Canby assumed that this would be an adequate garrison to maintain the fort if the anticipated invasion came from the Pecos. If it came up the Río Grande, all available troops would be rushed from Belén as planned.

Patiently Canby waited to see from which direction the Confederates would strike. Union troops at other points in the territory, principally at Fort Union, Santa Fé, and Albuquerque, were kept on the alert to move in any direction. Transportation and ten days' supplies were held in reserve to meet any emergency. Canby notified the governor that the militia should stand by to turn out at a moment's notice. He advised that some of the militia be used, if necessary, to reinforce Santa Fé and Fort Union. Canby had no intention of employing them in the field — their usefulness lay in replacing the regulars and volunteers that might be withdrawn from posts not immediately threatened by the army.

All citizens were asked to watch the roads and trails to prevent any enemy scouts, spies, or small parties from entering the country for purposes of capturing couriers, plundering trains, or other disruptive activity. As assurance that he would have at least several days' advance notice of the enemy's approach, Canby ordered all approaches to the country kept under close surveillance. On January 11 he reported that his scouts on the Pecos had seen no sign of Texans, but two regiments which had left San Antonio in November were not accounted for among those Confederate troops that had reached the Mesilla Valley. "This fact, more than any other," Canby mused, "gives probability to the reported invasion by the Pecos."[8]

While tensely awaiting the Confederate move, Canby was plagued by new troubles. During the second week of January he received information from private sources that the paymaster had been detained at Fort Leavenworth. If true, this meant that no funds would reach New Mexico until spring. He feared that if this information leaked out the volunteer forces would melt away by desertion, and the people of New Mexico would become even more apathetic than they already were. According to the Colonel, the natives, having little or no affection for the institutions of the United States, nursed a strong, but hitherto restrained, hatred for the Americans as a race. He also pointed out that Confederate sympathizers and agents from the very first had endeavored not only to keep this discontent alive, but to fan it into flames. It was in an effort to check such activity that he had suspended the writ of habeas corpus throughout the territory as early as August. The long-deferred payment of the volunteers, of course, would make them far more susceptible to the enemy's propaganda.

Unfortunately, the rumor of the paymaster's delay spread like wild fire among the citizenry and volunteers. Canby's fears were fully vindicated when a revolt broke out in a militia company at Fort Union, and another among two volunteer companies of the Second Regiment almost two hundred miles away at Camp Connelly, a temporary training base near Sabinal. The first revolt was quickly suppressed by the commander of Fort Union, but the second was not so easily managed, and about thirty mutineers fled to the mountains. Only stern measures prevented further outbreaks.

Hostile Indians had stepped up their plundering forays to such an extent that the governor wrote Canby for additional military protection. Realizing that the chief executive apparently had little or no grasp of the present military situation, the Colonel enlightened him in his reply: "The plan and scope of the Texan operations admits of the concentration of their entire force in one body, and permits them to assail the Territory with the great bulk of their force at any one of several points. Our own circumstances are widely different. We have an extensive country to defend and long lines of communication to protect, and it is barely possible to keep in hand a force that will not be inferior to that which the enemy is able to send into the country. It would be exceedingly unwise," Canby continued, " ... so to disseminate our forces that they would not be concentrated in season to meet invasion at any point that may be attempted."[9] In the face of reality, the departmental commander suggested that the governor raise a temporary force for the express purpose of fighting the Indians. Canby could neither arm nor supply such a body, but he did agree to detach as large a force as he could spare to accompany it on a retaliatory foray.

Although Canby's regular units were lacking sufficient officers, the most serious deficit, in regard to competency at least, lay with the volunteers. For several reasons Canby declined the suggestion by several of his subordinates that regular army officers be appointed to head the volunteer units. First, he needed the regular officers where they were. In the second place, and perhaps of more importance, the prejudice of the natives toward the Americans was too great. If the field officers were chosen altogether from the Americans, it could easily result in the delay, if not the defeat, of the organization of the volunteers. Canby preferred instead to select outstanding natives for commissions and hope for the best.

Harried by tremendous internal problems, Colonel Canby's mettle was put to the test when information arrived that Sibley's army was definitely moving upon him by way of the Río Grande. With 1,500 men he left Belén, reaching Fort Craig on or about January 31. At this critical moment the Union government was indeed fortunate in having such a capable commander in New Mexico.

Since his inauguration as governor of New Mexico on September 4, Henry Connelly had made fervent pleas to the territory's citizens in an effort to arouse them from their lethargy and to stimulate volunteer enlistments. Knowing that the natives cared little or nothing about the great national issue at hand, he directed his appeals toward reviving their hatred of Texans. His speeches, letters, and broadsides pictured Sibley's Confederate army as hardly more than a filibustering band of Texans bent on subjugation. To stimulate local patriotism, he reminded them that they had defeated the Texan invaders in 1841 when Texas claimed all of New Mexico east of the Río Grande, and he implored them to do it again by joining the volunteers.[10] It is difficult to ascertain how much effect, if any, Connelly's appeals had toward filling the ranks of the volunteer regiments.

Between Sibley's departure from New Mexico in May, 1861, and the eve of his invasion, important changes, aside from those purely military in nature, had come about. Of considerable interest was the seemingly altered attitude of former Congressional Delegate Miguel Otero who, it will be remembered, had been avowedly pro-Southern and a supporter of New Mexico's slave code.

Shortly after Lincoln's election, and while still in Washington, he revealed in a private letter that he did not believe the election of a Republican President sufficient grounds for secession. This letter was made public by its appearance in the December 8, 1860, issue of the Santa Fé *Gazette*, and it apparently had gone unnoticed by Southern zealots. Otero pointed out that should a dissolution of the old Union come about New Mexico would eventually have to join one of the two, three, or four republics which would be formed. If, and when, this time came, and if California and Oregon declared their independence, he personally advised that New Mexico join her destiny with those free Pacific states. This was certainly a far cry from his previous stand, and indicates that his former pro-slavery attitude had been a façade all along. Otero's influence among his people was great, and many of the Confederates had taken his support for granted. Even the ardently pro-Southern Santa Fé *Gazette* had changed its policy, as a result, it was said, of receiving a contract to publish official documents for a handsome fee.[11] Instead of advocating an immediate union with the South or the North, the editor now favored a policy of watchful waiting.

Lincoln's appointment of Henry Connelly to the governorship was criticized by some Unionists in New Mexico. Though a resident of the territory for thirty-three years, he was a Virginian by birth, and had later lived in Kentucky and Missouri. He had been a member of the legislature which passed the slave code. But though he might have favored slavery, or was, more properly, acquiescent toward that institution, he most certainly opposed secession. Probably as a result of the secession crisis, he came to develop antislavery sentiments. In November, 1861, he publicly stated that he considered the slave code to be contrary to the territory's feelings and interests. When the legislature convened in December, 1861, one of its first actions was to repeal the slave code. There was no opposition.[12] To all appearances, by the time of Sibley's invasion New Mexico had firmly taken her place by the side of the Union. Those who had warned all along that "as Missouri goes, so goes New Mexico," were correct.

New Mexico's changed attitude made the Confederate conquest of that area of even greater importance. At the peace conference following the cessation of hostilities, the Federal government might be reluctant to cede an area which was Union in sentiment. If Sibley could occupy the territory, Southern influence would again prevail there, and, perhaps of greater importance should the Confederacy win, the military occupation of the territory at the close of the war would certainly confirm its becoming a part of the new nation.

On receiving word from Canby of the impending invasion from the Río Grande, Connelly called up all the available militia in the territory. Though the legislature still had five more days before its session ended, the governor could not hold himself passively in the capital while exciting developments were brewing farther south. Fully aware that there was grave doubt concerning the courage of the natives when coming into contact with the Texans, he believed his presence at Fort Craig would set an example which would bolster native morale. He also noted that militia units coming from northern counties might hesitate to march south if he, the governor, remained safely behind in Santa Fé. At any rate, there were only a few unimportant laws left to pass, and since most of these were later sent to him to be signed before the legislature adjourned, he did not feel he had neglected his civil duties. Accompanied by Major James L. Donaldson, Captain Gurden Chapin, and James L. Collins, the territorial Indian agent, the governor set out on January 26 for the theater of war.

On arrival at Fort Craig the governor was delighted to find that an air of general enthusiasm prevailed. The militia were in high spirits and Colonel Canby had the entire confidence of his army. Intelligence reported that the Confederates were poorly armed and supplied, and though supposedly three thousand strong, their ranks had been seriously thinned by smallpox. Connelly's optimism grew apace as more and more volunteer and militia units poured into the post, thus assuring the Union of superior numbers. Only if the enemy received reinforcements, and this was highly unlikely, did the governor believe there could be the slightest danger of any disaster to the Union army. He exuberantly averred: "We will conquer the Texan forces, if not in the first battle, it will be done in the second or subsequent battles. We will overcome them."[13] Indian Agent Collins likewise noticed that the New Mexicans had turned out "with a spirit that is truly commendable. The best and most influential men in the Territory are here and will take part in the battle. It is an important event in the history of the Territory."[14] Even though Canby noted that the natives appeared to be animated by patriotism, his skepticism concerning their military abilities prevented his sharing the enthusiastic optimism of Connelly and Collins.

When all the available forces had concentrated at Fort Craig, Canby had an army totaling 3,810. Of these, about 1,200 were regulars[15] comprising five companies (B, D, F, I, K) of the Fifth Infantry, three (C, F, H) of the Seventh Infantry, three (A, F, H) of the Tenth Infantry, two (D, G) of the First Cavalry, four (C, D, G, K) of the Third Cavalry, Captain Alexander McRae's provisional battery of six guns (composed of Companies G, Second Cavalry, and I, Third Cavalry), and Lieutenant Robert H. Hall's provisional battery of two twenty-four-pounders. The native troops consisted of the First Regiment New Mexico Volunteers (now commanded by Colonel Christopher "Kit" Carson, Ceran St. Vrain having resigned), seven companies of the Second (Colonel Miguel E. Pino), seven of the Third, one company of the Fourth, two of the Fifth, Captain James "Paddy" Graydon's Independent Spy Company, and about one thousand hastily collected and unorganized militia. In addition, Captain Theodore H. Dodd's company of Colorado volunteer infantry had arrived in time to join Canby's army. Dubbed the "Foot Volunteers" for their long trek from Colorado, this unit eventually became Company A, Second Regiment Colorado Volunteers.[16]

Since he knew that the Confederate forces were mounted, Canby expected Sibley's main efforts would be directed toward crippling his transportation by attacking his wagon trains, impeding the operations of his troops by stampeding their animals, and/or engaging in night attacks. His commanders were to impress upon their men that such anticipated attacks could succeed only when the defenders were thrown into such confusion that the enemy could break through their lines. In this event they were to repel the Texans with the bayonet or the clubbed musket. There was to be no firing of weapons, since in the confusion the shots would more than likely endanger friend as well as foe. An old infantryman himself, Canby stressed the point that a foot soldier who is cool is more than a match for a horseman, and in groups they are safe against any number. In preparation for any emergency, the Colonel ordered that four days' rations be constantly carried in the company wagons, and the remainder kept loaded in the supply train. With his forces all assembled, and apparently in a high state of morale, Canby was as well prepared as possible to meet the challenge of the Army of New Mexico.

Shortly after Sutton's arrival at Fort Thorn, General Sibley issued the order for the Army of New Mexico to move up the Río Grande. Green's Fifth Regiment, accompanied by Teel's artillery, set out on February 7 as the advance. The remaining forces were scheduled to leave from day to day, and the whole army was to concentrate a few miles below Fort Craig.

The biting winter weather caused intense suffering among the Texans. One soldier complained that it was "as cold as any I ever felt in any land or country."[17] Mush ice in the Río Grande made water from that stream almost too frigid to drink. Oftentimes the supply wagons could not keep pace with the main body. When this occurred it meant that the men had neither provisions nor blankets to nourish and warm their chilled bodies during the night encampments.

By February 9 the Fifth had pushed to within thirty miles of Fort Craig. Being so near the enemy, Colonel Green ordered a strong guard around the camp, and cautioned his men to graze their horses carefully and to keep their weapons loaded and ready for use at all times. The next day the regiment moved several miles closer to the enemy bastion. While Major Samuel A. Lockridge took three companies on a reconnaissance around the post, the remainder of the regiment—"daily and hourly" expecting an attack—encamped in a cottonwood thicket. The following day the Fifth cautiously advanced several more miles. Camp was carefully laid out in a two-rank battle formation, and the howitzers were unlimbered in a commanding position on a nearby hill.

The men remained here during the twelfth, when they were joined by Pyron's command and one company of the Fourth. As the troops moved closer toward

Fort Craig the next day, the terrain became increasingly rough and hilly, prompting one soldier to grumble that "This country will be a tax to any government to which it may belong."[18] About an hour after making camp, a picket rushed in to report that the Federals were advancing upon them a few miles upstream. Immediately bugles blared and the troops raced for their horses. Proceeding upriver about four miles, the Confederates came in sight of a Union force drawn up in a skirmish line. Quickly the Texans maneuvered into battle formation. Most of the officers and men seemed cool and anxious for a fight; "Some were cursing the Yankees, some were careless and unconcerned, while others were almost praying for an attack."[19] Before a battle could materialize, the Federals withdrew to Fort Craig, leaving the Texans to hold their position until dark before returning to camp.

At eight o'clock on the morning of February 14, the Fourth Regiment and the squadron of the Seventh arrived at Green's camp. It had been a most unpleasant night march. Leaving their camps around midnight, the men had had to face a north wind with sleet and snow falling so hard "as to almost pelt the skin off" their faces.[20] That evening several companies, while on reconnaissance, had a minor skirmish with the enemy near Fort Craig and captured twenty-one New Mexican volunteers.

The bulk of the Army of New Mexico was now united into one body for the first time. The assembled forces consisted of the Fourth Regiment, which, because of Colonel Reily's absence, was under the command of Lieutenant Colonel William R. Scurry; the Fifth Regiment led by Colonel Thomas Green; five companies (A, B, F, H, I) of the Seventh, commanded by Lieutenant Colonel John S. Sutton; and Major Charles L. Pyron's command, which consisted of companies B, D, and E of the Second Regiment (Company A appears to have remained in the Mesilla Valley) and three independent companies of volunteers (Captain George M. Frazer's "Arizona Rangers," Captain John Phillips' "Brigands," and Captain Bethel Coopwood's "San Elizario Spy Company"). In addition there was Captain Trevanion T. Teel's Light Company B, First Texas Artillery, consisting of four guns, and two howitzer batteries of four guns each, commanded by Lieutenants John Reily and William S. Wood. Accompanying the army were a long supply train and thousands of draft and beef animals.

The exact number of men composing the Confederate invasion force is not known. When the three regiments were in camp above San Antonio, each had about nine hundred men, giving the brigade a total of twenty-seven hundred troops. As noted previously, however, only half the Seventh Regiment was with Sibley. Colonel William Steele had remained behind in the Mesilla Valley, charged with holding that area with an undetermined number of troops.[21] Captain Hunter and Colonel Reily had had a combined force of around one hundred when they set out for Tucson and Mexico, respectively. Disease had reduced the ranks, causing many sick and disabled to remain behind in hospitals. San Antonio and Houston newspaper accounts listed Sibley's actual invasion force at two thousand, while a correspondent for the New Orleans *Picayune* gave the number as twenty-three hundred, exclusive of Sutton's battalion.[22] It seems unlikely that it could have been more than twenty-five hundred.[23]

By February 15 the Confederates had reached a point about five to seven miles south of Fort Craig. Since reconnaissance indicated that the post was too heavily fortified to be taken by assault, Sibley determined to challenge Canby to battle on the open plain south of the fort. About one o'clock the following day, the bulk of the army (2nd, 4th, 7th, and five companies of the 5th) set out. For several days General Sibley had been so ill that he was unable to continue commanding. Colonel Thomas Green, the next ranking officer, therefore temporarily assumed charge of operations.[24] About a mile and three-quarters below the post, Green drew up his men in battle formation. The position he chose was a good one, for his line was protected by a low bank which ran east and west, nearly parallel to the fort. Detachments forming the extreme left occupied a range of low hills in that direction. With his battle flag gently waving in the breeze, Green tensely awaited the enemy's reaction.

At first Fort Craig appeared to be deserted, but in a few moments the "Stars and Stripes" was hoisted, and troops began pouring out of their quarters. Major Lockridge jokingly boasted to his men that he intended to make a shimmy out of that flag, averring that if he could get a wife as easily as he could that banner, he would never sleep by himself again.

When the Confederates first came into view, Canby believed they intended to assault his fort. When he perceived that this was not their intent, he ordered out a strong force to keep a watchful eye on them. This detachment consisted of the various companies of the Fifth, Seventh, and Tenth Infantry, the First and Second Volunteers, two cavalry units, and a battery of six guns. Since he had no confidence in the militia and but little in his volunteers, Canby flatly refused the Confederate challenge to a full-scale encounter. Rather he intended to bring on a battle only in a position where the native troops would not have to maneuver under the direct fire of the enemy. The plain south of Fort Craig certainly was not the desired place under those circumstances.

The Confederates remained in position for several hours. When it was evident that the enemy did not intend to fight, Green instructed his troops to return to camp. In the process of withdrawing, the column which had occupied the low hills on the left fell behind the main body. As these troops came down into the plain, Canby ordered his cavalry to charge. The Confederates, seeing the charge coming, began yelling and waving their hats at "Yankeedom" to beckon them on, for hidden in the ravine was their artillery. The Federals reined up and retreated in time to escape the murderous blasts of the cannon. Following this brief encounter, the Confederates continued their withdrawal uninterrupted, most reaching camp around eleven-thirty that night.

The enemy's refusal to fight in the open posed a dilemma for the Texans. Fort Craig was too strong to be stormed, especially since the light Confederate artillery could not be used for an effective bombardment. But worst of all, the commissary department reported that only a ten-day supply of food remained. Something would have to be done, and soon.

Green summoned a council of war, which, after due deliberation, developed a plan: the army would move to the east bank of the river, bypass Fort Craig, and then recross at the Valverde ford, some six miles above the post. Perhaps Canby, in an effort to prevent the recrossing, might be lured out to fight. The detour would be hazardous, involving as it did the crossing and recrossing of the frigid waters of the Río Grande. From Paraje, about eight miles south of Fort Craig, northward to a point almost opposite the post, the valley was bounded on the east by a basaltic mesa varying in height from forty to eighty feet. The pedregal was traversed by ridges of drifting sand—broken in places by protruding beds of lava—which were, in general, parallel to the river valley. The ravines between these ridges were natural covered ways which would conceal the movements of the Texans. Heavy sands, however, would make it difficult for the wagon train, and the route was entirely devoid of water.

During the seventeenth and eighteenth a furious wind from the southeast raised such a cloud of sand and dust that active operations by either side were rendered temporarily impossible. Early on the morning of February 19, the wind having abated, the Army of New Mexico retired down the river to the ford opposite Paraje. By three o'clock the entire command, including the wagon train and beef herds, had safely crossed and had set up a dry camp about two miles above the ford.

The Confederate movement across the river engendered great anxiety at Fort Craig, arousing conjectures by the score as to Sibley's intentions. Some were bitterly critical of Canby's unwillingness to fight when the Texans had drawn up below the fort several days before.[25] But those who knew their commander best realized that he would move against the enemy only when he thought the time was right.

Canby assumed that Sibley intended to move up from Paraje to occupy a bluff which was about one thousand yards across the river immediately opposite Fort Craig. This projection of pedregal held a slight command of his post, and if the Confederates planted artillery on its summit, they could easily shell the fort. To prevent such a possibility, Canby sent Colonels "Kit" Carson and Miguel Pino with their regiments to secure that strategic point. This was accomplished on

February 19, the native troops holding this position throughout the night and the next morning.

Daylight of February 20 found the Army of New Mexico in the saddle ready to move out. Since Captain George M. Frazer of the "Arizona Rangers" was somewhat familiar with the terrain, he was charged with the duty of leading the army around the mesa to the Valverde ford. For the utmost protection, the wagon train was placed in the middle of the column. Veering away from the valley, the long Confederate line proceeded up a large ravine, literally blazing a new road in the process. The Texans had hoped to reach the ford before nightfall, but the rocky pedregal and heavy sand made the going exceedingly difficult. Around four o'clock, after a march of only seven miles, the teams had become so exhausted that it was necessary to stop and make another dry camp. Many of the wagons, unable to keep pace, lay scattered for several miles along the route. A number of them were burned by Union patrols that night. Both men and beasts were now suffering severely from thirst.

When Canby concluded that the Confederates planned to bypass his post, he moved to contest, or at least to harass, their passage. With a command of both regular and volunteer cavalry and McRae's battery, he set out across the river. Carson's and Pino's regiments left their post on the bluff to join him. Impeded somewhat by the cumbersome pedregal, Canby moved slowly eastward toward where the Confederates were setting up camp.

The Texans, anticipating such an attack, had selected an ideal defensive location on a pedregal mesa. As Canby approached, he decided to attack even though he realized that the ground in front was not suited for cavalry or artillery. Cautiously he spread out his men and then threw skirmishers forward to draw the enemy's artillery fire so the guns' positions could be located. This maneuver was successful, and shortly four Texan howitzers were booming and echoing throughout the mesa. The bulk of the Union troops were brought into position without mishap, but Pino's men were so terrified by the blasts of the cannon that it was impossible to restore them to any kind of order. This development, as well as the approach of nightfall, prompted the Federal commander to discontinue the attack. To cover his withdrawal, and also to keep the Texans in position as long as possible, Colonel Roberts led his cavalry in a diversionary assault against the Confederate right. Under cover of this feint, Canby withdrew his forces safely. The volunteer infantry stayed behind to continue holding the strategic bluff commanding Fort Craig, while the artillery and cavalry crossed the river to the post. The Texans remained in their camp, which was in sight of Fort Craig, less than four miles away.

No further action took place that night except for the "raid" of Captain James "Paddy" Graydon. Long a resident of New Mexico, Graydon was probably the most colorful figure of Canby's command next to "Kit" Carson. Before the Federal troops evacuated Arizona, he had operated a saloon at Fort Buchanan. Later he recruited a company of Unionists who had been dispossessed and driven north by Southern sympathizers. To them, perhaps more than to the others, the present war was a personal matter. Graydon's Independent Spy Company served the fourfold purpose of spy, scout, police, and forager.

With Canby's permission, Graydon packed a dozen twenty-four-pounder howitzer shells in two wooden boxes. After lashing these on the backs of two old mules, he and three or four of his men crossed the river under cover of darkness and headed toward the Confederate camp. When within 150 yards of the enemy line, they lighted the fuses, drove the mules forward, and began a hasty retreat. On looking back, Graydon's party was horrified to see that the mules, instead of going toward the enemy, were following them! The shells soon exploded, bringing the Confederate camp quickly to arms. Graydon and his men were unharmed, and made their way back to Fort Craig, needless to say, without the mules.[26]

4

The Battle of Valverde

AT DAWN ON THE MORNING OF FEBRUARY 21, GENERAL SIBLEY, THOUGH STILL VERY WEAK, took to the saddle to personally direct the operations of his army. According to plan, Green's Fifth Regiment, Sutton's battalion of the Seventh, and Teel's battery launched a threatening demonstration against Fort Craig, while Scurry's Fourth Regiment, well-flanked by Pyron's battalion on the left, commenced marching up river to the Valverde ford. The movement was unfortunately delayed because of a stampede during the night of several hundred of the Fourth Regiment's mules. About midnight the frantically thirsty animals broke for the river in spite of all the guards could do, and were later captured by the Federals. Rather than alter his strategy because of this loss, Sibley abandoned about thirty wagons containing the tents, blankets, books, and papers of the Fourth Regiment.

With 180 men, Major Pyron set out at daybreak to reconnoiter the road leading to Valverde. The air was crisp and cold and the sky cloudy as he moved through the rough pedregal. After a march of about two and a half miles the Mesa del Contadero (generally known today as Black Mesa) loomed up on his left. Formed by the action of an extinct volcano, this basaltic eminence, which rose to a height of about three hundred feet, was roughly three miles long and two wide. Pyron passed around the northeastern end of it before moving directly westward to the river. As he approached the Río Grande the terrain immediately sloped down into a valley thickly studded in part by *bosques,* or groves, of cottonwoods. The river had changed its course, and the dry arroyo of the old channel formed more or less the eastern edge of the valley. Not far back from the river, rows of small hills and sand ridges ran northward for over a mile to another, but lower, mesa. The river broadened out here, becoming shallow and easy to cross. On coming in sight of the Río Grande, and seeing no enemy, Pyron dispatched a note to Sibley informing him that the road was clear. He and his men then leisurely proceeded to the river, for their horses had gone without water for over twenty-four hours.

Meanwhile, about sunrise Colonel Scurry had ordered Major Henry Raguet to take four companies, and with Captain Frazer's company of Pyron's battalion as guide, to set out as his advance. As an added precaution against surprise by the enemy, Scurry also threw out flanking patrols. By around eight o'clock the whole of the Fourth Regiment, including Reily's battery, was en route to the Valverde ford. Because of the poor system of command, the Colonel was unaware that Pyron had preceded him. When later informed of this, he instructed Raguet, some three miles ahead, to rein up and reunite with the main body. Shortly after this, Scurry received Pyron's message that the river was in sight and the road clear of the enemy. With a feeling of security, the Fourth continued its march around the Mesa del Contadero.

From across the river Canby easily saw through the Confederate feint against Fort Craig. Shortly before eight o'clock he detected Scurry's regiment proceeding northward in the direction of Valverde — the enemy's intentions were obvious. To prevent the Texans from reaching their objective, Canby sent Colonel Roberts with a force of regular and volunteer cavalry up the western side of the Río Grande with instructions to cross the river to hold the ford before the enemy could reach it. Roberts' immediate subordinates were Major Thomas Duncan, commanding five companies of regulars (C, D, G, K, Third Cavalry, and G, First Cavalry), and Lieutenant Colonel José M. Valdez in charge of four companies of the Third Regiment New Mexico Volunteers. Roberts was followed shortly by two sections of Captain Alexander McRae's battery (four guns), and Lieutenant Robert H. Hall's two twenty-four–pounders. Supporting the artillery were Captain David H. Brotherton's company of the Fifth Infantry, Captain Charles H. Ingraham's Company H of the Seventh Infantry, and two selected companies of New Mexican volunteers (Captain William Mortimore's of the Third and Captain Santiago Hubbell's of the Fifth). Canby had already sent Graydon's Spy Company and five hundred mounted volunteers under Colonels Miguel Pino and Robert H. Stapleton across the river opposite Fort Craig to watch the enemy's movements, as well as to impede his movements by threatening his flanks and rear. Most of the Federal infantry was already opposite Fort Craig, for they had remained across the river after Canby's unsuccessful assault against the Confederate camp the previous day.

After marching a short distance, Roberts instructed Major Duncan to advance rapidly to the ford with four of his companies. If the Texans had not arrived, he was to cross the river to hold the bosque on the extreme right of the ford which was bordered by the Mesa del Contadero. When the Major reached the ford, he discovered that two of Valdez' volunteer companies had reached it ahead of him. With these, as well as his own command, he crossed the icy Río Grande. No sooner had he gained the eastern bank than he sighted Pyron's force moving through the cottonwoods a few hundred yards to his left front. He quickly sent Lieutenant Claflin's Company G to see what the Texans were up to.

After watering their horses, the Confederates started back across the valley the way they had come. When Pyron spied the approach of Claflin's company, however, he immediately set out in pursuit through the heavy bosque. When he had come to the bank of a wide slough—actually the lower end of the old river bottom—he saw the rest of Duncan's command arrayed ahead with the river to their backs. Without a moment's hesitation Pyron ordered his men to dismount so as to take position behind the protective cover of the trees and the bank of the slough.

When Claflin came galloping back to report that the Confederates were hot after him, Duncan, surmising that the Texans greatly outnumbered him, took up a defensive position, instead of attacking. He quickly dismounted his troops to deploy them behind sand hills, logs, and a few scattered trees. The horses were dispatched about a hundred yards to the rear toward the river where they would be protected somewhat by a low sand ridge there. Duncan was determined to hold his position between the Texans and the river until Roberts could cross over to support him with the artillery and infantry. Hostilities commenced around nine o'clock.

Upon being confronted by the enemy, Pyron dispatched Captain John Phillips to relay the news to the commander of the Fourth Regiment. When Scurry learned of the situation, he ordered his men to gallop to Pyron's support as fast as their horses could carry them, lest the Major be overwhelmed before they could arrive. With Phillips leading the way, the Fourth approached the battleground about ten o'clock. Scurry instructed his men to dismount and to advance on foot to take position behind a low sand bank on Pyron's right. Frazer's company rejoined Pyron, and Reily set about unlimbering his howitzers. The fighting now began in earnest.

Across the river Colonel Roberts awaited the arrival of his approaching artillery and supporting infantry. From his vantage point, he observed a body of Texans, with a piece of artillery, moving down through the cottonwoods toward the Mesa del Contadero. It was obviously their intent to turn Duncan's right flank, while extending their own left to the river. Quickly he notified the Major to throw some skirmishers into the heavy timber to drive the enemy back. Duncan had already dispatched Captain Edward Treacy's Company D into the area to repel small reconnoitering parties which had been probing it. On receipt of Roberts' intelligence, he sent Captain George W. Howland's Company C to Treacy's support. After a spirited clash of several minutes, the Texans were driven back. They soon rallied, however, to vigorously renew their assault. McRae's and Hall's batteries, having set up on the west bank about four hundred yards opposite Reily's Confederate guns, commenced firing shot and shell into the bosque, while Brotherton's infantry company crossed to reinforce Duncan's command. With the combined artillery and small-arms fire, the duel for the bosque raged ever hotter. Seeing that Reily's light howitzers were no match for the heavier metal of the enemy, Scurry ordered the battery to withdraw to the rear.

Around eleven o'clock Captain Teel galloped up with one section of his battery under Lieutenant James Bradford. Earlier that morning Teel's battery had been protecting the wagon train as it moved toward the ford. Bradford's two guns had led the advance while Teel remained with the section bringing up the rear. As the battle began assuming greater proportions, Sibley ordered the battery to the front. Leaving the rear section in charge of Lieutenant Jordan W. Bennett and Joseph H. McGuinness (spelled "McGinnis" in the *O. R. A.*) with orders to follow immediately, Teel loped to the head of the train to take Bradford's section to the field. The Captain set up the two guns near the center of the Fourth Regiment and soon began shelling both the left of the enemy line and the artillery across the river. The Federals responded by training their fire on his battery, an action resulting in the death of one cannoneer and the wounding of two others. This left only five men to work the guns. To add to the confusion, a bomb exploded nearby and set the grass on fire. The intrepid Teel not only held his position, but seized a rammer to help his men load the pieces. Seeing his predicament, Scurry ordered Reily's command to join Teel and assist in the effective working of the guns. By this time Bennett and McGuinness had arrived on the scene. Assuming from the heavy firing on the left that Major Pyron was hard pressed, Scurry sent Teel to his support with these guns which had just come up. He also ordered Major Raguet, with four companies, to maintain the left, while he stayed on the right with the remainder of his regiment and two guns under McGuinness to check an apparent enemy movement to turn his right flank.

As Canby observed that the Confederate movement toward Valverde was becoming more determined, he recalled Captain Henry R. Selden's column from across the river opposite the fort to reinforce Roberts. Selden's column consisted of two battalions under Captain P. W. L. Plympton (Companies C and F, Seventh Infantry, Companies A and H, Tenth Infantry, and Dodd's company of Colorado volunteers) and four companies under Captain Benjamin Wingate (Companies B, D, F, and I, Fifth Infantry). Shortly after Selden set out, Canby also ordered "Kit" Carson's First Regiment (eight companies) to the scene. These reinforcements reported to Roberts around noon. The Colonel instructed Selden to take his men farther up the river where he was to cross over to engage the enemy with the bayonet. There was no ford above, but because of the low stage of the river, Selden's men crossed (in water up to their armpits) selecting step by step their foothold among quicksands and against the strong current of the Río Grande. Roberts had received an erroneous report that some five hundred enemy cavalry had forded the river farther up to threaten his flank and rear.

To check any such maneuver, he ordered Carson's regiment to take position in a bosque higher up the west bank near the main road leading to the north. Meanwhile, Selden's men had forded the river and had re-formed to assault the extreme Confederate right.

As Scurry was preparing to check the enemy movement on his right, Major Lockridge came up with several companies of the Fifth Regiment. Shortly after Scurry had directed him to support the left, Colonel Green reached the field and assumed command about one o'clock. Green placed most of his companies between Pyron on the left and Scurry on the right. Three of his companies under Lieutenant Colonel Henry C. McNeill were dispatched to the extreme left near the north point of the mesa to bolster the Confederate line against the heavy enemy assaults.

Near noon General Sibley had ordered Green to discontinue the feint against Fort Craig and take his regiment to the battlefield. The wagon train stretched for miles, and large numbers of Federals (the regiments of Pino and Stapleton) threatened its safety. Before advancing, Green left a protective force consisting of Sutton's battalion of the Seventh and two companies (C and H) of his own regiment. With several companies, Major Lockridge set out as the advance, followed closely by Green and the others. "In consequence of severe and prolonged illness and weakness resulting from it,"[1] Sibley could stay in his saddle no longer. He consequently relinquished his command to Green, sending his aides and other staff officers to report to him on the field. Although the battle had raged most of the morning, Sibley had at no time gone to the front. It was Scurry who had commanded the actual battle operations until relieved by Colonel Green.

With the extension of the battle line, Teel found it necessary to detach his guns to support the long front better. Bradford went to the extreme left flank with one piece to bolster Pyron. With one gun, McGuinness took position to the right of Lockridge's battalion soon after that officer arrived at the scene. Bennett set up in the center of the right flank, while another unlimbered at the extreme right. The light howitzers came into action again, with Reily installed on the left wing and Lieutenant Woods on the right. While the battle raged on the guns changed positions from time to time as circumstances required.

Duncan's command and the artillery had poured such a terrific fire into the Confederate left that Bradford was forced to abandon his gun. It was left in an exposed position at the foot of the Mesa del Contadero where it had been set up in an unsuccessful endeavor to disable the battery across the river. Shortly afterwards Major Lockridge arrived with three companies, and Pyron and Bradford's commands were withdrawn to the right. Lockridge pointed out the disabled gun to Raguet who immediately ordered Captain Andrew J. Scarborough and part of his company of the Fourth to the rescue. Since the horses belonging to the weapon had been either killed or wounded, the men had to pull the gun back by hand. As they gallantly labored to bring the piece to safety, the enemy shelled them, killing one and wounding several others. Undaunted by the fire, the Texans succeeded in getting the gun safely within their line. The weapon was put to use by three of Reily's men and a few others until Raguet ordered it silenced because of lack of gunners. It was left double-shotted for instant use in anticipation of an enemy assault.

Selden's command, on the Union left, vigorously launched its attack while Duncan, on the right, continued his assault. Both efforts were heavily supported by artillery fire. As Selden's men advanced toward Scurry's position, Captain Willis L. Lang and about forty of his lancers charged. The extreme Union left, which Lang assaulted, was composed of Dodd's company of Colorado volunteers. Dressed in gray uniforms similar to those of the New Mexicans, Lang may have mistaken them for natives and accordingly charged recklessly. The Coloradoans reserved their fire until the lancers had come in close, and then sent a devastating volley into their midst. The Texans reeled back in confusion and disorder. Lang himself fell mortally wounded. This company suffered more loss of life than any other of the Army of New Mexico. This first of modern wars had obviously made lancers obsolete. Though Lang's charge was completely repulsed, it did have the effect of bringing the Federals within close range of the Confederate line. The small-arms fire of Hardemen's and Crosson's companies and the raking barrages of Teel's two guns, shattered Selden's assault, forcing him back with considerable loss. The Confederate right was now secure.

The Federals at the same time had far better luck on their right. So heavy was the fire of Duncan's men, and particularly the artillery across the river, that Lockridge and Raguet called upon Green for additional support. When the reinforcements did not come, they were forced to fall back to the protective cover of the more pronounced old, dry river channel about a hundred yards to their rear. This was done by companies after the artillery and the wounded had been removed.

Colonel Roberts now felt secure in crossing his artillery to the east bank. This was accomplished in short order, and soon the guns were firing into the Confederate line again. McRae's four pieces took position on Selden's right rear, guarded by Ingraham's company of regular infantry and by Hubbell's and Mortimore's volunteers. Hall's battery, supported by Brotherton's company of regular infantry, set up to the left of Duncan's command on the right.[2] As a result of these changes, the Confederates were compelled to alter the positions of their batteries in order to render more effective resistance. After a spirited artillery duel, the Confederates' guns ceased fire, and a lull ensued. It seemed that the Federals were now assured of victory.

About two-thirty o'clock Roberts learned that Colonel Canby was on his way to the field with reinforcements. "The 'wear and tear' of the morning required repair, both in men and horses."[3] Some of the troops had been engaged in continuous combat for over five hours. Since there was now a lull in the fighting, and with Canby to arrive shortly to assume command, Roberts allowed his men to eat lunch and to fill their cartridge boxes. During this time the artillery remained vigilant, firing occasionally on any enemy who showed himself.

Shortly after noon Canby decided to go to the battleground to assume personal command of his fighting forces. By now, of course, the enemy's plan was completely obvious, and Fort Craig was no longer in imminent danger. A Confederate detachment across the river from the post, estimated by Canby to be around five hundred men, did, however, pose a possible threat. Before setting out with Company G, First Cavalry, and the remaining section (two guns) of McRae's battery, the Colonel took the precaution of detailing two companies of volunteers, Colonel Manuel Armijo's regiment of militia, and some detachments of regulars to guard the fort. He also ordered Pino's volunteer regiment from across the river to escort the ammunition train to Valverde.

Canby reached the field shortly before three o'clock, and was received with enthusiastic cheers from his troops. The lull in the hostilities enabled him to spend nearly an hour in conference with Roberts and other field officers, and in making a personal reconnaissance of the battleground. Though the superior fire power of the Federal artillery had driven the Texans back, the position they now held behind the high western bank of the old river bed was one of great natural strength. The bank of the dry channel and the numerous sand hills running parallel in front of it not only protected their guns and men from Federal fire, but to a great extent also concealed their movements. Canby was convinced that a direct, frontal assault upon the Texan line would not only prove costly, but very likely would end in failure. Up to this time Union arms had been successful, and, of the regulars and Colorado volunteers, only ten men had been killed and sixty-three wounded. The great problem now was how to drive the Texans from their strong position. After due consideration, Canby devised an admirable tactical maneuver to envelop the Confederate left and drive the enemy from the field. His plan was simple: using his own left as a pivot, the center and right of his line would press forward to smash the enemy left. Once the left had been shattered, his troops would be able to enfilade the Confederate position behind the old river bed. Thus enveloped, and with small-arms fire and Hall's artillery, the Texans would be driven from the field in disorder.

As the day was growing short, Canby quickly ordered his troops into position to carry out his enveloping strategy. McRae's battery, forming the pivotal left, was moved about 150 to 200 yards to the left front, putting it about 850 yards from

Hall's artillery on the right. Its support (Ingraham's company of regulars and two of volunteers) was increased by Plympton's four companies of regulars and Dodd's Coloradoans, who took position in back of the support already there. Colonel Pino's Second Regiment, which was now approaching, was ordered to cross the river as the reserve for the left as well as an additional support for McRae's battery (now increased to six guns with the addition of the section Canby brought to the field). When "Kit" Carson requested that his regiment be utilized, Canby ordered his men to cross the river and, with Selden's regular infantry, form the center. Hall's twenty-four–pounder, with its infantry support, and Duncan's dismounted cavalry composed the right. Forming the cavalry reserve was Captain R. S. C. Lord's company of regulars merged with Claflin's and Valdez' New Mexican volunteers. Shortly after McRae's battery had taken position the guns opened up on the Confederate line. The Texans responded immediately with a devastating barrage of canister from two of their hitherto concealed guns—McRae's new position proved to be dangerously exposed. The battery supports meantime had formed to the left of the guns and behind them in a line parallel to the river. Lying in a prone position, the support was protected from the enemy artillery fire.

Not long after Roberts had crossed his artillery to the east bank, Sutton reinforced the Confederate line with four companies. Sutton's men had been engaged in protecting the wagon train, and all thought for a time that the Seventh would have no share in the conflict. As the battle increased in severity Sutton was ordered to the front with all his available force. After detaching three companies (A and H of the Seventh and C of the Fifth) to remain with the train, he moved out at a gallop with the others (B, F, and I of the Seventh and H of the Fifth). Lockridge met him on the field and directed him to take position on the left.

When the Federal batteries, having crossed the Río Grande, began sending renewed showers of round shot, grape, and shell into his line, Green concluded that only by a daring frontal assault could he win the day. The main emphasis of the charge would be directed toward the two Union batteries. Since they were so far apart, the attack would have to be executed simultaneously by two storming parties. Under the protective cover of the old channel, Green set about gathering and re-forming his men. The attack directed at McRae's battery was to be carried out by dismounted troops of the Fourth and Fifth Regiments, parts of Sutton's and most of Pyron's battalion. The artillery of Teel, Reily, and Woods would serve as the support. Teel placed his guns in battery on the extreme right flank as a reserve. Should the charge be unsuccessful, he would be in an excellent position to shell the enemy as a cover for the retreating Confederates. When the attack was launched on the right, Major Raguet (Lockridge had been in charge of the left, but had now gone to the right to engage in the attack there) was instructed to lead four companies of the Fourth (B, E, G, H) and one of the Fifth (D) in a cavalry assault against Hall's battery. Raguet ordered his command, numbering around 200,[4] to align in a single rank—tense feelings of anxiety gripped the men as they awaited the signal to charge.

When informed of the strategy to turn the Confederate left, Duncan asked Canby for another company of infantry to join that of Brotherton's in support of Hall's battery. The Colonel promptly complied by dispatching Ingraham's regulars, which heretofore had been with McRae's guns. With Hall's twenty-four–pounder safely bolstered, Duncan felt confident in throwing all his dismounted cavalry forward as skirmishers. Canby had just about completed arrangements all along the line for executing his enveloping maneuver, when suddenly the Confederates took the offensive.

With the roar of cannon, a hail of small-arms fire, and Rebel yells, Raguet's determined cavalry bravely dashed across the field toward Hall's battery. Taken by complete surprise, Canby hastily ordered Wingate's battalion of the Fifth Infantry to aid in repelling the attack. "Kit" Carson's regiment, which had just crossed the river, was attracted by the firing and also rushed to the right. When the Confederates had galloped to within 150 yards of the Union line, they received a deadly discharge of rifles and musketry from Duncan's skirmishers and the battery's infantry support. As Carson's volunteers raced to the scene, Raguet's men passed diagonally across their front about eighty yards away. Carson's whole command thereupon sent destructive volleys into the Texans while, almost at the same moment, a shell from Hall's gun burst in their midst. The Confederate assault was completely shattered. As Raguet looked back toward his men, nothing but chaos met his eyes. The squeals of wounded horses and the groans of those who had fallen from their saddles were evidence enough of the failure of his assault. As his men reeled back in utter confusion, he ordered them to retreat to the safety of the old channel, from which they had come. The rout was so complete that most of the cavalrymen did not stop at the channel but continued on to protective sand banks farther to the rear.

Raguet's ill-fated cavalry charge, launched against far superior numbers, had been a costly failure in one respect. Nearly one-fifth of the men and horses involved had been either killed or wounded. Captain Marinus van der Heuvel, one of the most distinguished heroes of the day, was lost. It is possible that Colonel Green may have meant this offensive on the left to serve mainly as a feint to cover the larger movement on the right. Not only had Duncan's command and Hall's battery and support rushed forward, but the whole Union center had merged with the right in hot pursuit of Raguet's Confederates. In chasing the Texans such a great distance, the Federals consequently left a great gap in the center of their line—a gap which would prove fatal to Union arms that day.

About the same time Raguet led the assault on the left, the main body of Confederates charged on the right. The objective lay some four hundred fifty yards ahead over an open plain thinly interspersed with cottonwoods. At the command, "Up boys, and at them!" the determined Texans leaped over their protective sand bank and rushed toward the battery, unmindful of the storm of grape, canister, and musket balls sent hurling against them. Covering their assault were well-aimed barrages from their own artillery. As the Texans saw the flashes from McRae's guns, they would hit the ground and fire their small arms, and when the artillery charges had passed over, they would spring up to advance again in the same fashion. The employment of such tactics kept the casualty rate at a minimum, at the same time leading the Federals to believe their guns were doing far more damage than they actually were.

When Canby saw the attack coming, he hastened to inform the battery's supports. Lying in protected positions behind the guns, the men were unable to see the approaching danger. The fire of the Confederate batteries was so intense that the volunteers flatly refused to advance to defend the battery. Canby got off his horse and used every exertion possible to urge them to action. Even McRae left his post for a moment to run back to implore them "for God's sake to assist him in maintaining his position and to save his guns."[5] But the increased firing and the onward surge of the "terrible Texans" with their Rebel yells, threw such fear into the already terror-stricken natives that they broke and fled in wild disorder. In racing to the river, they passed through Plympton's battalion, carrying part of that command with them. Many of the regulars and Coloradoans maintained their composure and rushed into the battery to engage in a gallant and desperate attempt to repel the enemy.[6] For a moment their spirited defense hurled back the Texans' advance units. At this juncture Captain Lord's small cavalry reserve came from the right with the intention of charging. On nearing the battery, however, Lord found himself exposed to the fire of both friend and foe alike. Wheeling to the left, his men retreated to the rear amid the confusion.

The main Confederate storming party, in an effort to completely envelop the battery, had deployed in an advancing crescent formation nearly a half-mile in length. Armed with double-barreled shot guns, muskets, and revolvers, the Texans poured a lethal barrage into the battery. The group of Confederates closing in from the Union right took full advantage of a clump of cottonwoods in that area. Moving cautiously from tree to tree, these sharpshooters picked off the cannoneers. As the Texans converged upon the stilled artillery, they fell upon the Union gunners, who were armed with revolvers, and the infantry, who were equipped with muskets, in a fiercely savage, bloody, hand-to-hand encounter. Captain McRae and Lieutenant Lyman Mishler were killed at their pieces. Colonel Sutton, while leading his men, fell mortally wounded within twenty paces of the battery. Major Lockridge, also at the head of his column, fell at the mouth of the enemy's guns, but lived long enough to see victory achieved. The superior numbers of the Texans, coupled with their ferociously intrepid determination, drove the stubborn defenders into retreat. McRae's gallant battery lost nearly half its number in killed, wounded, and captured. At this critical moment, Captain Wingate's battalion arrived on the "double-quick" from the right and fired into the Texans. So stunned were the Confederates by this unexpected action that they momentarily reeled back. As a result, Canby now hoped that the battery, and with it the fortunes of the day, would yet be saved. Such was not to be the case, for the Texans quickly re-formed to smash this new Union threat. With the wounding of Wingate and the killing of his second in command, the shattered Federal battalion retreated in disorder.

When Colonel Roberts, in charge of the right, perceived the situation, he ordered all his available troops to speed to the left. But his men had been over-zealous in their pursuit of Raguet, and were now too far away to be of assistance. It did not take Canby long to realize that a prolongation of the battle would only increase the casualties without changing the result. Quickly he instructed Selden to cover the retreat on the left, while Roberts took charge of the withdrawal on the right. The Union troops who had repulsed Raguet and then had successfully pursued him, believed that they had won the battle. It came as a shock to hear the bugle sound retreat.

On seizing McRae's battery, the Confederates turned the six pieces around and began using them on their late owners. Captains Hardeman and Walker manned several guns on the right while Lieutenant Raguet of Reily's battery took charge of another. Undaunted by the lack of a rammer, Raguet used a flagstaff instead. Within a matter of minutes Captain Teel came forward with his guns to join in the cannonading. With the Federal forces in wild flight in front, Green quickly turned his attention to the Union right. According to his account, "We charged them as we had those in front, but they were not made of as good stuff as the regulars, and a few fires upon them with their own artillery and Teel's guns, a few volleys of small-arms, and the old Texas war-shout completely dispersed them. They fled from the field, both cavalry and infantry, in the utmost disorder, many of them dropping their guns to lighten their heels . . . Our victory was complete."[7]

Canby's version differed somewhat, particularly in regard to the manner in which the retreat was carried out. Though under heavy fire, Selden's infantry successfully covered the orderly withdrawal of the regulars on the left, while Roberts accomplished the same on the extreme right. The native New Mexicans were, according to Canby, the ones who fled pell-mell. On the west bank those volunteers and militia who had escaped from the battle were scattered in every direction. The men of Pino's Second Regiment, for example, were so terror-stricken that no efforts of their officers, nor of Canby's staff, could restore them to any semblance of order. In contrast, the regulars were easily re-formed and marched back to Fort Craig. Under the protective cover of Selden's infantry, and later of the regular cavalry, most of the stragglers were gathered up and returned to the post.

Fearing an attack upon his fort, Canby ordered the beef herd, and all other property, brought into its confines. Aside from McRae's battery of six guns (three six-pounders, two twelve-pound field howitzers, and one twelve-pound mountain howitzer), Canby asserted that nothing was abandoned on the field except some tents and fixtures of the field hospital left behind for the wounded, and one wagon from which the escort of volunteers had cut loose the mules to flee to the mountains.

Shortly after the enemy had retreated across the river on the Confederate right, Major Raguet and five mounted companies arrived on the scene. Two of these (E and H of the Fourth) had engaged in the charge on the left, while the other three had been guarding the wagon train. After falling back considerably beyond his original point of departure following his ill-fated assault, Raguet had attempted to re-form his ranks. With as many of his command as he could gather, and after instructing Lieutenant Woods to set u his one gun between the enemy and the wagon train—still moving northward some distance beyond—Raguet set out to join in the action on the right. Why he did not stay where he was and launch a counterattack or, at least, prepare to stiffen resistance to the Federal onslaught, is not clear. If the Federals were as successful in advancing on their right as it appears, and if the Confederate attack on the Union left had been hurled back, Raguet's leaving could have easily resulted in the loss, or capture, of a good part of the train, as well as the enfilading and consequent turning of the whole Texan line. Apparently the main charge of the Texans on McRae's battery had virtually halted the Union advance on the right. At least it is certain that Colonel Roberts did immediately order the bulk of his forces to rush to the support of the left. Perhaps, Raguet, on perceiving this development, felt justified in leaving to join in the chief assault on his right.

With the arrival of the five "fresh" mounted companies, Scurry received Green's permission to lead them across the river to pursue the flying foe. When the column reached the opposite bank, Scurry was ordered back, for a flag of truce had been dispatched by the Union commander. For some time the Confederates interpreted this as meaning that the Federals intended to surrender. Canby had sent it, however, for the purpose of ceasing hostilities to enable the dead and wounded to be removed and cared for. By now darkness had settled over the field of Valverde. In the first full-scale encounter, the Army of New

Mexico had emerged victorious. Nevertheless, for a long time victory had been, as one soldier put it, "hanging on a thread."[8]

Sibley reported that his forces on the field did not exceed 1,750 in number (Second Regiment, 250; Fourth Regiment, 600; Fifth Regiment, 600; Seventh Regiment, 300). At all times the Texan officers were in the thickest of the fight setting sterling examples of bravery to their men. Throughout the engagement Scurry's cheering voice was heard above the din of battle, while Green was noted for his calm, cool, and discriminating courage. The gallantry of Lang, Pyron, McNeill, Heuvel, Raguet, Ochiltree, Lockridge, and a host of other staff and field officers, coupled with the heroic endurance and unfaltering courage of the volunteer soldiers of Texas, marked February 21 as a day of valor. Proudly Sibley wrote the adjutant general that "For the first time, perhaps, on record batteries were charged and taken at the muzzle of double-barreled shot-guns, thus illustrating the spirit, valor, and invincible determination of Texas troops. Nobly have they emulated the fame of their San Jacinto ancestors."[9]

Sibley admitted that the victory of Valverde should have resulted in the capture of Fort Craig, but that Canby's flag of truce had prevented further action that day. Several other factors, however, account for the failure of the Texans to follow up their victory. Aside from the five companies which arrived with Raguet, the bulk of the Confederates were dismounted, thoroughly exhausted, and in no condition to chase the enemy further. If Scurry had pursued with his five companies, Canby undoubtedly would have counterattacked with his reliable and numerically superior regulars. The coming of nightfall also played a part in discontinuing further military operations.

Considering the numbers involved, the battle of Valverde had been won at a heavy cost. Green gave the losses as 36 killed, 150 wounded, and 1 missing—roughly 8 per cent of Sibley's whole force:

Second Regiment (Pyron): 4 killed, 17 wounded, 1 missing
Fourth Regiment (Scurry): 8 killed, 36 wounded
Fifth Regiment (Green): 20 killed, 67 wounded
Seventh Regiment (Sutton): 2 killed, 26 wounded
Teel's battery: 2 killed, 4 wounded[10]

Most of the wounded and dead were brought into camp that night, "and many were the salutations of friends who had not seen each other during the day."[11] The losses sustained prompted Sibley to write the adjutant general that "It will be necessary, to secure our purpose, to re-enforce me largely from Texas at as early a day as possible. The force we had to contend against amounted to near 6,000 men."[12] It is possible that the General may have purposely exaggerated the numbers comprising Canby's force in order to motivate the adjutant general to expedite the sending of reinforcements. At any rate, Sibley now realized that the conquest of New Mexico would not be as easy as he had prophesied.

The Federal losses were even greater than those of the Confederates: 68 killed, 160 wounded, and 35 missing.[13] The Federals suffered their greatest casualties at McRae's battery and in fording the river in retreat. Although he was undoubtedly exaggerating, a Texan correspondent described the Río Grande as being "literally dyed with blood."[14]

Canby was outspoken in his condemnation of the native troops, pointing out that his previous doubts concerning their worth were now fully vindicated. According to the Union commander, Pino's Second Regiment, which had orders to cross over to form part of the reserve and to serve as an added support to McRae's battery, had failed miserably. Only one company and part of another actually forded the stream. In his first official account of the battle, Canby listed the refusal of this regiment to rush to the support of the left wing as the immediate cause of defeat. This criticism seems unduly harsh. On the basis of Colonel Pino's report and other evidence, the regiment was in the process of crossing when the Confederates struck, sending the battery's supports fleeing down upon those of the regiment who had just emerged from the ford. There is no doubt concerning the cowardice of Mortimore's and Hubbell's volunteer companies. These native troops did refuse to rush to McRae's defense, and did break and flee from the field, but so did many of the regulars. Canby was far less critical of his regulars than were others who witnessed the action.[15] Although it is a fact that most of the natives had behaved badly under fire, it is nonetheless true that many of the regulars were equally guilty.

In closing his official report, Canby added a note of optimism by saying, "The troops are not disrupted by this result, as all are satisfied that we have inflicted greater losses upon the enemy than we have suffered ourselves and that the ultimate result of the contest will be in our favor."[16] But equally certain was the editor of the Mesilla *Times* who noted: "This battle . . . is generally considered in this valley to have decisively ended military operations in New Mexico. The remaining [Federal] force can make no considerable stand against our arms, and the garrison of Fort Craig will soon be compelled to capitulate for want of supplies."[17]

5

Onward to Albuquerque and Santa Fé

SIBLEY AND CANBY AGREED TO A TWO-DAY TRUCE TO ALLOW FOR THE CARING OF THE wounded and the burying of the dead. Agonizing moans and groans filled the air about the Confederate camp near the battlefield as the surgeons busily dressed wounds and provided for the comfort of the injured as best they could. The deceased were wrapped in blankets and interred in trenches near the scene of conflict. The sound of rifle fire from the direction of Fort Craig indicated that the Federals were also "burying many a poor soldier far from his relatives and the home of his youth."[1] Throughout the day after the battle many New Mexican militia and volunteers drifted into the Confederate camp to surrender and be paroled.

In their hasty retreat from the battlefield the Union soldiers had discarded much equipment. Groups of Texans scouring the area later gathered about 250 stand of small arms, numerous well-filled cartridge belts, and many canteens and haversacks containing food and drink—enabling them, half-starved as they were, to eat "sumptuously . . . on Yankee light bread and other delicious eatables."[2] But even with this addition, Sibley's commissary glumly reported that only a bare five days' rations remained.

Many Confederates believed that the enemy violated the two-day truce by gathering up small arms from the battleground and carrying them off in their dead wagons. Technically, the Texans had won the field and were only allowing the Federals to remove their dead and wounded. Sibley maintained that one of Hall's twenty-four–pounders which had been abandoned in the river was recovered by the enemy during the truce period. Green reported his certainty that the Federals had at the same time picked up a company flag and guidon belonging to his regiment. Since most of these alleged violations had occurred during darkness, the Confederates had been unable to prevent them.

The day following the battle Sibley sent Scurry and Captain Denman W. Shannon under a white flag to demand the capitulation of Fort Craig. Though these officers and gentlemen offered honorable surrender terms, Canby politely refused. After spending some time in refreshment and conversation, the Confederates returned to their camp. During the course of the interview Canby had referred to the flags from the Fifth Regiment as trophies of the fight. Upon learning of this Colonel Green surmised that Canby must not have known how they had been obtained, "as he would not have spoken of stolen flags as trophies."[3]

After Valverde much disaffection came to reign within Confederate ranks. The Texans had hoped to capture everything they needed from the Federals. To be sure, they had won a victory at Valverde, but the resources of Fort Craig were not forthcoming. The country about them was barren and destitute of food, not even producing enough grass for their horses. Many came to curse Sibley for their plight. This prejudiced feeling, though possibly intensified by Sibley's not being a Texan, arose primarily because he had failed to continue commanding his troops during the battle. Many accused him of being drunk most of the time, and a coward at heart. Some extremists actually believed he was involved in a deliberate plot to turn them over to the enemy![4] With morale at such a low ebb, the officers found it increasingly difficult to maintain discipline.

When Canby refused to surrender, the Confederates held another council of war to determine their next move. Some of the more daring officers favored an attack on the post. But Scurry and Shannon, having been inside Fort Craig, pointed out that it was too strongly defended to be taken either by an assault or by a siege. Others believed that the Army of New Mexico was too small to conquer the territory, and so should withdraw to the Mesilla Valley. After all views had been discussed, the council reached its decision: Fort Craig would be left unmolested and the army would continue its northward march. Sibley believed that the capture of supplies at Albuquerque and Santa Fé would eradicate disaffection in the ranks, as well as make possible the continuation of the campaign. If the Confederates were successful in the north, Canby's isolated garrison would eventually be forced to capitulate anyway. To have turned back now would have meant the end of Sibley's dream, after a fruitless expenditure of time, money, and men. From the first the campaign had been a gamble; the decision to continue was simply another calculated risk. As one of Sibley's more optimistic officers viewed the situation, "If we can subsist our men and horses, there is very little doubt we will be conquerors of New Mexico, and have it in our power to establish Southern principles in the Territory."[5]

On February 23 the Army of New Mexico forded the Río Grande and proceeded northward about five miles before encamping. While en route, the Texans seized the goods of a store belonging to the Stapleton Ranch. The following day as the men remained in camp, those wounded who had since died were given a proper military burial, and several Union prisoners captured at Valverde were released on parole. That evening Sibley instructed Lieutenant Colonel McNeill to take five companies of the Fifth Regiment (about four hundred men) and two pieces of artillery to occupy the town of Socorro.

After his defeat, and with the Texans still occupying the battlefield, Colonel Canby saw three possible courses of action. (1) He could attack the Confederates again, and thus submit the major part of the Federal army in New Mexico to the chances of battle. (2) He could abandon Fort Craig and, by circumventing the Texans, march his troops rapidly northward. Once above the enemy, he could impede their progress, as well as strengthen his army by uniting his column with the Federal detachments in the north. This course would entail the destruction of many supplies at Fort Craig, the abandonment of an important strategic point, and the leaving behind of his sick and wounded. (3) He could retain Fort Craig while awaiting the reinforcements he had previously requested from outside the department. Once they arrived he would be in a position to launch concerted operations which, if successful, would compel the Confederates to retreat down the Río Grande. The garrison at Fort Craig would then be able to cut off their escape. Furthermore, while Sibley was involved in the north, the troops at the post could intercept any reinforcements coming from Texas, and might even be able to take the offensive against the small Confederate force in the Mesilla Valley. Canby discussed these various plans with his commanders and the key territorial officials, including the governor. All agreed that the third one was the best.

At first Canby felt certain that the Confederates would assault his post just as soon as the truce period expired. He consequently hastened to strengthen his defenses. Within the fort were far more troops than necessary, and in case of a siege, so many men would be a detriment because of limited commissary supplies. Since the militia were the least valuable, he concluded to "disembarrass" himself of them by sending them away. This would leave a garrison of about 1,100 regulars, plus the several regiments and detachments of volunteers. From the latter, he hoped to organize a picked force of partisans to harass the Texans with surprise flanking attacks.

Canby believed that if the expected Confederate assault were unsuccessful, or did not materialize, the enemy would continue his march upriver. During the night following the battle, he dispatched instructions to his subordinate in the north to remove all government property from the path of the enemy, and to destroy the remainder to prevent its capture. To avert the possibility that detachments of Texans might rapidly move ahead to seize such supplies before the northern commander could act, Major James L. Donaldson, Canby's chief quartermaster, volunteered to carry out the order in the area beginning immediately above the Confederate encampment. In the hope that the militia might yet serve some useful purpose, Canby instructed the officers before they left to remove all livestock, grain, and any other supplies in private hands which might be of use to the enemy. Canby concluded that "If there be any consistency of purpose or persistence of effort in the people of New Mexico, the enemy will be able to add but little to his resources from a temporary occupation of the country."[6]

On February 22, under cover of darkness, the militia detachments filed westward from Fort Craig toward the mountains. According to plan, they were to move northward through the foothills and, when safely above the Texans, reunite on the Río Grande. During the course of the march, however, great numbers of them deserted and returned to their homes. Major Donaldson and Governor Connelly left with the militia. On reaching the river the next morning, they were alarmed to learn that McNeill's advance was moving rapidly toward the supply depot at Polvadera, some fifty miles above Fort Craig. Fortunately for their cause, the provisions there were quickly gathered up and sent northward to safety. Several days later Donaldson arrived in Santa Fé and immediately set himself to the task of carrying out Canby's instructions. Governor Connelly entered the capital on February 27 accompanied by several militia officers.

Colonel Nicolás Pino commanded one of the militia detachments which left Fort Craig on the night of February 22. After he had advanced as far as Lemitar, an express overtook him with instructions to fall back to Socorro. Apparently he was to repel any enemy foraging parties until all property could be removed or destroyed. Reaching Socorro at dusk on February 24, Pino selected quarters for his command of 280 men, posted a security guard south of town, and sent his horses out to graze. Hardly had he completed these arrangements when word came of an approaching enemy. Quickly he alerted his command to prepare for action.

On nearing Socorro, Colonel McNeill stationed the bulk of his force on a strategic elevation southwest of town. To prevent the Federals from escaping, he sent Captain Frazer with a detachment around the town to secure the road leading north. He then fired a cannon ball over the village as a warning. From that moment on—about eight o'clock—the Union militiamen began to desert and to hide. They had obviously had enough of the "terrible Texans" at Valverde.

As the Federal command began to disintegrate, Major Charles Wesche, a member of the governor's staff attached to Pino's force, sent an urgent appeal northward for reinforcements. In company with the adjutant, he also visited the homes of some of the influential Mexicans in a vain effort to get them to rally to the town's defense. His entreaties fell on deaf ears. One Don Pedro Baca probably best summed up the sentiments of the natives when he replied that "the United States Government was a curse to this Territory, and if the Texans would take and keep possession of New Mexico the change could only be for the better."[7] Completely disheartened, the Major returned to Pino's headquarters to relate the attitude of the citizenry.

Shortly after firing the cannon, McNeill demanded Pino's unconditional surrender. Failure to comply, he pointed out, would result in an immediate attack upon the town with the consequent imperiling of the lives of innocent civilians. To play for time until the hoped-for reinforcements arrived Pino agreed to discuss the matter at a conference. In order to spare the townspeople, Pino proposed that his troops meet the Confederates at daybreak on the plain south of town. After a lengthy discussion, McNeill finally agreed to this suggestion if the Union colonel could give his word of honor that he had not written anyone, nor had in any way given notice of the Confederate approach. Since Pino tried to evade the question, McNeill considered the conference at an end.

Several times during the discussion, McNeill had suggested that Pino visit the Texan camp. He could then see for himself that the numerical superiority of the Confederates made resistance futile. Pino at length accepted the invitation, and shortly he saw "the long line of rebels." With only a handful of men remaining, and with apparently no relief on the way, Pino had no choice. He surrendered his command, or what remained of it, at two o'clock A.M. on February 25. After the negotiations had been completed, most of the native troops came out of their hiding places to take the oath of neutrality.

Aside from prisoners, the Confederates captured a large supply of ammunition and about 250 small arms (mainly Mississippi and Minié rifles and muskets and a few Sharp's rifles). From these ordnance additions, Captain McCown armed his company. Heretofore, his men had been equipped with lances, but Valverde had taught the uselessness of such antiquated weapons in modern warfare.

The following day McNeill dispatched two companies under Captains Jordan and McCown northward to Lemitar and environs to look for government property. At Lemitar the party confiscated the goods of a store belonging to Governor Connelly, and secured a large quantity of corn from a government warehouse. Continuing on to La Joyita, they appropriated the stock—mainly clothing—from another establishment owned by a Federal employee. After these successful foraging operations, Jordan and McCown rejoined the main army, which by now was nearly opposite La Joyita.

While Jordan and McCown were carrying out their mission, McNeill and Dr. E. N. Covey, the medical purveyor, set about readying suitable quarters in Socorro for the Confederate sick and wounded. In searching about the village, they fortunately discovered numerous supplies and a large quantity of medicines. Shortly the bulk of the Army of New Mexico arrived and encamped above town. On February 27, while most of the troops rested in camp, the approximately two hundred sick and wounded were transferred to the general hospital.

During the battle of Valverde, many of the Fourth Regiment's horses had been killed, leaving half that body afoot. Lack of forage and overwork also had resulted in the loss of many mounts. In order to make the army as a whole more efficient, the men of the Fourth were asked to turn over their remaining horses to the quartermaster to be reapportioned to those needy units which were to remain mounted. Since the horses were the soldiers' private property, their permission was necessary for such a change. Colonel Scurry, orally backed by General Sibley, promised his men that the government would reimburse them for their mounts at their appraised value. He emphasized that since the horses would probably die from the rigors of the campaign anyway, it would be a wise measure to get rid of them now while they could receive compensation. The Colonel's words apparently had the desired effect, for according to Sibley, "without a dissenting voice" this proud cavalry regiment took the line of march as a strong and reliable regiment of infantry.

However, contrary to what Sibley reported, the men did not take kindly to becoming infantry. There was probably nothing more degrading to a proud Texan than being reduced to the status of a foot soldier. Unaccustomed to walking, and loaded down with gear, the troops discovered that a march of ten miles made them so sore and tired that they were scarcely able to drag themselves along. The fact that the rest of the army rode caused "considerable growling among the boys."[8]

On the last day of February the Army of New Mexico resumed its northward march from the vicinity of Socorro. With commissary supplies now all but exhausted, the men faced the unhappy prospect of having nothing to eat but coarse beef. The only ray of encouragement was that the Federal depot at Albuquerque was reputedly filled with supplies of all descriptions. Once these items were captured, all would be well. To prevent the Union troops from removing or destroying these all-important stores, Sibley ordered Major Pyron to take two hundred men and march rapidly ahead.

As the main Confederate army pushed onward, they traversed country characterized by small farms and villages clustered along the river. Grass and wood, nevertheless, continued to be scarce, for the land was exceedingly barren. At times the men were compelled to gather dried cow chips for use as fuel. In at least one instance, they directed a village alcalde to furnish firewood. To one soldier this part of New Mexico had the appearance of a "desolate old waste farm."[9] The intense cold and the destitute nature of the land prompted another to remark that the territory obviously was "never intended for white folks." In fact, he disgustedly continued, the "first man that ever came to the country ought to have been killed by the Indians."[10] By March 3 the army was just about out of provisions, yet it was still some thirty miles to Albuquerque—the "promised paradise."

During the afternoon of March 1 Captain Herbert M. Enos, assistant quartermaster in charge of the Albuquerque depot, heard that about four hundred Texans had entered Belén, only thirty-five miles to the south. Lest the supplies at his depot be captured, he ordered his men[11] to load the most important military stores—primarily ammunition and ordnance—into wagons as quickly as possible. In obedience to Donaldson's instructions he planned to destroy all property which could not be carried away. About six o'clock that evening an express rode in to report that a Confederate advance detachment of fifty men had reached Los Lunas, about twenty miles below, and had confiscated a civilian-owned train carrying government supplies. Having by now completed the loading of the strategic matériel, Enos dispatched these wagons at once to Santa Fé. He and part of his command remained behind at the depot to await further developments and, if necessary, to destroy the rest of the supplies.

Though the Texans made no appearance during the night, Enos knew they would not be long in arriving. Despairing of reinforcements coming to his support from Santa Fé, he ordered the destruction of the government property at six-thirty that morning. Since he had so few men, and with time being of the essence, he considered it impractical to carry the goods outside to be burned. Rather, he instructed his men to set fire to the buildings housing it.[12]

This destruction would have been complete had it not been for the natives. Fully aware of what was to take place, they had waited anxiously all night for the opportunity to plunder whatever they could lay their hands on. The flames had hardly begun licking at the warehouse when a horde of men, women, and children rushed inside to carry out molasses, vinegar, soap, and candles from the subsistence department, and such items as saddles, carpenter tools, and office furniture from the quartermaster section. The small band of soldiers were powerless to stop them. Enos believed that even had he been able to carry the supplies outside to be more effectively burned in piles, the natives would have overpowered him and saved the property for the Confederates.

Escorted by New Mexican volunteers and militia, Enos set out from Albuquerque with five wagons carrying the soldiers' baggage. While encamped near the Indian village of Sandía, about twelve miles north, a band of native Union deserters attacked the train, and drove off three wagons. It was only because of the quick thinking and bravery of the wagon master that the other two were not lost as well. Enos learned later that six wagons and teams which had gone to the mountains for fuel on the morning of March 1, and which had been later ordered to move to Santa Fé by way of Galisteo, had been attacked and captured by deserters.

As Pyron's advance approached Albuquerque on March 2, large columns of smoke told the tale of Enos' destruction of supplies. Once again the Texans' hopes of capturing large stores of needed goods were doomed to bitter disappointment. Several days after Pyron's arrival, Richmond Gillespie rode into town bearing a dispatch from a Dr. F. E. Kavenaugh, commanding the military post of Cubero. Gillespie reported that the Federal depot there was well supplied with war matériel (originally intended for use against the hostile Navajos), and requested that an adequate

Confederate force be sent to secure it. Seeing an opportunity to compensate partially, at least, for failure at Albuquerque, Pyron detailed Captain Alfred S. Thurmond[13] to Cubero with twenty-five men of his Company A, Seventh Regiment.

Cubero, a Mexican village of approximately five hundred inhabitants, was located about sixty miles west of Albuquerque. Captain Francisco Aragón, with a command of forty-two natives, three regulars, and an American surgeon, was in charge of the depot. Apparently Major Donaldson, in carrying out Canby's orders to remove or destroy all property, had forgotten about Cubero. The only American civilians in town were Kavenaugh, the owner and operator of a local store, Gillespie, George Gardenhier, and R. T. Thompson. All four were staunchly pro-Southern, and had made no secret of their sentiments. Fully cognizant of the native attitude toward the war, they decided to seize the depot for the South. At nine o'clock in the morning of March 3, Kavenaugh, in "command" of his three companions, demanded in the name of the Confederate States that Aragón surrender his post. Having no desire to fight for a cause in which he had no interest whatsoever, Aragón yielded without a struggle. After taking charge, Kavenaugh dispatched Gillespie to carry the news to Confederate authorities in Albuquerque (Kavenaugh assumed that by now the Texans had occupied the town). Gillespie's lone mission was extremely dangerous, for the route between Cubero and Albuquerque was in the realm of the hostile Navajos. Kavenaugh paroled Aragón's command and provided them with enough arms (20 muskets and 40 cartridges each) and transportation to carry them safely to Albuquerque. On arrival there, they promised to turn over this equipment to the Confederate commanding officer.

Captain Thurmond reached Cubero about two o'clock P.M. on March 5. The following day Kavenaugh formally relinquished his "command." The depot held invaluable quantities of quartermaster, commissary, ordnance (including 60 small arms and 3,000 rounds of ammunition), and medical supplies, requiring twenty-five wagons to carry the stores to Albuquerque. The outstanding bravery of Kavenaugh, Gillespie, Thompson, and Gardenhier had rendered the Army of New Mexico an inestimable service.

Meanwhile the main body of the army crossed the Río Grande to the east bank and continued its northerly advance. At an unidentified village (probably Peralta), the Texans were welcomed by ex-Territorial Delegate Miguel Otero and his South Carolina-born wife. As a gesture of their sympathies, the couple accepted Sibley's invitation to accompany the army to Albuquerque. Apparently Otero was now officially pro-Southern again.

On March 7 the Confederates encamped at Spruce M. Baird's[14] ranch, and the following day entered Albuquerque in triumph. At a formal ceremony in the town plaza, thirteen cannon roared a salute as the Confederate banner was raised to flutter in the crisp New Mexican breeze. About a week after establishing temporary headquarters at Albuquerque, Sibley issued the following proclamation in the hope of gaining the support of the native population and of weakening the Federal army:

TO THE PEOPLE OF NEW MEXICO:

The signal victory which crowned our arms at Valverde on the 21st of February proves the truth of the assertions contained in my first Proclamation in regard to our powers and ability to accomplish the purposes therein declared. Those of you who volunteered in the Federal service were doubtless deceived by designing officials and interested citizens. The militia were driven to the field by force of arms. Under these circumstances I deem it proper and but just to declare a complete and absolute amnesty to all citizens who have, or may within ten days lay aside their arms and return to their homes and avocations.

The conduct of this army since its entrance into the Territory of New Mexico attests the honesty and integrity of our purpose, and the protection it has and can afford to the citizens of the country.

Return then with confidence to your homes and to your avocations, and fear not the result.

Given at Albuquerque under my hand this 13th day of March 1862.
(Signed) H. H. Sibley
Brig. General
Commanding.[15]

The results of the proclamation were disappointing. Sibley lamented that the "ricos," or wealthy citizens, had been so "completely drained by the Federal powers," that they had no choice but to support and follow the Union army "for dear life and their invested dollars. Politically they have no distinct sentiment or opinion on the vital question at issue. Power and interest alone control the expression of their sympathies."[16]

Two notable exceptions were Rafael and Manuel Armijo, the wealthiest and most respected native merchants in the territory. Manuel, as a member of the militia, had been "compulsorily" present at the battle of Valverde. When Sibley entered Albuquerque, both brothers came forward to pledge their allegiance to the Confederacy. As evidence of their sincerity, they placed their stores, containing goods amounting to $200,000, at Sibley's disposal.

Sibley ordered the confiscation of several stores in Albuquerque which were operated by sutlers for the Union army. All persons who had taken any government property prior to the arrival of the Texans, were ordered to turn it over to Confederate authorities. At Carnuel Pass, about fifteen miles east of Albuquerque, a small party of Texans captured a train of twenty-three wagons loaded with provisions destined for Fort Craig. Designating Albuquerque as his depot of supply, Sibley noted that the goods secured at Cubero, Albuquerque, and Carnuel Pass would provision his army for about three months.

With Enos' arrival from Albuquerque, and the knowledge that the Confederates were advancing steadily, Major Donaldson concluded to abandon the capital and withdraw to the safety of Fort Union. Several factors prompted this decision. Having only a small number of troops, and with Santa Fé virtually surrounded on all sides by hills, he knew he would not be able to defend the town. The most valuable supplies in the department—at least $250,000 worth—were now at Santa Fé. To insure their safety, he prepared to send them to Fort Union. To protect this train of 120 wagons adequately, his entire command would have to serve as escort.

As the Major set about preparing to evacuate the capital, he made certain that little would remain for the Confederates. Two warehouses containing large stores of flour were put to the torch. Two large stacks of hay in the government corral were about the only things left behind, for to have set them afire would have endangered nearby buildings. Donaldson even ordered the flag pole cut down so the Confederates would not be able to raise their banner on it.

On March 4 he called his soldiers into line and set out for Fort Union. With the capital left undefended, and its capture by the Texans imminent, Governor Connelly left with the troops. He later established his executive department at Las Vegas, about thirty miles southwest of Fort Union. Donaldson's command comprised about two hundred men, consisting of several detachments of regular infantry and cavalry and a company of Colorado volunteers captained by James H. Ford.[17] An undetermined number of New Mexican volunteers commanded by Lieutenant Colonel Manuel Chávez also formed part of Donaldson's force. By the time the column had reached Fort Union, all the natives, except Chávez and a few of his officers, had deserted along the way.

The army wives in Santa Fé, including Mrs. Canby, were not permitted to accompany the troops. Before their departure, Donaldson's men left the ladies with an adequate supply of foodstuffs. For several days following the abandonment of the capital, the local Mexicans so eagerly commenced plundering what had been left behind that the American women feared for their safety. Fortunately the natives—who "stood in great fear"[18] of Texans—had a scare put into them by the arrival of two Texans from Fort Union. Immediately the warning,

"Tejanos! Tejanos!" rang throughout the town. The two men had been arrested previously in Santa Fé as spies, but had been released when the Federal troops concentrated at Fort Union. Their timely appearance completely overawed the natives, thus allowing the soldiers' wives to breathe freely again.

Shortly after occupying Albuquerque, Major Pyron dispatched eleven Arizona volunteers to Santa Fé, about seventy-five miles distant. On March 4 Union intelligence reported that they had reached Algodones. Although now only fifty miles from Santa Fé, they did not reach the capital until March 10. If the Union report was correct, it is a mystery as to why it took six days for the scouts to cover this relatively short distance. Perhaps the Arizonans halted, awaiting information that Pyron's larger force was following behind, before continuing on to Santa Fé.

When the eleven Arizona volunteers entered town, some started seizing the goods belonging to the Union wives. As luck would have it, Captain Ford's wife was acquainted with the officer in charge. At her request he ordered his men to cease their pilfering at once, and to respect the ladies' property.[19]

On March 13 Major Pyron came into Santa Fé with seventy men. It appears that he had remained in Albuquerque with most of his command until the arrival of the main body of the army. Santa Fé, the second oldest town in what is now the United States, was formally occupied for the Confederacy.

With the outbreak of the war, the formerly pro-Southern Santa Fé *Gazette* advocated a neutralist policy, but as the conflict progressed, it became staunchly pro-Union. As a result of the turmoil occasioned by Donaldson's abandonment of the capital, the paper suspended operations. Desiring to publish Sibley's "Albuquerque Proclamation," Pyron seized the *Gazette* printing plant and sent the following note to the editor:

SANTA FE NEW MEXICO,
March 22th 1862.
Mr. John T. Russell

Sir. You deliver to the barrer [sic] the keys of the printing of the Santa Fe Gazett [sic].

C. L. Pyron C. S. A.
Maj. Comd'g Santa Fe.[20]

The day following the seizure, copies of the proclamation were printed and distributed throughout the town.

A day or so after Sibley arrived in Albuquerque, he sent the bulk of his army eastward into the mountains where grass and wood were plentiful. Here the men and animals could rest and recruit before commencing the march against Fort

Union. An important strategic purpose behind this eastward movement was to maintain a vigilant lookout on the mountain road leading from Fort Craig to Fort Union to prevent the Federal forces from forming a junction.

The severity of the winter weather minimized rest and recuperation. A soldier of the Fifth Regiment considered this mountainous country—as he did New Mexico in general—to be entirely worthless. The officers of his detachment were apparently as disgusted as he, for they were "drunk all the time, unfit for duty—incompetent to attend to their duty."[21]

So furiously did the icy wind blow at times that one Texan was led to comment that "the sand and gravel . . . [flew] in a manner that I never saw before. I would compare it to a description that I have seen of the sand storms of the great desert of Sahara."[22] Unfortunately the men of the Fourth Regiment had no tents to protect them from the weather, since these had been left in the wagons abandoned near Fort Craig. A four-inch snow on March 12 caused such intense suffering that Colonel Scurry quartered his troops in a small Mexican village, the huts of which afforded some comfort against the bitter cold.

Having secured all available supplies in Albuquerque after a stay of about two weeks in the area, Sibley decided it was time to move against Fort Union. Major John S. Shropshire (formerly Captain of Company A, but promoted to replace Lockridge) received orders to take Companies A, B, C, and D of the Fifth up the river road to reinforce Pyron at Santa Fé. Fort Union could be reached from the capital by following the Santa Fé Trail. The remaining six companies of the Fifth were ordered in from the mountains and concentrated at Albuquerque. Being somewhat crippled in transportation, they were to remain momentarily in Albuquerque to check any movement which might come from Fort Craig along the river road. Scurry in command of the Fourth Regiment and the battalion of the Seventh[23] (now under Major Powhatan Jordan), was to proceed by way of Galisteo either to Santa Fé or to where the Santa Fé Trail entered Apache Canyon. By following this mountainous route, part of which comprised the main road from Fort Union to Fort Craig, Scurry would be able to intercept Canby should that officer attempt to unite his forces with those at Fort Union.

Sibley considered Fort Union to be the key to the entire territory. If that post fell, he would seize invaluable supplies (provided they were not first destroyed by the Federal garrison), Canby would be helplessly cut off from aid, and virtually the whole of New Mexico would be in his hands. If such took place, what next? President Davis' instructions stated that Sibley was to drive the Federals from New Mexico and then establish a military government. He made no reference to additional territorial ambitions. But would Sibley, and, indeed, Richmond, be content simply to occupy New Mexico for the remainder of the war? Did the Confederacy have designs on the neighboring territories of Colorado and Utah, and the state of California? According to Teel's postwar statement, Sibley, personally at least, looked upon the New Mexican campaign as a means to an end—the end being the capture of California and the annexation of northern Mexico.

Sibley's plans for operations after the fall of Fort Union can be only surmised. From a military standpoint, it seems logical that in order to secure New Mexico, he would have had to pacify Colorado. The possibility of gaining recruits and supplies, as well as control of the gold fields there, offered additional incentives. After a Confederate conquest of Colorado, the Mormons of Utah would probably have sided with the Confederacy, for they had been at odds with the Federal government for some time. If it was Sibley's aim to move into Colorado, he might have planned to set out for that area immediately after the fall of Fort Union, or to have backtracked first in order to force Canby to surrender.

On the other hand, Sibley may have had no designs on that territory. After the fall of Fort Union, Sibley's army, enriched by captured matériel and possibly by recruits from the Southern sympathizers of Colorado, would have been strong enough to force Canby to capitulate. The road to California would then have been open. But whatever might have been Sibley's ultimate ambitions for the West, everything hinged upon the surrender of Fort Union.

Exactly how Sibley planned to capture Fort Union is not at all clear. Apparently he did not know that the post had been moved from its old location and rebuilt as a strong fortification with bomb-proof quarters about a mile out in the valley. This new post was far better constructed for defensive purposes than was Fort Craig. Yet Sibley had refrained from an assault upon the latter bastion because he lacked heavy artillery. Laying siege to Fort Union would have involved a costly expenditure of time which the Confederates could not afford. Even with the captured and confiscated goods from Albuquerque, Cubero, and Santa Fé, they were still seriously short. If Fort Union was as well supplied as supposed, the garrison might hold out until reinforcements arrived from some other quarter.

Whether or not Sibley knew about the recently constructed post, he apparently calculated that the Union commandant would automatically surrender when his relatively large Confederate army invested the fort. The Federal garrison at this time was a small one—so small that perhaps the troops would have been inadequate to man the defenses successfully against an assault. As long as this situation prevailed, all was well for the Texans.

6

Colorado Volunteers at the Skirmish of Apache Canyon

THE BEHAVIOR OF THE NATIVE SOLDIERS DURING AND AFTER VALVERDE CONVINCED FEDERAL officialdom in New Mexico that such forces could not be relied upon for future operations against the enemy. Canby gave formal sanction to this belief when he sternly warned his officers, "Do not trust the Mexican troops."[1] It seemed clear that if New Mexico was to be held in the Union, American soldiers would have to be employed. In appealing for such reinforcements outside the territory, Canby and his subordinates repeatedly pointed out the inadequacies of the natives.

Major Donaldson recommended that since the New Mexicans had such a traditional fear of Texans that they would not face them in the field the best thing to do would be to disband them entirely. Captain Gurden Chapin, Canby's adjutant, caustically noted that the Mexican soldiers were "worse than worthless," and in effect actually aids to the enemy. To bolster his contention he pointed out that large numbers of militia and volunteers were surrendering to the Texans, who, after taking their arms and equipment, directed them to return to their homes. Even Governor Connelly, who had written glowing letters about the merits and spirit of the native soldiers before Valverde, had altered his opinion. Dejectedly he informed Washington that the militia had all dispersed and gone home to prepare their fields for the coming harvest. This, he frankly admitted, was by far the best use that could be made of them. The bands of native soldiers who had taken to the mountains and were now engaged in robbing and plundering defenseless citizens posed a much more serious problem.

Even before Valverde, Canby had urgently appealed to the governor of Colorado for reinforcements. Though only one company of volunteers had arrived from that quarter in time to take part in the encounter, Canby's pleas were ultimately answered. On February 10 Major General David Hunter, commanding the Department of Kansas, to which Colorado was attached, instructed the governor to send all his available forces to Canby's relief. Twelve days later the First Regiment Colorado Volunteers set out from Denver for New Mexico.[2] When writing Canby that the regiment was on its way, the governor expressed the conviction that these inexperienced troops would prove efficient and that "their enthusiasm and patriotic bravery . . . [would] make amends, and more than that, for their lack of active service in the past."[3]

Several of Canby's officers feared that the Coloradoans would not get to New Mexico in time, or if they did, they felt it would take more than a "green" regiment to secure the safety of the territory.[4] In requesting Major General Henry W. Halleck, commanding the Department of the Missouri, to dispatch at least two additional regiments of infantry and a battery of rifled cannon, Captain Chapin pointed out the importance of holding New Mexico in the Union; to him the conquest of New Mexico was a great political feature of the rebellion. He warned that once the Texans had captured the territory they would augment their forces and then extend their conquest to Mexico and southern California. Success would win the Confederacy great prestige abroad, and might even result in diplomatic recognition. It was therefore imperative, in the captain's opinion, that this invasion be checked immediately.

Colonel Gabriel R. Paul, the commander of Fort Union and Canby's second-ranking officer, reported that the defeat at Valverde had resulted in a precarious position for the military and chaos and general panic throughout the country. According to him many civilians whose homes were in the path of the enemy were fleeing for safety. To insure an adequate consideration of New Mexico's plight and need for reinforcements, he instructed Major Donaldson to proceed at once to Washington where he was "to represent the interests and wants of the department" and to "enter more fully into details."[5]

As the Confederates advanced unimpeded, Colonel Paul set about concentrating at Fort Union all Federal forces in the northern district. Once the Colorado regiment, or any other, reached him he hoped to organize and equip a column to march southward to join Canby's command. He felt that once the Federal troops were united they might have a good chance of driving the Texans from the land. On March 9 he dispatched his plan to Canby by special messenger. His strategy called for his leaving Fort Union on March 24. By taking a back road, thus avoiding the Río Grande Valley and the Confederates, he calculated that his column would reach the village of Antón Chico two days later. Here he would await the coming of Canby's troops from Fort Craig. He planned, should the Texans attempt to thwart this junction, to continue southward until he met Canby. While awaiting his commander's certain approval, Paul hastened to complete the organization of his column.

Near dusk on March 11 the First Regiment Colorado Volunteers came in sight of Fort Union. The valley in which the post lay was about four miles wide and bounded on the east and west by timbered ridges. Running through the valley was a small, stagnant, alkali stream. On a gentle swell about a mile from the west side of the valley was the post: a simple fieldwork of moderate size with bastioned corners surrounded by a dirt parapet and ditch, with a slight abatis at exposed points. Although the armament was poor—consisting mainly of howitzers—the ammunition supply was considered adequate for any situation. Forming part of the works were bomb-proof quarters capable of sheltering five hundred men and all the fort's supplies. The old post lay to the west below a two-hundred-foot rocky ridge. It was built of adobes, logs, slabs, and lumber without any apparent order. Within a few days after their arrival the Coloradoans were issued arms and clothing in preparation for the coming trial with the Texans.

When Colonel John P. Slough, the commander of the volunteer regiment, appeared at Fort Union, Paul was mortified to learn that the Coloradoan's commission was senior to his.[6] As ranking officer Slough immediately assumed command of all forces at the post and planned to carry out the junction with Canby according to Paul's original plan. While Slough was engrossed with completing details for the march southward, a dispatch from Fort Craig arrived on March 21. Though Canby had approved of Paul's plan earlier, he now had changed his mind. In the belief that Fort Union was too valuable to be abandoned at this time, he instructed Paul (he did not know that Slough had assumed command) to concentrate all his forces at the post and there remain until reinforcements reached him from Kansas, Colorado, or California. When large enough numbers arrived which would give him an army adequate to operate directly against the enemy, Canby directed him to notify Fort Craig at once.[7]

Canby intended to retain Fort Craig as long as possible, for, as previously noted, it was ideally situated to cut off any supplies coming to Sibley from the Mesilla Valley and to block any contemplated Confederate retreat down the river. Canby was in no need of immediate help, for the post was stocked with enough food and supplies to last until April 10. He realized that should he consider it necessary to abandon the fort his command would have to unite with Paul's as soon as possible. Until that time—and Paul would be informed when this would take place—he ordered his second in command not to move from Fort Union. In addition Canby suggested that while Paul was awaiting sufficient reinforcements he harass the Confederates with raiding forays. Such operations would involve only a relatively few men, and if successful they would seriously impede the Texans' movements as well as destroy some of their supplies.

Differences of opinion quickly developed between Paul and Slough concerning the interpretation of Canby's instructions. The matter was undoubtedly intensified by Paul's jealousy and Slough's apparent lack of tact. Slough realized that garrison duty at Fort Union certainly was not improving the restless mood of his undisciplined men—most of whom were hardy, individualistic miners. This awareness, as well as his desire to reap laurels, probably were the main reasons which motivated him to interpret Canby's orders loosely. The Coloradoans had come to New Mexico to fight, and Slough made it plain that they would do just that.

In reply to Paul's vigorous protests, Slough insisted that Canby's orders were not only "to protect Fort Union, but also to harass the enemy." He reasoned that by marching his command to the vicinity of Bernal Springs, forty-five miles southwest of Fort Union, both ends could be accomplished. At that point the Federals would be between the enemy and the post. Since Bernal Springs was on the only road to Fort Union, the post would be as much protected as if the troops remained there. Certainly Bernal Springs would be a much better point from which to launch raiding operations against the enemy. Paul was so upset by Slough's decision that he wrote the adjutant general in order "to throw the responsibility of any disaster which . . . [might] occur on the right shoulders."[8] Fearing the worst, he also asked Washington for several batteries of the best cannon and reinforcements to the amount of four thousand men.

Governor Connelly was fully aware of the "little discord in relation to the movement . . . from Union," but since he was anxious for offensive action, he sided with Slough. He believed that this action "would curtail the limits of the enemy, and mayhap lead to the expulsion of the enemy from the capital,"[9] which was now reported to be occupied by only one hundred men with two pieces of artillery. Another reason for Connelly's defense of Slough's plan was his belief that the Texans were preparing to leave soon by way of Fort Stanton and the Pecos River. The governor reported that the Confederates had not behaved with the moderation that had been expected, desolation marking their progress on the Río Grande from Fort Craig to Bernalillo. Hearing reports that exactions and confiscations were the order of the day wherever the Texans went, he concluded that the enemy must be planning to depart soon, otherwise they would not be antagonizing the native population in such a manner.

About noon of March 22 Colonel Slough and his command sallied forth from Fort Union, leaving only a handful of regulars and volunteers to garrison the post. The column, numbering 1,342 men, consisted of the following units:

First Regiment Colorado Volunteers, 916 men
Captain W. H. Lewis' battalion, U. S. Fifth Infantry, and Captain James H.
    Ford's Colorado company, 191 men
Captain George W. Howland's detachment, U. S. First and Third Cavalry,
    150 men[10]
Captain John F. Ritter's regular battery (two twelve-pounders and two six-
    pounders), 53 men
Lieutenant Ira W. Claflin's regular battery (four twelve-pound mountain
    howitzers), 32 men[11]

Two days later Slough reached Bernal Springs. Ironically, he named the temporary encampment Camp Paul in honor of the commander of Fort Union.

Though Slough staunchly maintained that he was adhering to Canby's instructions, what the departmental commander considered compliance with his orders might be another matter.

While occupying Santa Fé, Major Pyron apparently learned that Federal troops from Fort Union were marching toward the capital. Since Shropshire's four companies of the Fifth had recently joined him, he considered his force large enough to launch a counter-offensive. With 250 to 300 men and a section (two guns) of Teel's artillery, Pyron set out from the capital on March 25.[12] He encamped that night at Johnson's Ranch (present-day Cañoncito), which was located near the mouth of Apache Canyon. At this point the Santa Fé Trail wound its way through the southern extremity of the Sangre de Cristo Mountains by means of Glorieta Pass. The pass—the western portion of which was called Apache Canyon—was around seven miles in length, narrow at both ends, and about a quarter of a mile wide at the middle.

Meanwhile on the same day, Colonel Slough, having set up camp at Bernal Springs, selected Major John M. Chivington to lead a raiding party to Santa Fé. Chivington was a colorful character. Born in Warren County, Ohio, on January 27, 1821, he migrated to Illinois in 1848 and joined the Illinois Conference of the Methodist Episcopal Church. He later transferred to the Missouri Conference and became a missionary to the Wyandotte Indians in Indian Territory. He moved to Colorado in 1860 where he held the post of presiding elder of the Rocky Mountain District. When the First Regiment was being formed, Governor Gilpin offered him the position of chaplain. Chivington refused, stating that if he went into the army, he would have to have a "fighting" commission. As a result, the governor awarded him the field rank of major.

About three o'clock in the afternoon of March 25, Chivington set out from Bernal Springs with instructions to proceed as far as he could that night before encamping. He was to remain at his camp during all of the following day. When nightfall came he was to march rapidly to the capital and fall upon the small enemy garrison. His party, totaling 418 men, consisted of 180 infantrymen and 238 cavalrymen:

Colorado Volunteers:
Company A, Captain Edward W. Wynkoop, 60 men
Company D, Captain Jacob Downing, 60 men
Company E, Captain Scott J. Anthony, 60 men
Company F (mounted), Captain Samuel H. Cook, 88 men

Regular Cavalry:
Company E, Third Cavalry, Captain Charles J. Walker, 50 men
A detachment of the Third Cavalry, Captain George W. Howland, 50 men
Sections of Companies D and G, First Cavalry, Captain R. S. C. Lord, 50 men

Chivington continued his forward movement until he reached Kozlowski's Ranch about twelve o'clock that night. Learning from the owner that Confederate pickets were in the neighborhood, he ordered his troops to encamp. Kozlowski's Ranch was situated about twenty-seven miles from Santa Fé and approximately thirty-five from Bernal Springs. It was located on the Santa Fé Trail near the Pecos Indian ruins and had served for many years as a hostelry. Near the main house was a grove of cottonwood trees which shaded a fine spring of water flowing from crevices in the sandstone rock. To the rear of the ranch was a small scrub-cedar–covered rise, on which Chivington instructed his men to set up camp.

In an effort to secure more information concerning the disposition of the Confederates, the Major sent Lieutenant George Nelson of Company F with twenty men to capture one of the enemy's pickets, who reportedly were at Pigeon's Ranch, five miles ahead. When Nelson arrived at that place and discovered that the Texans had already left, he decided to return to camp. As luck would have it, the Union detachment got between the pickets and their main force. It was just about dawn, and, because of the obscurity, the four well-armed and well-mounted Confederates mistook Nelson's party for their own. Riding into the midst of the Federals before realizing their mistake, they surrendered without a struggle. One of them, Lieutenant McIntire, had been on Canby's staff at the battle of Valverde, but shortly afterward had left the Union ranks to join Sibley. Another, Captain Hall, had been a resident of Denver City before leaving to enlist in the Southern army. An outraged Coloradoan asserted that "Being a Northern man, I can conceive no excuse for his conduct. He never should be allowed to taint the fair soil he has disgraced by his silly and despicable treachery."[13]

After interrogation at Kozlowski's Ranch, the prisoners were sent under a small detail to Bernal Springs. Undoubtedly Chivington learned from them, or at least deduced, that a sizable body of the enemy was nearby. He therefore discarded his original plan and decided to march forward to engage the Texans in a daylight battle.

On the morning of March 26, after his men had finished eating breakfast, Chivington set out on the Santa Fé Trail. His infantry led the advance while the cavalry brought up the rear. As his men leisurely made their way along, scouts kept coming in to confirm the fact that the Texans were somewhere ahead. The command passed by Pigeon's Ranch and continued up the canyon about a mile and a half, where it reached the summit of the divide around two o'clock. As the advance guard descended the slope, it passed through a narrow gulch where the trail made a short turn. Here in the midst of a thicket of trees and bushes, the Federals unexpectedly ran into the Confederate advance. Caught so completely off-guard, the Texan lieutenant and his thirty men surrendered without firing a shot. A Federal soldier came charging back to the main body with the captured officer, shouting, "We've got them corralled this time. Give them h——l, boys. Hurrah for the Pike's Peakers."[14]

Instantly the infantry closed ranks and the cavalry took open order by fours and rushed forward for about three-quarters of a mile. Knapsacks, canteens, overcoats, and other impediments were flung along the road as the Federals made ready for the expected encounter. On turning a short bend, the men entered Apache Canyon proper and sighted the main body of Texans about four hundred to five hundred yards ahead.

Major Pyron had marched only a few miles from Johnson's Ranch when he suddenly found himself confronted by the enemy. The capture of his advance guard had, of course, deprived him of any warning. Though taken by surprise, his response was immediate. He ordered the formation of a skirmish line and the unlimbering of his two six-pound howitzers. Within a matter of minutes his artillery was throwing grape and shell at Chivington's men. Supporting the battery was a mounted company which displayed a red flag emblazoned with a white star, the emblem of the Lone Star State.

The blasts from the Confederate howitzers temporarily threw the Federals into confusion. Aside from some of the regulars, the men had never been under fire before. As soon as he had formed a battle line across the canyon, Chivington attempted to calm his troops by addressing them on the importance of the contest. Just then a shell came screaming through the air and a "hundred voices" cried, "look out there Maj the d——d rebels are shooting at you with their cannon."[15] Chivington bowed politely as the missile passed over his head, prompting his men to laugh at his "chivalry." After a hasty survey of the terrain and the situation, Chivington decided to employ enveloping tactics. Companies A and E under Wynkoop and Anthony deployed to the left while Downing's Company D went to the right. The men had instructions to climb up the mountains which formed the sides of the canyon to get beyond the elevated range of the Texan howitzers, as well as to be in a better position to fire into the enemy's line. Chivington ordered Captain Howland to retire with the cavalry to the rear, where he was to hold himself in readiness to charge whenever it appeared that the Confederates might retreat. In obedience, Howland's regulars fell back, though in a disorderly manner, leaving Company F in front. Several shells whizzed over the heads of the cavalrymen who responded by crowding to the left to get out of range. "All was confusion. The regular officers in command of the cavalry plunged wildly here and there, and seemed to have no control of themselves or of their men. Everyone was talking—no one talking to any purpose. Major Chivington was placing the infantry in position, and Cook's cavalry awaited orders, while the shells went tearing and screaming over them."[16]

The Confederate battery maintained its fire for only a short time. Though the howitzers had close range, the rough, rocky, and wooded terrain all but nullified their effectiveness. In addition, the Confederate line came to be imperiled by the galling fire from those Federals who had deployed up the mountain sides. Seeing that his position was untenable, Pyron ordered his men to prepare to retreat. The gunners quickly limbered their howitzers and withdrew down the canyon closely followed by the remainder of the command.

According to Chivington's plan, Howland should have charged with his cavalry at this opportune moment. His failure to do so enabled the Confederates to fall back in safety. With this, the first phase of the skirmish of Apache Canyon came to a close.

About a mile and a half down the trail from the first scene of conflict, the canyon made an abrupt turn to the left and then resumed its old direction, leaving a high, steep, and rocky bluff—like the bastion of a fort—squarely in front of the advancing Federals. At this point, also, an arroyo, about fifteen feet wide and as many deep, crossed the canyon floor. It was here that Major Pyron decided to set up his new line of defense. Upon a small mound below the bluff and behind the protective arroyo, he set up his artillery. He also formed a skirmish line which went out well up the sides of the canyon, including the top of the bluff. The road approaching the Confederate position was rough, narrow, and crooked, making it quite difficult for cavalry operations. With his troops entrenched in this strong, natural location, Pyron anxiously awaited the Federal attack.

Chivington's cavalrymen cautiously followed the Texans down the road until they had come to within about an eighth of a mile of the Confederate line. Here they halted behind the protective covering of a projection from the canyon wall while the infantry companies were collected and regrouped. After surveying Pyron's new position, Chivington decided to employ the same successful enveloping tactics as before. Downing's Company D again deployed to the right, while Wynkoop's Company A and Anthony's Company E moved to the left. Since Pyron now had his skirmish line well up both sides of the canyon, Chivington deemed it necessary to increase the numbers involved in his enveloping maneuver. Consequently all the regular cavalry were ordered to dismount and to come forward to fight as infantry. Lord's detachment joined Company D on the right, while Walker's and Howland's supported Wynkoop and Anthony on the left. Captain Cook's Coloradoans of Company F remained mounted and formed the reserve, with instructions to be ready to charge as soon as Chivington gave the signal. If the Major was not in a position to signal, and if Cook saw the Confederates limbering up their howitzers preparatory to retreating, he was to charge immediately on his own initiative.

As the second phase of the battle commenced, Major Chivington proved an inspiring sight to his men:

. . . with a pistol in each hand and one or two under his arms, [he] chawed his lips with only less energy than he gave his orders. He seemed burdened with new responsibility, the extent of which he had never before realized, and to have no thought of danger. Of commanding presence, dressed in full regimentals, he was a conspicuous mark for the Texan sharp shooters. One of their officers taken prisoner averred that he emptied his revolvers three times at the Major and then made his company fire a volley at him. As if possessed of a charmed life, he galloped unhurt through the storm of bullets, and the Texans, discouraged, turned their attention to something else.[17]

The Confederate howitzers commanded the road, but again the rocky and scrub-covered terrain rendered them far less effective than they should have been. After about an hour's fighting, Captain Downing's skirmishers on the right had almost succeeded in flanking the artillery, forcing Pyron to order his men to prepare to withdraw.

When Chivington observed the artillery limbering up, he shouted to Captain Cook. Almost before the order to charge left the Major's mouth, Cook, with his sword gleaming in the sunlight, dashed down the canyon with his men following as fast as their horses would carry them, "fearful lest . . . [they] should win no share of the laurels that were to crown the day."[18] As the cavalry approached the steep, rocky bluff, the Confederates fired into their ranks. Captain Cook was struck in the thigh with a ball and three buckshot, but he was able to stay in his saddle to continue leading the charge. About two hundred yards further down, however, his horse stumbled and fell on him, badly spraining his ankle.[19] Lieutenant Nelson now assumed command. When the men came to a bend in the road where the small-arms fire was heaviest, they halted a moment to fire a few shots from their revolvers at the rocks above, and then dashed around the point. Ahead lay the fifteen-foot arroyo. When the Confederates saw the charge coming, they immediately tore up a small bridge which spanned the arroyo, hoping to prevent the Federals from crossing. The undaunted Coloradoans, however, galloped onward and leapt over the gulch into the midst of the retreating enemy. Only one horse failed to make the jump. Part of the cavalry under Nelson continued down the canyon after the artillery, while two units under Lieutenant William F. Marshall remained behind charging back and forth through the shattered Texan line. The artillery proved to be too fleet-footed, so Nelson shortly returned to help in the mopping-up operations. While the cavalry was charging through the Confederates, Captain Downing gained the rear of the enemy and attempted to cut off his retreat. By pouring a destructive fire into the Texans from the rocks on the hillside, he drove many of them up a small canyon on the left side of the main one. Here Wynkoop and Anthony were able to take a large number of them prisoners. The Colorado infantry came down the sides of the canyon like a "parcel of wild Indians, cheering at the top of their lungs."[20] About half an hour after the cavalry had launched its charge, the Confederates had been completely routed. The battle was over.

During the latter phase of the fighting, two "Pike's Peakers," as the Confederates called the Coloradoans, captured fifteen Texans. As the Confederates were being disarmed, someone cried out, "Shoot the s——s of b——s." One of the captors immediately responded, "No, I'm d——d if you do! I'm d——d if you do! You didn't take 'em. I took these prisoners myself, prisoners of wah. Fall in thar, prisoners! Forward, double quick,"[21] and away he went to the rear with them. As the captives were marched off the field they "saw some men with their heads shot nearly off, and some with their arms or legs shot off, and one poor man . . . lying against a tree, with his brains all shot out."[22] Even in remote New Mexico war was hell.

It was now sundown. Since Chivington did not know how near the Texans' regiments might be, and had no cannon to oppose theirs, he gave up plans for further pursuit and sounded "assembly." As stillness settled over the battlefield, the Federals gathered up the dead and wounded, including several belonging to the Confederates. The command then returned to Pigeon's Ranch, where a hospital was set up and the men went into camp. From here Chivington dispatched a messenger to Bernal Springs informing Slough of the events which had taken place and urging him to come to his assistance at once.[23] Acting as a rear guard, Captain Walker's Company E, Third Cavalry, remained on the field until 9:30 that night before retiring to join the main body.

After being overwhelmed in the second brief encounter, Pyron fell back to his former camp at Johnson's Ranch. Late that evening he sent a flag of truce to Chivington, who agreed to his request for a cessation of hostilities until 8:00 A.M. the next morning in order to allow ample time for the burying of the dead and the caring of the wounded.

Pyron's force had been soundly beaten by superior numbers—the first defeat the Confederates had suffered since they began their campaign. A Texan enlisted man recorded the losses as four men killed and six wounded. In addition the Federals had taken seventy or so prisoners, seven of whom were commissioned officers.[24] Completely routed, and with approximately a quarter of their original force captives of the victorious Yankees, there was truly no joy at Johnson's Ranch that night.

The Federals sustained a loss of five killed, fourteen wounded, and three missing. Captain Cook "was all shot to pieces, but his usual fortitude remained with him. The ghastly smile with which he endeavored to make light of his wounds to cheer his boys betrayed his agony."[25] Lieutenant Marshall, who had come to lead the victorious cavalry charge, accidentally shot himself while breaking a prisoner's loaded rifle which he foolishly had held by the muzzle. His death within a few hours "cast a shadow athwart the glories of the day."[26]

So ended the skirmish of Apache Canyon. Though the action was a relatively small one, the "green" Colorado volunteers had proven their mettle and had taken on a new feeling of confidence. One exuberant member of Company F boasted that darkness alone had kept them from making the victory even more decisive.

During the morning of March 27 the Federals buried their dead in an open field a quarter of a mile down the canyon from Pigeon's Ranch. Since the well at the ranch proved inadequate to meet the needs of both men and horses, Chivington fell back to Kozlowski's Ranch where the water was plentiful. From there Captain Lord's cavalry company escorted the captured Confederates to Fort Union.

7

The Battle of Glorieta Pass

According to Sibley's strategy for moving upon Fort Union, Colonel Scurry, commanding his Fourth Regiment[1] and the battalion of the Seventh, was to proceed northward by way of Galisteo. After distributing rations and sending his sick to the general hospital recently established in Albuquerque, Scurry set out on March 21. The road, much of which was mountainous, would make travel difficult, but a compensating feature was that timber abounded and firewood would be available at camping stops. The weather had turned somewhat milder during the day, but it was still exceedingly cold at night.

As the Fourth neared the village of Real de Dolores in the Ortiz Mountains on March 24, the Texans spied a flag waving in the distance. At first the men thought that the enemy was ahead, but on closer scrutiny, they found the banner to be a white rag which a Mexican had placed on his housetop as a sign of neutrality. Real de Dolores was the most interesting hamlet in which the men had yet encamped, primarily because it possessed a smelter for gold and silver ore. Though the mill was not then in operation, all around the bases of the nearby mountains were ore diggings—sights which fired the imaginations of many. Perhaps New Mexico had some good features after all!

From Real de Dolores the road gradually left the mountains to emerge into a vast, barren plain. The distant mountains, gleaming white with snow, presented a picturesque sight as the men wearily trudged along. Near dusk on March 25 the Fourth arrived at Galisteo and encamped. The Seventh, which was following some distance behind, did not come in until late the next day. Galisteo, another of the small, but numerous New Mexican villages, was approximately twenty-five miles south of Santa Fé.

As Scurry's troops were resting in camp late in the afternoon of March 26 (the Seventh having arrived a few hours before) a cloud of dust approached from across the prairie. As it came nearer, it proved to be a man on horseback who loped up to Colonel Scurry's tent with a paper in his hand. Shortly after the messenger had delivered his dispatch, the Colonel gave him another, and he was off again. The appearance of the express naturally aroused the interest of the rank and file. One soldier who was standing nearby candidly prophesied, "Hell is brewing and not a mile off."[2]

The messenger had come from Major Pyron, who reported that he was engaged in sharp conflict with a greatly superior enemy about sixteen miles away in Apache Canyon. No sooner had the express left than Scurry, hat in hand, came down the line telling his men of Pyron's critical condition and the necessity of moving to his assistance at once. Within ten minutes the column was formed and ready to march. It was sunset as the troops set out directly across the mountains to the scene of battle. All packing and loading of the wagons was left to the teamsters, for time was of the essence. Since the direct route would be too difficult for the wagons to follow, the train, guarded by one hundred men under Lieutenant John W. Taylor, was to proceed by the regular road.

The night was bitter cold, and in some places the snow was ankle-deep. Only by marching along as fast as possible could the men keep warm. Not far from Apache Canyon the jaded teams were unable to pull Teel's two artillery pieces up a very steep hill. The men thereupon tied long ropes to the cannon, and after an hour or so of tedious labor, managed to pull them over the crest. About three o'clock in the morning the column reached Pyron's encampment. Scurry's men immediately set about gathering wood to build fires to warm their chilled bodies. Completely exhausted, they lay on the cold ground without blankets to sleep until daylight.

The truce to which Pyron and Chivington had agreed was due to expire at eight o'clock that morning. As soon as daylight permitted, Scurry—who had assumed command by virtue of his rank—thoroughly examined the terrain in and around Johnson's Ranch. He found the area admirably suited for defense. The canyon walls were so steep that he felt an attack could come only from down the trail. He formed his men in a battle line across the road a few hundred yards below the ranch where the canyon made a bend, and planted his artillery on a hill in front of the ranchhouse. By eight o'clock he had completed the disposition of his troops and was ready to receive the expected Federal onslaught.

Near noon the wagon train arrived, and the hungry men, though still remaining in battle formation, set about cooking refreshments. The warm food put them in a much better humor, but they were still quite weary from the previous night's march. Throughout the day and during the night, the Texans maintained their position, but the enemy did not make an appearance.

The next morning, March 28, Scurry had come to the end of his patience. If the Yankees would not come to him to fight, he would go after them. When his troops had finished breakfast, he told them to put what remained in their haversacks, for they were moving out and would not return until night. After posting a small guard for the wagon train, Scurry marched down the Santa Fé Trail through Apache Canyon. He had under his command parts of all four regiments of the Army of New Mexico. His own Fourth consisted of nine companies under their respective officers (unless designated otherwise, all were captains):

Company B — Lt. James B. Holland (Scarborough was too ill to command)
Company C — George J. Hampton
Company D — Charles M. Lesueur
Company E — Charles Buckholts
Company F — James M. Crosson
Company G — Julius Giesecke (promoted to replace Marinus van der Heuvel)
Company H — William L. Alexander
Company I — James M. Odell
Company K — William W. Foard
Major John S. Shropshire commanded four companies of the Fifth:
Company A — Lt. Pleasant J. Oakes (Shropshire's former company)
Company B — Lt. John J. Scott (Captain Lang was mortally wounded at Valverde)
Company C — Denman W. Shannon
Company D — Daniel H. Ragsdale
Major Powhatan Jordan led the battalion of the Seventh:
Company B — Gustav Hoffman
Company F — J. F. Wiggins
Company H — Isaac Adair
Company I — James W. Gardner

Major Charles L. Pyron commanded a detachment of about one hundred men of the Second Regiment which included one independent company (Captain John Phillips' "Brigands"). In addition, Scurry had three pieces of Teel's artillery in charge of Lieutenant James Bradford (the fourth gun was left at Johnson's Ranch to aid in guarding the train). There is some dispute as to the number of Confederates Scurry commanded as he launched his offensive. Sibley, who was not there, stated that Scurry had one thousand men. The San Antonio *Herald* of May 3, 1862, agrees with Sibley. Scurry reported, however, that because of sickness, the posting of details, and other causes, he had only six hundred soldiers fit for duty. In listing the units in his official report, he failed (with the exception of the "Brigands") to mention Pyron's command. If Pyron's men were not included in Scurry's total, and assuming that aside from this his total was correct, then the effective Confederate force was probably closer to seven hundred.

Shortly after Colonel Slough received Chivington's dispatch describing the skirmish of Apache Canyon, he determined to advance to Kozlowski's Ranch.

Leaving Bernal Springs about noon on March 27, he reached Chivington's camp about two o'clock in the morning. After a thorough briefing by Chivington, and learning from spies that the Confederates at Johnson's Ranch now numbered a thousand, Slough formulated an offensive plan involving a two-columned movement. While his main force of almost 900 men followed the Santa Fé Trail toward the Confederate encampment, Chivington, with about 430 men, was to take a mountainous trail which would bring him to the heights overlooking Johnson's Ranch. Both would then converge upon the enemy. Engaging the Texans in a full-scale battle was, of course, contrary to Canby's instructions. Slough later justified his aggressive actions by claiming to be reconnoitering in force with the sole intention of "ascertaining the position of the enemy and of harassing them as much as possible."[3]

Between eight and eight-thirty o'clock on the morning of March 28, the Federal column left Kozlowski's Ranch. Captain Charles J. Walker's Company E, Third Cavalry, led the advance, while the baggage train of one hundred wagons brought up the rear. At nine-thirty, about two miles down the road, Chivington's detachment parted from the main body to take the trail which ran to the left of the canyon and nearly parallel to it. Slough continued on about three miles to Pigeon's Ranch where, by ten-thirty, all his command had arrived.

Pigeon's Ranch was the largest hostelry on the trail between Santa Fé and Las Vegas. It was called "Pigeon's" Ranch after the nickname given to its Franco-American owner, Alexander Vallé, who had a peculiar style of dancing at fandangos. The ranch was situated at the eastern end of Glorieta Pass in a narrow defile, and the buildings, the trail, and an arroyo took up practically all the space in the canyon. In back of the main living quarters was a double corral in which loaded wagons were brought in for protection. Attached to it were sheds with stalls for draft animals. A formidable adobe wall ran from the sheds back to a ravine and then surrounded a yard in which teams were kept and fed. After the skirmish of Apache Canyon, Chivington had fallen back to the ranch and established a hospital for his wounded before moving on to Kozlowski's.

The various detachments of Slough's force halted upon reaching Pigeon's Ranch, the cavalry having arrived about an hour and a half before the infantry. Some of the soldiers rested, while others visited their comrades in the hospital. Many filled their canteens, for there was not another well except at the western end of the pass where the Texans were encamped. As the men leisurely passed the time, they were totally unaware of the enemy's approach.

Colonel Scurry had proceeded about six miles down the canyon from his camp when his scouts reported the Federals ahead in force. Coming to the head of his column, he discovered that the most advanced enemy pickets were about a half mile west of Pigeon's Ranch. Hastily he instructed his mounted troops, who had been leading the column, to retire slowly and quietly to the rear, where they were to dismount and return to fight on foot. Scurry then formed his men in a battle line which ran across the canyon from a fence on the left up into a pine forest on the right. He sent his three pieces of artillery forward to a slight elevation, where they shortly opened fire with grape and shell. The fighting began somewhere between ten-thirty and eleven o'clock. It would not end for six hours.

Slough's force consisted of five companies (C, D, G, I, K) of Colorado infantry and Captain John F. Ritter's battery of two twelve-pounders and two six-pounders under the immediate command of Lieutenant Colonel Samuel F. Tappan, Lieutenant Ira W. Claflin's battery of four twelve-pounders, Captain George W. Howland's detachments of the First and Third regular cavalry, and Company F, the only mounted unit of the Colorado regiment.

As soon as Slough arrived at Pigeon's Ranch with his infantry, he sent Howland's cavalry forward to reconnoiter. They had advanced no more than six or seven hundred yards when pickets dashed back to report that the Texans were taking position in the timber just ahead. Captain Walker, whose company was in the lead, quickly moved into a pine forest on his left to dismount so his men could skirmish on foot.

Meanwhile most of the Federals were still resting at Pigeon's Ranch when news came that the Texans were about eight hundred yards away. Immediately the bugles sounded "assembly," and the startled men seized their weapons and fell into line. At Slough's command, Tappan's battalion and the batteries rushed ahead about four hundred yards to take position. But before he could complete the arrangement of his forces, the Confederate artillery opened fire, cutting the tree tops over their heads. Scurry had taken the Union troops by surprise, and from the beginning of the battle to its end, Slough would have to fight a defensive action.

Both Union batteries unlimbered on a slight elevation in, and to the left of, the road. Ritter's guns rushed up just about the time that Walker's cavalry had commenced skirmishing. Setting up on his right, they soon were returning the Confederate fire with gusto. Colonel Slough came to the front, and, in a hoarse voice, ordered Downing's Company D to the left, while Captain Charles Maile's Company I[4] was sent to the right—both were to occupy the hillsides as skirmishers. Captain Richard Sopris' Company C was to support Ritter's guns, while Company K under Captain Samuel M. Robbins protected those of Claflin. These supporting units took position in the road at a spot where they were sheltered from enemy fire by the brow of a hill. Slough also instructed the cavalry, most of whom were now dismounted, to support the field pieces. Company G, the rear guard, was about a mile back with the wagon train.

About the time that Colonel Scurry had set most of his men into position, he spied the two enemy companies advancing upon his right and left fronts.

Hurriedly he dispatched Major Pyron to check them on the right while, after placing the center in charge of Major Raguet, he hastened to the left with the remainder of his troops. As the battle became general, the deafening roar of the artillery and the unceasing rattle of small arms was accompanied by yelling and cheering from the combatants.

When the Federals of Company I deployed to the right, they passed an open field commanded by Scurry's artillery. Though they suffered severely from the fire, they reached their assigned position. Shortly after Scurry had formed his left wing, he observed Company I moving down a gulch which ran through the center of the open field to his left. The "Pike's Peakers" were proceeding under cover of the gulch with the obvious intention of flanking the Confederate left and gaining their rear. As rapidly as possible, Scurry's men crossed the fence, and though under a heavy enemy barrage, raced two hundred yards across the field to the gulch.

Lieutenant John Baker had led the forward division of Company I. When he reached a point almost opposite the Texan battery on the higher ground to his left, he drew his sword and shouted, "Let's capture the guns!"[5] The words had barely left his lips when he was fatally struck down. Armed with pistols and knives, Scurry's men jumped into the gulch to engage the enemy in a deadly hand-to-hand conflict. After a few moments, the Federals broke and retreated in wild confusion. Meanwhile Pyron had checked the enemy on the right, and Raguet's force had charged down the center.

The Federals now fell back about three or four hundred yards to form a new line of defense in front of Pigeon's Ranch. Claflin's guns took position on an eminence to the left, while Ritter set up farther to the rear and south of the road. Company F posted themselves on a rocky point opposite Claflin's battery. Captain William F. Wilder's Company G had been acting as rear guard, but on hearing the sound of battle, the unit dashed to the front to join Company C in supporting Ritter.

Ritter's position soon proved untenable. He was exposed to a galling small-arms fire, his ammunition wagons were too far away, his guns were ineffective against the Texans, who were advancing from tree to tree and from rock to rock, and finally, with the exception of one platoon, all his supports were withdrawn to other locations. Before he could limber up and return to the road, one of his lieutenants was fatally wounded. It was only with great danger that he was able to extricate himself from his precarious position and set up in front of Pigeon's Ranch. At this new location one of Ritter's guns blew up a Texan limber box and disabled a Confederate howitzer by striking it squarely in the muzzle with a round shot. This excellent marksmanship was due to the skill of Private Kelly of Company E, Fifth Infantry. Companies D and I picked off the Confederate gunners which, combined with Kelly's deadly accuracy, put the Texan artillery temporarily out of action. Lieutenant James Bradford, in charge of the Confederate pieces, was wounded and borne from the field. With no other artillery officer present, the three guns were withdrawn to the rear before Scurry was aware of it. Actually the artillery was not of great importance except in the center of the line. The rugged terrain precluded a battle of the "bushwhacking" variety, and it soon became evident that small arms would decide the outcome.

After the Confederate charge had driven the Federals back to their new position, Scurry paused to regroup his somewhat scattered and disorganized forces. He also directed that the two serviceable howitzers be returned to the front. When he was ready to advance again, he found that the Federals had taken cover. He did not know whether their main body was behind the long adobe fence that ran across the canyon in front of Pigeon's Ranch, or whether it was behind a large ledge of rocks farther to the rear. In an effort to locate their position, Scurry used his two howitzers to probe the Union line.

While the Federal batteries were still occupying their second position, Slough, Tappan, and Captain Gurden Chapin climbed a hill on their right to reconnoiter. After viewing the field from this vantage point, they agreed that the hill on their left should be occupied at once. If flanked in that direction, the Texans would be able to gain their rear and destroy the wagon train. Furthermore, entrenched skirmishers on the hill would serve as supports for the batteries below. Slough selected Tappan to take twenty men from Company C for this purpose. Tappan, however, believing this not to be a large enough force, also took the police guard of seventy men. Within a short time, he had posted his ninety infantrymen on the summit of the hill which was in front and to the left of the batteries below. His skirmish line, extending for nearly three-quarters of a mile in a half circle, was nearly at a right angle from the road where the wagon train was drawn up. His position not only commanded a view of part of the valley, but the rough terrain afforded his men excellent protection from enemy fire. Tappan remained in this strong location during the rest of the battle. Occasionally small parties of Texans would attempt to ascend the hill, only to be repeatedly driven back.

From his position, Tappan saw Scurry assembling his men after their first charge. Fearing that the enemy was preparing to assault the batteries, he rushed to warn Slough. The Federal commander was already aware of Scurry's action. Believing that Tappan's hill would bear the brunt of the attack, Slough warned him to hold his position at all costs. Slough was momentarily expecting Major Chivington to attack the Texan rear. When this occurred, he planned to charge in front while Tappan attacked the flank. Such a maneuver might easily shatter and destroy the enemy.

While his battery was probing the Union line, Scurry sent Major Shropshire to the right to move up among the pines to find and attack the enemy. Major

Raguet, with similar orders, was dispatched to the left, to be followed shortly by Pyron. As soon as he heard the sounds of their guns, Scurry planned to charge down the center. When, after the lapse of sufficient time, he heard nothing from the right, Scurry left his center in charge of subordinates and went to see what was delaying Shropshire's assault.

Following instructions, Major Shropshire had set out at the head of his column to find the Union line in the pine forest. As he and Captain Denman Shannon moved cautiously ahead, they unsuspectingly came within a few paces of Tappan's skirmish line.[6] Private George W. Pierce of Company F, Colorado volunteers, fatally shot Shropshire and took Shannon prisoner. The Confederate column attempted to charge forward, but was sent reeling back with a loss of several killed and wounded. When Scurry learned of Shropshire's death and repulse, he took charge of the right himself. But instead of attacking Tappan, he assaulted the enemy line in front of the ranch.

Before the second Confederate charge, Captain Chapin had ordered Ritter's battery across the ravine to the right side of the canyon. Claflin's howitzers followed shortly. On taking charge of the Confederate left, Majors Raguet and Pyron exhorted their men to take the enemy's guns as they had at Valverde. Encouraged and shouted on by their officers, the Texans launched their assault. Taking advantage of the terrain as much as possible, they moved forward singly and in squads. The Federal gunners waited until they had come within fifty yards and then opened fire "like a regiment of Mexican dogs roused by the stranger at midnight. One man shoved in a charge with his arm, another fired her off, and the four pieces played the liveliest Yankee doodle ever heard."[7] The artillery, coupled with the small-arms fire of the battery supports, temporarily hurled the Texans back.

Soon some Confederates ascended a rocky hill on Ritter's right and commenced pouring a destructive rifle and musket fire into his midst. Before he could move his battery out, he lost one gunner killed and three wounded. The Texans now rallied and renewed the charge, but on closing in on the spot where the guns had been, they found only a few dead and wounded Federals. Ritter's battery had taken a new position, selected by Chapin, in front of the deep ravine, thus affording the supports complete protection. The supply train was in the road about forty yards to the left. Though Tappan was still holding his position firmly, the main Federal line had now been driven from the ranch to a ledge of rocks to the rear. It was here that the "Pike's Peakers" made their final and most desperate stand.

Heedless of the storm of grape, canister, and shell, the Confederates savagely pressed onward, determined to capture the enemy's guns. They had almost succeeded when a large body of Federal infantry rushed up to save them. With this the conflict reached its peak. The Confederate right and center had now united on the left. "Inspired with the unalterable determination to overcome every obstacle to the attainment of their object,"[8] the Texans fell madly upon the enemy. But the iron courage of the Federal infantry momentarily repulsed them, allowing the artillery time to escape. Once the batteries had got safely away, the Union infantry broke ranks and fled from the field.

Tappan now considered it dangerous to hold his position any longer. With Slough driven down the canyon a considerable distance, the Texans would be able to cut him off. Quickly ordering his men to withdraw, Tappan managed to overtake the main column about two miles back from the battlefield.

The Confederates attempted to renew their assault, but were forced from extreme exhaustion to halt. Apparently they had been too severely repulsed to rally in time to pursue their retreating enemy. It had been an extremely hard-fought contest. As Alexander Vallé later noted, " . . . ze foight six hour by my vatch, and my vatch was slow!"[9]

After the Federals had fled the field, Scurry galloped up to ask his men for a white handkerchief, for he wanted to send a flag of truce to tell "them damned Yankees" to come back and pick up their dead and wounded. Since no one responded, the Colonel bellowed, "God Damn it, tear off your shirt tail, we have got to have a white flag."[10] One soldier had just picked up a beautiful white silk scarf which a "Pike's Peaker" had dropped in his haste to leave. As he looked about, the Texan decided there was not a shirt tail in the crowd that would do for a white flag. In fact, most of them would have been better suited for battle flags! Such being the case, he reluctantly handed Scurry his prized scarf. Although the Colonel promised to return it, the soldier lamented that that was the last he saw of it.

Scurry's flag-bearing messenger had to go all the way to Kozlowski's Ranch before he could find a Union Officer empowered to send back details. Slough agreed to a one-day truce, and within a few hours a Federal detachment returned to Pigeon's Ranch. Working throughout the night, they removed their dead from the field and nursed their wounded.

Scurry boasted that the battle of Glorieta Pass had proved conclusively that few mistakes had been made in the selection of his officers. Always in the front leading their men in the thickest of the fight, all the field officers had been either killed, wounded, or scratched by enemy missiles. Scurry himself had been a sterling example. His cheek had twice been brushed by a Minié ball, each time just drawing blood, and his clothes had been torn in two places from enemy fire. Throughout the fighting he had moved among his troops encouraging them on and telling them to give the Federals "Hell." As one soldier later noted, "if he called using bullets Hell they . . . got plenty of it."[11] But Scurry was not one-sided in his praise. He commended the valor of the enemy, whom he described as the flower of the United States army.

In this encounter the Confederacy lost four of as "brave and chivalrous officers as ever graced the ranks of any army."[12] Major Shropshire had been killed early in the day, while Major Raguet had fallen from his horse mortally wounded while taking part in the last and most desperate charge. Raguet survived long enough, however, to "know and rejoice at . . . [the] victory, and then died with loving messages upon his expiring lips."[13] Captain Charles Buckholts and Lieutenant Charles H. Mills had conducted themselves with distinguished gallantry throughout the fight; they, too, near its close, fell.

"Of the living," Scurry observed, "it is only necessary to say all behaved with distinguished courage and daring."[14] From the field of battle, he proudly issued the following:

HEAD-QUARTERS, ADVANCE DIVISION, ARMY OF NEW MEXICO.
Cañon Glorieta March 28 1862.
General Order
No. 4

Soldiers—You have added another victory to the long list of triumphs won by the Confederate armies. By your conduct you have given another evidence of the daring courage and heroic endurance which actuate you in this great struggle for the independence of your country. You have proven your right to stand by the side of those who fought and conquered on the red field of San Jacinto. The battle of Glorieta—where for six long hours you steadily drove before you a foe of twice your numbers over a field chosen by themselves, and deemed impregnable, will take its place upon the roll of your country's triumphs, and serve to excite your children to imitate the brave deeds of their fathers, in every hour of that country's peril.

Soldiers—I am proud of you. Go on as you have commenced, and it will not be long until not a single soldier of the United States will be left upon the soil of New Mexico. The Territory, relieved of the burdens recently imposed upon it by its late oppressors, will once more, throughout its beautiful valleys, "blossom as the rose" beneath the plastic hands of peaceful industry.

By order of Lieut. Col. W. R. Scurry,
Commanding.[15]

Unfortunately the poetically optimistic Scurry had won at best a pyrrhic victory. While his men were driving the enemy from the field, Chivington's detachment struck a blow which, in the words of a contemporary, pierced the Confederates' "vitals and drew from thence the life blood."[16]

At nine-thirty that morning, Chivington had left Slough to take the mountainous trail along the rim of the canyon. His force of about 430 men was composed entirely of infantry.[17] Captain William H. Lewis commanded the first battalion, which included two companies (A, G) of his own U.S. Fifth Infantry, Company B of the Colorado regiment, and Ford's company of volunteers. Captain Edward W. Wynkoop headed the second battalion of three companies (A, E, H) of the First Regiment.

Since Chivington was totally unfamiliar with the terrain, Lieutenant Colonel Manuel Chávez and James L. Collins served as guides. Chávez was a member of an old, distinguished native family. He had won honors fighting Indians, and had been with Canby at Valverde. When Donaldson evacuated Santa Fé, he was one of the few New Mexican volunteers who did not desert on the way to Fort Union. Indian Agent Collins had also been at Valverde. Leaving with the militia afterward, he had become Slough's volunteer aide-de-camp. While leading a flanking party during the skirmish of Apache Canyon he advanced too far and was captured. He remained a prisoner only a short while, for he was released soon after Captain Cook launched his cavalry charge.

The detachment continued down the rough, rocky trail for about eight miles, and then turned off to go directly over the mountains to Johnson's Ranch. Near one-thirty in the afternoon the Federals reached the edge of an eminence overlooking the Confederate encampment. "You are on top of dem!"[18] Chávez pointed out to his commander.

A Texan picket stationed on the crest was captured before he could sound the alarm. With the enemy unsuspecting of his presence, Chivington was able to spend some time observing the situation one thousand feet below. All was in plain view: the ranch buildings, the Santa Fé Trail, the wagon train, and a few soldiers leisurely milling about. Chivington noted that a field piece was set up on one of the higher hills, and that about two hundred men were guarding the camp.

After a conference with his officers, Chivington agreed upon a plan of attack.[19] Captain Lewis was to lead the assault, while Chivington remained on the heights to gain an overall view of the action. Before Lewis left, Chivington advised that should an ambush develop, he would sound recall from the mountain. As the Captain set out, he remarked to Asa B. Carey, a fellow officer, that "they would never hear that signal."[20]

When the Federals had gotten about a quarter of the way down the steep mountainside, the crashing of loosened rocks rolling down the precipice aroused the Texans below. Many Confederates seized what horses and mules they could and dashed off down the Santa Fé Trail toward Glorieta. Others manned the field piece and were soon firing, though ineffectually, toward the mountain. Cheering and yelling at the top of their lungs, the Federals reached bottom safely, reformed into ranks, and went into action. With thirty men Wynkoop deployed to disable the six-pounder. As a volley from his rifles killed three gunners and wounded several others, Captain Lewis' men fearlessly charged up the hill. On seizing the howitzer, Lewis spiked it with an iron ramrod, jammed an iron ball into the muzzle, and sent it tumbling, carnage and all, down the hillside. The limber box was also destroyed. Meanwhile the rest of the command had surrounded the wagons and ranch buildings. By now the Confederate rear guard had been scattered, leaving the train and camp in Federal hands.

Undoubtedly Chivington overestimated the number of Texans guarding the camp, most of whom were either sick and wounded, or cooks and drivers. According to a postwar statement credited to the captain in charge of the camp, two companies of Germans which had been assigned as guards had earlier left their posts. Hearing the reverberating thunder of the cannon down the canyon, they rushed to join the battle, for they had "enlisted to get glory by fighting, and not in guarding mules and provisions."[21] If this account is true, had these two units remained at camp to unleash their bellicose feelings against the attacking Federals, Chivington's raid might have ended in failure.

The Confederate train was heavily loaded with ammunition, clothing, commissary items, forage, and surgical supplies. Since the Federals were unable to carry off the booty, all the wagons, most of which were overturned, were set afire and burned on the spot.[22] During the pillage one of the wagons containing ammunition exploded, severely wounding one soldier. He was the only Union casualty.

The Federals freed five of their men who had been taken prisoner during the forenoon at Glorieta. They had been sent to the rear under guard and arrived at camp during the action. It was from them that Chivington and his commanders first learned of the general engagement down the canyon.

With the destruction of the train, Chivington ordered his men to ascend the mountain. He had learned that a large enemy force was approaching from Galisteo, and he did not want to risk being caught in the canyon.

On the way up the mountainside, it was discovered that four heavily loaded wagons hidden behind a hill outside the main camp had been overlooked. Four volunteers returned to burn them, and within an hour had completed their task. In addition to destroying the train, the Federals killed three Texans, wounded several others, and captured seventeen, including two officers. About thirty horses and mules were also taken from a nearby corral.[23]

During the height of the assault, Reverend L. H. Jones, chaplain of the Fourth Regiment, was shot and seriously wounded, even though he had held a white flag in his hand. This, plus the real or rumored order that Chivington had instructed his men to shoot the seventeen Texan prisoners if the Federals were attacked on the return march, prompted the outraged Scurry to cry, "These instances go to prove that they [the Federals] have lost all sense of humanity in the insane hatred they bear to the citizens of the Confederacy, who have the manliness to arm in defense of their country's independence."[24]

After Chivington's command had marched three or four miles, Lieutenant Alfred S. Cobb rode up with a dispatch from Slough ordering his immediate return to support the main body, which was steadily being driven back by the Texans. Cobb also informed the Major that the enemy was in possession of the trail he was following. Since darkness had set in, it would have been next to impossible for Chivington to have found his way back to camp. Chávez was unwilling to accept the responsibility of guiding the party over any other trail than the one they had used. At this crucial moment, Padre Ortiz, a Catholic priest who had joined the party at the top of the mountain, came forward to offer to lead the detachment. The priest was from a small village near the Pecos ruins and was familiar with the mountainous territory. Riding a white horse, the padre led the column over a pathless route. Chivington, who had dismounted, stumbled along while leading his horse. Almost total darkness added to the confusion as the command felt its way through the rugged mountains. Finally Padre Ortiz brought the column out on the main road near the Pecos ruins, and Chivington set out for Kozlowski's Ranch.

Near ten o'clock that night Chivington came in sight of the Federal camp fires. Not knowing for certain whose camp it was, he called his men to halt. "Fall in, every man in his place; fix bayonets," cautioned the Major. "I don't know whose camp it is, but if it a'nt ours we'll soon make it so. Forward, keep close."[25] On coming within hailing distance of the guard, Chivington found it to be Slough's. Tired and weary, his exhausted troops plodded into camp for a well-deserved rest.

The battle of Glorieta Pass, called the battle of Pigeon's Ranch by the Federals, was a relatively small engagement in point of numbers involved. The casualties, however, attested to the ferocity with which it was fought. Scurry's losses were thirty-six killed and about sixty wounded. Of the killed, twenty-five were from the Fourth Regiment, two from the Fifth, eight from the Seventh, and one from the artillery. The Federals also claimed to have taken twenty-five Confederate prisoners, among whom were three captains and eight lieutenants.

There is some disagreement concerning the Union figures. Colonel Slough reported twenty-nine killed, forty-two wounded, and about fifteen prisoners. Tappan, however, stated that in his command alone there were twenty-nine killed, sixty-four wounded, and thirteen prisoners. Nine later died of their wounds, raising the number of dead to thirty-eight. Hollister, in his account of the battle, lists forty-six killed, sixty-four wounded, and twenty-one prisoners.

Chivington's rear guard foray more than compensated for Slough's defeat on the main battlefield. In fact, the destruction of the wagon train was the decisive action of the New Mexican campaign.[26] It was discouraging, indeed, when the Texans learned that, though they had won the battle of Glorieta Pass, they had lost the victory at Johnson's Ranch.

8

The Decision To Evacuate New Mexico

THE DAY AFTER THE BATTLE COLONEL SLOUGH, CONSIDERING THE HORSES OF HIS COMMAND so worn out as to be an encumbrance, ordered a small guard to take them back to Fort Union. News of the order spread like wildfire throughout the camp, for his men interpreted it as meaning he was planning to move against the Confederates again. Great was the dismay of many, and "It was somewhat amusing to see the various aches, ills, etc., with which some of the boys . . . were instantly attacked."[1] Obviously the lure of "Santa Fe had lost its charms," for "any sacrifice of manhood" was preferable to risking another battle with the Texans. Before the horses were ready to start, however, Slough countermanded the order.

Slough was convinced that the Confederates were too strongly entrenched in the canyon to be assaulted by his force. Consequently he decided to fall back to Bernal Springs. Had he been a man of greater nerve and daring, he would have launched an attack. Surely he was aware that as a result of the battle and the destruction of the supply train Scurry was in a destitute condition. Slough's failure to assume the initiative resulted in the loss of a golden opportunity to deliver a knockout blow against the greater part of the Army of New Mexico.

During the morning of March 29, while the Federals were busy bringing in their wounded and burying their dead, Colonel Scurry sent in another flag of truce asking for a continuation of the armistice until eight o'clock the next morning. He felt that it would take that long to provide adequately for the needs of his wounded. Slough agreed, for it made little difference how many armistices were accepted, since he had already decided to fall back to Bernal Springs. After completing arrangements for the comfort of the wounded, Slough's column set out about two o'clock that afternoon. Fresh graves near the field of conflict and a crowded hospital at Kozlowski's Ranch attested to the horrors of the battle the day before.

The road from Kozlowski's Ranch to San José ran between the base of a mountain and the Pecos River. It was beautiful country, but as the Federal column sadly moved along, the men failed to appreciate its aesthetic qualities. They were too engrossed in other matters: "half glad to escape the renewal of yesterday yet revolting at the idea of backing out before . . . [they] were well whipped."[2]

The day after Slough's arrival at Bernal Springs, a messenger from Canby arrived with orders to fall back to Fort Union. Slough could do nothing but obey, for the instructions were explicit. In his official report to the adjutant general Slough asserted that his action at Glorieta was taken solely for the purpose of annoying and harassing the enemy as Canby had ordered. Canby, nevertheless, considered Slough's movement from Fort Union a breach of orders. Rather than face the possibility of a court-martial Slough resigned his commission—to take effect on April 9—and relinquished his command to Colonel Paul.[3] No doubt Paul rejoiced at finally winning out over his rival.

At dusk on April 2 Slough's column arrived at Fort Union. The Federals had been gone eleven days and had fought two battles. After this brief, but arduous, campaign, the men welcomed an opportunity to rest and recuperate.

The day after the battle was a hard one for Scurry's haggard troops. Some hungrily picked up kernels of corn, which the horses and mules had wasted in the corral, and parched them over campfires. Tired, hungry, left with their ammunition nearly exhausted and their supply train destroyed, the Texans were in no condition to follow up their shallow victory.

As did the Union Soldiers, the Confederates spent the morning burying their dead and attending their wounded. They had no picks or shovels, but when the Federals finished interring their dead, they graciously loaned their tools to the Texans. That evening the bugle called the troops into line, and Scurry told his men of their grave situation. All their wagons and supplies had been burned, and the sick that had remained with the train had been taken prisoner. Since Santa Fé was the only place where supplies and transportation could be obtained to help replace what had been lost, Scurry ordered his troops to fall back to the capital. After making certain that the wounded were taken care of as satisfactorily as possible in the hospital established at Pigeon's Ranch, the Confederates set out for Santa Fé, about twenty-two miles distant.

Scurry reached the capital early the next morning, but members of his command continued to straggle into town throughout the day—"Some rode, some walked and some hobbled in."[4] As quickly as possible, Scurry secured food and quarters for his tired and hungry troops. Shortly after his arrival, he wrote Sibley a report of all that had taken place. He urged the General to dispatch supplies of ammunition, for as soon as possible he wanted to go after the enemy again. He also warned that he had heard from three different sources that Canby had left Fort Craig on March 24.

When Major Pyron had first set out to meet the Federals on March 25, Mrs. Canby had urged all Union ladies to make preparations for receiving any men who might be wounded in the impending clash. She set the example by setting up beds in empty rooms, and preparing soups. When some of the women protested that it might be Confederates who would have to be cared for, Mrs. Canby snapped, "No matter whether friend or foe, our wounded enemy must be cared for and their lives saved if it is possible; they are sons of some dear mother."[5]

When the Texan casualties were brought in, Mrs. Canby nursed and cared for them as if they were her own sons. Her large home became a hospital, and she personally saw that no one suffered from neglect. Since there was a shortage of ambulances, she contrived the idea of nailing tent cloths across wagon beds, so as to form hammocks. This made the rough trip to Santa Fé much easier. The wounded who could not be brought to town became her special charge. Her carriage could be seen every day on the road bearing either her, or some needed items for the men at the field hospital.

Needless to say, Mrs. Canby's loving care endeared her to the Confederates. One Texan maintained that that Christian lady "captured more hearts of Confederate soldiers than the old general [Colonel Canby] ever captured Confederate bodies."[6] Several months later when a large group of convalescents was preparing to leave, the soldiers unanimously passed the following resolution:

RESOLVED, That we should be doing violence to our feelings were we to leave this place without expressing to the ladies of Santa Fe and, through them, to those who have aided them in their mission, our proformed [sic] gratitude for the delicate kindness which has been shown to many of us in suffering and sickness, and the attention and courtesy which has been extended to all.[7]

Although every effort was made to care for the men, privations and hardships, intensified by a climate much colder than their own, caused many Texans to fall prey to disease. Pneumonia particularly gave the grave as many as did the fight. Day after day the hospital wagon with its silent load wended its way along the mountainside to inter its contents on the lonely plateau. Only a few months before these men had been hale, and hearty, and filled with optimism as they left the sunny soil of Texas to begin the New Mexican campaign.

On March 31 Captain W. H. Lewis of the Fifth Infantry and Captain James H. Ford, Colorado volunteers, came into Santa Fé under a flag of truce to negotiate an exchange of prisoners. Since they could reach no agreement with Scurry, they left that afternoon without accomplishing their mission.

That same day the Confederates had the good fortune to locate a large amount of property belonging to the Indian agency. These supplies had been intended for the Navajos, but the hostility of that tribe had prevented their distribution. Before leaving Santa Fé, Superintendent James L. Collins had placed the supplies in a storeroom at the agency, the door of which had been carefully sealed, plastered over, and whitewashed. The Texans had suspected that property of this nature was somewhere in the capital and had made frequent investigations to find it. Since it was so well hidden, they must have been informed of its whereabouts. As a result the Confederates gained a valuable supply of blankets and other articles which they sorely needed. Some of the goods were of no value to them; these they attempted to sell to the townspeople at nominal prices.

Meanwhile Green's six companies of the Fifth Regiment, which had temporarily remained in Albuquerque, were either ready to depart, or were already under way for Santa Fé.[8] Upon learning of the battle of Glorieta Pass, Green broke camp immediately, and at about three o'clock in the morning of March 30 set out on a forced march to the capital.

Sibley, though still in Albuquerque, was preparing to leave shortly for the scene of active operations.[9] News of the skirmish of Apache Canyon reached him on the night of March 29, and early the following morning a courier came in to report the battle of Glorieta Pass. To celebrate the victory Sibley ordered his brass band to strike up "Dixie," to which the soldiers in the town responded with a loud, boisterous, general cheer. Sibley and his staff left for Santa Fé shortly thereafter, and apparently caught up with Green's column. Before leaving, the General ordered two guns from Reily's battery to join Green. To protect the depot, he left a small guard supported by the battery's four remaining guns.

On April 4 Green's regiment reached Santa Fé, and here Sibley found his "whole exultant army assembled."[10] The General praised Scurry for having taken care of everything that should have been done: the sick and wounded had been cared for, and the loss of clothing and transportation had largely been made up from Federal supplies and confiscations from local merchants.

But conditions were far from satisfactory. The Confederates had occupied the capital for nearly a month, and the forage and supplies in the general area were rapidly being exhausted. While in Santa Fé Sibley ordered his brigade quartermaster to seize the funds of the territorial treasury. Apparently Governor Connelly and other Union officials, in their haste to leave, had forgotten about the treasury. The amount Sibley confiscated is not known, but it probably was not great.

Regardless of what goods and money had been seized in and around Santa Fé, the fact remained that the loss of Scurry's train had caused irreparable damage, particularly in regard to ammunition. The result was that the plan to move upon Fort Union had to be temporarily set aside. The great question of "what to do now?" pressed heavily upon Sibley and his staff. Santa Fé was untenable, the army was still suffering from lack of supplies, and rumors reported Canby's advance from Fort Craig. The situation was critical. In desperation Sibley had written both the adjutant general and the governor of Texas for immediate aid.[11] It was clearly evident to Sibley that only with additional men and supplies could he successfully conclude the campaign.

After careful consideration, Sibley and his staff decided that while awaiting the hoped-for reinforcements, the whole army should occupy Manzano, which lay on the eastern side of the Manzano Mountains. This village, intermediate between Fort Union, Albuquerque, and Fort Craig, would enable the Texans, by means of patrols, to keep a watch on the movements of the Federals. Since Manzano was on the road to Fort Stanton, communication could be kept open with the Mesilla Valley. In addition, and equally important, it was hoped that the brigade would be able to live off the land in and around the village. When reinforcements arrived, Sibley could then move upon Fort Union and bring the New Mexican campaign to a glorious conclusion. However, should such aid not be forthcoming, making evacuation necessary, the road from Manzano to the Mesilla Valley would be an advantageous one, for there would be little danger of an attack from either of the Federal armies.

Hardly had the Confederates made the decision to move to Manzano when the plan was completely upset by the receipt of "rapid and continuous" pleas from Albuquerque for immediate reinforcements. Canby had definitely set out from Fort Craig and would soon be before Albuquerque!

Frantically Sibley issued orders for the whole army to rush southward to bolster the garrison and protect the supply depot. The Fifth Regiment, encamped just below Santa Fé, set out first on April 7. After a strenuous forced march, Green's men came into Albuquerque on the night of April 9, only to discover the next morning that Canby had withdrawn from the area. On the tenth the rest of the army arrived.

When the Confederates abandoned the capital, they left behind a surgeon and several attendants to care for approximately one hundred sick and wounded soldiers in the hospital. Some of the citizens of Santa Fé who sympathized with the Southern cause decided to leave with the Texans rather than face the consequences of a Union reoccupation. William Pelham and Alexander P. Wilbar, both ex-surveyors general of the territory, and a Mr. Clemens were among those who chose to cast their lot with the Confederacy. When Governor Connelly returned to the capital to resume his duties, the Santa Fé *Gazette* caustically remarked that "the only memento . . . [the Texans] left for our worthy Chief Magistrate was some of Sibley's proclamation's [sic] and empty champagne bottles."[12]

The crisis had come. The Army of New Mexico was caught between two better equipped and better supplied Federal forces which would shortly unite, giving the enemy numerical superiority. The Texans were fairly well clothed, but they had only about twenty days' full rations left. Possessing from thirty-five to forty cartridges per man, they might have enough ammunition to engage one Union army, but not both. Under these circumstances, the great decision Sibley had to make as he put it, was "whether to evacuate the country or take the desperate chances of fighting the enemy in his stronghold (Union), for scant rations at the best."[13] It did not take the Confederates long to decide that evacuation was the only reasonable course of action. Orders were issued to move out as quickly as possible so as to avoid another major clash with the Federals. Knowing that Fort Craig was now garrisoned by a small force of volunteers, the Texans intended, as a parting gesture, to attack and destroy that post on their way down the Río Grande.

Since there was an acute shortage of artillery ammunition, Sibley considered it expedient to abandon some of his howitzers. This would lighten the load on the draft animals, and the carriages would serve as needed transportation for baggage. To keep the guns (eight brass howitzers) from falling into the hands of the enemy, Sibley ordered them secretly buried in town.[14] The six pieces captured at Valverde were retained, for the Confederates attached great sentimental value to them.

On the morning of April 12, about three miles below Albuquerque, the Fourth Regiment, the battalion of the Seventh, Pyron's command, and part of the artillery crossed over by ferry and by ford to the west bank of the Río Grande. Green was to follow, but on discovering that there was too much quicksand for his heavy wagons, he decided to continue down the east bank some twenty miles to a better ford at Peralta. The remainder of the army proceeded southward to Los Lunas, nearly opposite Peralta, and went into camp to await him.

The extremely sandy nature of the road on the east bank greatly impeded Green's speed. Getting as far as Judge Baird's ranch, seven miles below Albuquerque, the first day, he finally reached Peralta the following evening. Instead of attempting to ford the river that night, he determined to camp at Governor Connelly's ranch and cross over in the morning.

Meanwhile at Fort Craig, Canby flushed with anger as he read Colonel Slough's dispatch informing him of the skirmish in Apache Canyon and his intention of moving against the Texans with his entire force. As yet Canby had not learned of the results of the battle of Glorieta Pass, and he feared that his subordinate's impetuosity might not only endanger the Federal army in the north, but place the whole territory in jeopardy as well. Indeed, as already seen, Slough had been driven from the field at Glorieta, and his defeat would have been disastrous had not Chivington saved the day by burning the enemy's supply train at Johnson's Ranch at the mouth of Apache Canyon.

Prompted by Slough's rashness, Canby determined to leave Fort Craig immediately to join forces with those in the north. A messenger was dispatched to order Slough—if it was not already too late—to fall back to Fort Union to await further word concerning the junction.

There were two main routes which Canby could take. One ran through Abó Pass and up the eastern side of the mountains. The other was the river route to Albuquerque, and from there eastward through Carnuel Pass and up the eastern side of the mountains. Canby chose the latter, for he believed the Texans would least suspect he would use it. Furthermore, if he could occupy Albuquerque without serious loss, he intended to hold the town until a junction could be effected. By uniting his troops below the Confederates, he would be in a strategic position to cut off their retreat. Should Albuquerque prove to be too heavily defended, he planned to make a demonstration against the town anyway. Such a feint might draw the Confederates from Santa Fé. While they were being deceived, he could quietly move out and unite his column elsewhere without fear of opposition. He felt confident that once his forces were combined he could drive the Texans from New Mexico, at least from the area north of Fort Craig. He planned, if reinforcements arrived from the east, to leave an adequate occupation force in the north while he proceeded with the bulk of his army to drive the Confederates from the Mesilla Valley. In contemplating such an offensive operation, Canby pointed out that the New Mexican volunteers could not, of course, "be relied on for any purpose of this kind."[15]

On April 1 Canby sallied forth at the head of a column of 860 regulars, 350 volunteers, and four pieces of artillery. Left in charge of Fort Craig was "Kit" Carson with seven companies of his First Regiment, two of the Second, and one of the Fourth Regiment New Mexico Volunteers. Before leaving, Canby warned that though the Confederates in the Mesilla Valley were not strong enough to attack the fort openly, they might attempt to take it by surprise. To guard against such a possibility, Carson was to exact the most unremitting vigilance from his men. Fort Craig was to be held "to the last extremity."[16]

As Canby's command proceeded northward, the road became increasingly soft and sandy. It was only with the greatest difficulty that the men were able to keep rolling the heavy field pieces and the wagons, which were loaded to the brim. To avoid wearing out the draft animals, they made frequent rest stops.

When just below Socorro, a messenger, "Doc" Stracham, rode up with a dispatch from the northern district. This was the first that Canby had heard about the battle of Glorieta Pass. In the plain below town, Canby formed his men in a hollow square and read the dispatch aloud. When the troops learned that the destruction of the enemy supply train had caused their retreat to Santa Fé, the whole column, "from the commanding officer down to the lowest private in the rear rank,"[17] gave three rousing cheers which rang throughout the countryside.

When the Texans in charge of the hospital in Socorro heard the shouts, they assumed Canby was planning to storm the town. Quickly they hoisted a hospital flag, and a delegation came out to tell the Colonel that the few Confederate soldiers in town were serving only as guards and nurses for the sick and wounded. After assuring them that he was not going to molest them, Canby re-formed his men and continued on toward Albuquerque.

Shortly before reaching the sandhills north of Socorro, several infantrymen who had been drinking whiskey got out of hand. A particularly troublesome trooper was seized and tied behind a wagon. The sergeant of the guard, taking pity on the fellow, who was too drunk to stand, offered to untie his hands and let him lie in the feed trough to sober up, if he promised to behave himself. The soldier readily agreed, but no sooner were his hands free, than he jumped up, jerked out the sergeant's pistol, and shot him through the breast. The drunken soldier was quickly overpowered, and at camp that night he was tried by a field court-martial. The next day the column filled three sides of a square, while the prisoner, his eyes bandaged, was placed in a chair at the open end. After reading of the sentence came the command "Fire!" and a squad of mounted riflemen pierced his body with six bullets and "sent him into eternity for his rash act."[18]

The afternoon of April 8 Canby arrived before Albuquerque to find a Confederate force occupying the town. To determine the size of the garrison and the location of their guns, he ordered an immediate demonstration.

The exact number of Texans who defended Albuquerque is not known, but it was probably in the neighborhood of two hundred men.[19] Sibley, upon leaving for Santa Fé, had left Captain William P. Hardeman in charge of a force made up of detachments from his own Company A, Fourth Regiment, and Walker's Company D, Second Regiment, in addition to one six-pounder and three twelve-pounder mountain howitzers of Reily's battery. Augmenting the command were Captain Coopwood and a number of his men who had come into Albuquerque from Mesilla on April 1.

When his pickets reported Canby's advance from Fort Craig, Hardeman immediately sent dispatches to Santa Fé. Although realizing he would be overwhelmingly outnumbered, he was determined to hold out until relief arrived. In preparing for Canby's assault, Hardeman set up the artillery at various locations along his line of defense—a particularly strong point being at Armijo's mill in the eastern part of town. Throughout the ensuing attacks, Reily and his cannoneers skillfully executed rapid changes of position so as to present a greater front and thus deceive the enemy as to their actual numbers.

Canby planted his four pieces of artillery in a large irrigation ditch about one mile east of Armijo's mill. After the battery's supports had deployed along the protective cover of the ditch and behind a low embankment on its west side, Captain Graydon's Spy Company, bolstered by the regular cavalry, launched the exploratory foray. The resulting skirmishing, though often sharp, was on the whole hardly more than a series of harmless maneuvers. Several shots from the

Confederate six-pounder did nothing more than throw sand into the eyes of Canby's battery supports. But as the balls bounced harmlessly over the artillery, they kept rolling, forcing the cavalrymen in the rear to take refuge near some buildings. In attempting to dodge one of these missiles Major Thomas Duncan lost his balance in the saddle and fell to the ground, seriously injuring himself. He was to be the only casualty in the skirmish of Albuquerque.

After the artillery duel had gone on for some time, several citizens of Albuquerque slipped out to inform the Federals that the Texans would not allow the people to seek refuge. Since the Union guns were doing far more damage to defenseless citizens than to the enemy, Canby ordered his artillery to cease fire. Near the end of the day, Canby called off the probing attack, and ordered his men to fall back about two miles to some temporary entrenchments which had been thrown up. The firm Confederate resistance had convinced him that Albuquerque was too strongly defended to be taken by assault.

Canby had hoped to occupy and hold Albuquerque until the junction with the troops from Fort Union could be effected. Thwarted in this, he now turned to the other alternative. He would continue the demonstration the following day as a feint to draw the Confederates from Santa Fé, and then quietly move out. If this maneuver was successful, he and the troops from Fort Union could unite without fear of enemy opposition to either column. What Canby did not know, though, was that the Confederates were racing to the defense of Albuquerque.

Sharp skirmishing, without casualties, and less Federal cannonading characterized the action throughout April 9. At sundown Canby instructed his men to build the customary campfires. When darkness set in, the Federals began loading their baggage wagons. Leaving behind only buglers, drummers, and fifers, Canby's command stealthily made its way eastward toward Carnuel Pass. At eight o'clock, with the campfires burning brightly, the musicians played "tattoo." Immediately after, they mounted their horses and, in company with a small escort, caught up with the column.

The Federal departure from Albuquerque had been carried out none too soon. In fact, Canby had come perilously close to a premature clash with the whole Confederate army. Later, during the same night in which Canby had left, Thomas Green's Fifth Regiment had come into Albuquerque, followed the next day by the remainder of the army.

The reaction of the Texans at dawn of April 10, after discovering that Canby had withdrawn, can only be conjectured. Undoubtedly the majority were relieved. Not only would it mean no more fighting, but it would probably result in their evacuation of hated New Mexico. Canby's wily maneuver, however, had robbed the Texans of their last chance to regain the initiative. Had Canby tarried just one day longer, he would have been faced by all the Army of New

Mexico. Victory for the Texans would have meant the capture of Canby's train of desperately needed commissary and ordnance supplies. Sibley's men would then have been in an even stronger position than before to move against the forces at Fort Union. Defeat would surely have resulted in the surrender of the Confederate army. But regardless of that possibility, the opportunity to conquer New Mexico for the Confederacy had slipped away with Canby's quiet nocturnal departure for Carnuel Pass.

Canby's column marched throughout the night of April 9 and part of the following day. Passing through Carnuel Pass between the Sandía and Manzano mountains, the Federals finally halted at the village of San Antonio, about twenty miles east of Albuquerque. The day after Canby reached this point a messenger from Colonel Paul arrived from Las Vegas—a junction could now be accomplished at any point. Leaving nothing to chance, Canby decided to await at San Antonio the arrival of the Fort Union column. From this vantage point he could keep an eye on the movements of the Texans, who, from all indications, were preparing to leave the territory.

On the morning of April 5 Colonel Paul ordered the troops at Fort Union to be ready to march within an hour. Coming "like a dash of cold water . . . Letters were cut short in haste, poker took wings and vanished, blankets and effects were bundled, the herd brought in, adieux said."[20] After frenzied efforts by all to comply, it was soon learned that only the infantry were to set out that day.

When the Colorado infantry had assembled, Major Chivington briefly explained matters: Canby had left Fort Craig, and the troops at Fort Union were to march southward to unite with him in order to drive the Texans from the land. Near dusk the infantry set out. Company F of the Colorado volunteers and Claflin's battery left the post the next morning, and overtook the infantry at Las Vegas. Later that night Colonel Paul, escorted by Captain Lord's company of the First Cavalry, arrived in camp. His command probably consisted of twelve hundred men.[21]

By three o'clock in the afternoon of April 7, Paul arrived at Bernal Springs and went into camp. He remained here the next day while cavalry detachments were sent out to locate the whereabouts of the enemy. Company F proceeded to Kozlowski's ranch, where the Union hospital was set up. On arrival the Coloradoans were attended by about one hundred paroled Texan prisoners who had recently been released from Fort Union and were on their way to rejoin their commands. Conversations between the two groups naturally developed. One volunteer was so exasperated by the Texans' defensive arguments that he came to the conclusion "that a war of extermination is all that will ever restore American unity. They hate us intensely. Kindness is accepted only as their due and as food for their haughtiness. Nothing can cure their insane prejudice against Northern men, whom they habitually stigmatize with every base epithet known to the vocabulary of abuse. All they want is the *power* to inflict a worse servitude on us than that which the unfortunate negro suffers."[22]

On April 9 Paul left Bernal Springs. Seven miles away at San José he was met by Major Alexander M. Jackson and Lieutenant Colonel Henry C. McNeill, who had ridden up in a carriage bearing a white flag to propose an exchange of prisoners. Since they would consent only to an even exchange "between Mexicans and Whites," Paul refused to negotiate. According to a Union observer, both Jackson and McNeill were under the influence of liquor and acted in an "insolent and threatening" manner, forcing the Federal commander to be "somewhat peremptory" with them. When the Texans found out that they could not deal with Paul, they departed.[23]

A few hours after leaving San José, Paul received intelligence directly from Santa Fé that the Confederates had evacuated the capital and were retreating to Albuquerque. During the late afternoon of the next day, the Federal column reached Kozlowski's Ranch, where Paul decided to encamp while his cavalry checked the validity of the previous day's news. Captain Howland was sent to Santa Fé, while Company F proceeded toward Galisteo.

It was a miserable day as the Coloradoans set out. It was snowing and the wind blew directly into the men's faces as they rode along. Shivering from the cold and dampness, the company finally reached Galisteo, but there was no sign of the Texans. From all appearances it seemed that the Confederates were evacuating the country as reported. A trooper candidly observed that "As they have bought up with Confederate scrip all the army supplies in this section, the soundness of their judgment in not returning here is evident."[24]

Captain William Nicodemus, passing through Galisteo on his way to contact Paul, at first did not know whether to take the Coloradoans for cowboys or skinners. The men soon convinced him, however, that they were Union soldiers, whereupon Nicodemus informed them of Canby's demonstration against Albuquerque and his subsequent movement to San Antonio. The distance from Galisteo to Canby's camp was about forty miles.

Company F was ordered to continue on to Pino's Ranch, twenty miles west of Galisteo, for further reconnaissance. But after a march of eighteen miles, a messenger overtook them with an order to fall back to Galisteo. "Ten hours in the saddle for nothing is enough to excuse an oath in the mouth of the mildest Christian on the sod,"[25] cried a disgusted volunteer. This incident, plus the real or imagined preference given to the regulars, caused this individual to sarcastically state that "If there is a disagreeable task to be performed, or danger to be encountered, they call on us; but if a town is to be occupied after the enemy has gone, the regulars come in. Howland's company went into Santa Fe yesterday and had their spree while we were marched out twenty miles across the prairie and back as if we needed exercise."[26]

Colonel Slough had accompanied the column from Fort Union, and on April 12, his parting address was read to the assembled First Regiment. Slough claimed that his motives had been pure, and he referred to the engagement in Apache Canyon as proof of his earnest effort to save the territory for the Union. He humbly expressed regret for his direction of operations whenever he had failed to give satisfaction. The former commander closed his remarks by asking the men to remember that they "were Colorados, men and Americans, and could not afford to do anything to dishonor"[27] themselves. In the morning he set out for San Antonio to talk with Canby personally. In company with two other officers who had resigned their commissions, he left shortly afterwards for Denver City.[28]

On April 12 Captain Howland confirmed that, except for about 250 sick, wounded, and deserters, the Confederate army had evacuated Santa Fé and had fallen back to Albuquerque. On entering the capital city the Union soldiers had been received with public demonstrations of joy. Exuberantly Colonel Paul wrote Governor Connelly at Las Vegas he could return to the capital whenever he desired.

With the Confederates now concentrated at Albuquerque and apparently planning to leave the territory, the way was clear for Paul to move southward to unite with Canby. Early on the morning of April 13 the stillness was rudely broken by the drum and bugle calling Paul's men to rise and prepare for the hard march ahead. At two o'clock, before many had even finished breakfast, the column started moving out. For the first few miles the road wound about hills covered with scrub pine. Soon the trail passed through a cactus-studded plain which stretched out in every direction except in the west, where it was bounded by a broken chain of mountains. Through occasional gaps in these mountains the blue and hazy peaks of more distant ranges could be seen. Thirty miles from Galisteo the road approached the mountains and then passed up a canyon toward the head of Carnuel Pass. Near nightfall Paul's column reached the village of Tijeras where Canby had his camp nestled among the densely timbered hills of the Pass. Canby had moved his forces from San Antonio to Tijeras, about six miles further toward Albuquerque.

Footsore and weary, Paul's men straggled in to make camp. They had been on the road for fourteen hours and had traveled a distance of over forty miles without food. Some of the horses were so jaded that they had to be led into camp, "and they will probably never leave it,"[29] mused one of the exhausted volunteers.

With Slough's resignation, Lieutenant Colonel Tappan had temporarily taken charge of the First Regiment. Shortly after making camp, Tappan presented Canby with a petition signed by all the regiment's officers asking that Chivington be appointed colonel. The following day Canby complied by issuing a temporary order to that effect, an action later confirmed by the governor of Colorado.

With his forces finally united and numbering around twenty-four hundred men, Canby was ready to move against the enemy, who was now retreating down the river from Albuquerque. On the afternoon of April 14 the Federals marched through Carnuel Pass to the mouth of the canyon, where they halted briefly to eat. From this point they could see the Río Grande, which, at that distance, appeared to be "a silver thread glistening under the slanting beams of the setting sun."[30] After emerging from the canyon, Canby veered southward, following the road which angled toward the river. Near ten o'clock that night, the Federals struck the Río Grande about one mile above the village of Peralta.

The men of Green's Fifth Regiment who were encamped at Peralta were totally unaware of Canby's approach. From captured pickets and from spies, the Federals attempted to learn the condition of the Army of New Mexico. Apparently the Texan enlisted men were badly demoralized, while at the moment their officers were carousing at a fandango. To be sure, in the distance Canby's ears were "saluted with the 'sound of revelry by night.' The violin was in full blast, accompanied by other and more noisy instruments."[31] Obviously the officers were celebrating their leaving despised New Mexico.

Most of the Federals impatiently awaited orders to attack. But Canby had other plans; so the wagons were drawn up and camp made. Chivington offered to capture or disperse the Texans with his Colorado regiment alone. Canby, however, was well aware that Green held a strong defensive position, and so knew better than to risk an engagement. During the remainder of the mild, moonlight night, the troops watched and waited, hoping to surprise the Texans in the morning.

9

The Retreat from New Mexico

THE NEXT MORNING THE FEDERAL AND CONFEDERATE TROOPS WERE STARTLED BY A "thrilling" reveille from Canby's bugles, followed shortly by the "stirring strains of Dixie thrust upon the deathly quiet by the brazen throats of Sibley's Brass Band."[1] All thoughts of a surprise attack were now at an end, and by daylight, both camps were in motion.

During the previous evening seven Confederate wagons had bogged down hub-deep in sand about two or three miles from Green's camp. The mules were so exhausted that the Texans had no alternative but to stop where they were.[2] Accompanying the train were Judge Spruce M. Baird and his family.[3] In fact, one of the seven wagons contained Baird's household goods and other articles of personal property. Lieutenant James A. Darby and thirty-four men of Company I, Fifth Regiment, supported by one brass howitzer, served as the train's escort.

The next morning the Texans started out toward Peralta, unaware of the enemy's presence. When the train was about equidistant from the Confederate and Union camps, Canby dispatched a force of infantry and cavalry to capture it. On seeing the Federal cavalry speeding toward him, Darby quickly commanded his men to take defensive positions. The Texans could have abandoned the overloaded wagons and have easily made it safely to Green's camp. Judge Baird and his family, who were riding in an ambulance, did so, as apparently did several of the escort. Undoubtedly Darby trusted that Green, seeing his plight, would come to his aid. With the unlimbering of the howitzer, the others took cover under the wagons, and leaned on their "trusty rifles" to await the attack.

When the Union cavalrymen had come within two hundred yards of the train, they quickly dismounted to deploy as skirmishers. As they advanced, the Texans fired, but the Federals "hit the dirt," fired back, and rose to advance further. These tactics were continued until they were within fifty yards of the Texans when, with a loud yell, they rushed the train. At that moment about a dozen Confederates stepped out in view, dropped their weapons, and hoisted a dirty handkerchief on a ramrod. The others took "leg bail" and were either shot down, captured, or allowed to escape. Perhaps Darby could have held out longer, but two companies of Union infantry were rapidly coming to the support of the cavalry. With no help in sight from Green's camp, he considered it useless to resist. The Union infantry arrived on the scene in time to witness the surrender.

In this brief engagement, the Confederates suffered four killed and six wounded, while most of the remaining escort were taken prisoner.[4] The only Union casualty was wounded so severely that he died within a few days. Besides Baird's property, the train carried quartermaster and commissary supplies. In addition to the seven wagons, the Federals captured the howitzer, seventy mules, ten to fifteen horses, and various miscellaneous equipment. The howitzer was limbered up and the prisoners forced to haul it in. On the way back the Federals met Captain Claflin who took charge of the cannon and was soon using it against its late owners.

Meanwhile Colonel Green, greatly surprised to learn of Canby's presence, dispatched a messenger to Sibley's camp across the river about four miles below. Though Green's whole force numbered only about 550 men, supported by four howitzers, he occupied a strong defensive position. Canby maintained later that it was the strongest in the territory outside of Fort Union.

The village of Peralta was a two-mile stretch of adobe houses, thick adobe fences, raised ditches, and groves of large cottonwood trees. Governor Connelly's residence, where Green had set up his temporary headquarters, was surrounded on all sides for a half mile by a low, heavy growth of trees. Only the main road leading to the house could be used for wagons or artillery. Numerous wide irrigation canals ran parallel to, and across the road, while adobe walls enclosed the cultivated fields.

When Canby ordered the column after the wagon train, Graydon's Spy Company began feeling out the enemy by galloping into Peralta to fire a few shots. On Graydon's return, Canby opened a furious, but harmless barrage against Green's position. Hardly had the first twenty-four-pounder burst over the Texans, than they responded with the guns they had taken at Valverde. This was the first time these weapons had been put to use since their capture. The first ball the Texans fired fell short, bounced over the enemy, and buried itself in loose sand behind. The next, after making a high arc in the air, came whizzing in, and crashed among a pair of battery wheel mules. The ball tore away the whole face of the saddle mule, and struck the off-wheeler on the head. Both animals fell to the ground not knowing what had hit them. With their guns in range, the Texans began pouring shells into the midst of the Federal train, compelling Canby to pull his wagons back further to the rear. Though the Union guns continued their barrage, they were so ineffectual against the entrenched Texans that Canby ordered them to cease fire.

After the force which had captured the Confederate wagon train had returned, Canby ordered the bosque in front of Peralta cleared of the enemy. Two columns under Paul and Chivington, with a section of artillery in the center of each, started toward the Río Grande, their objective being to approach Peralta from the protective cover of the trees along the river. This position would also enable them to command the ford, and thus prevent Sibley from sending reinforcements to Green. On the way, the columns halted several times to probe the Confederate line with their artillery. The Texan battery was located in a superb position, for it was on higher ground and sheltered by the bank of a large canal. Having the Federals' exact range, they forced the two columns to keep moving. The Union cavalry, as one Coloradoan saw it, was "here, there and everywhere; now preparing to charge, now on foot advancing as skirmishers; always about to do something but never doing it."[5] It must not be forgotten, however, that there was much prejudice and rivalry between the regulars and the volunteers.

Paul and Chivington were under the impression that Canby would assault the other side of town while they attacked from the river. Anxious to close in and take Peralta by storm, Paul intended to send his infantry forward while his cavalry charged on the right. Chivington's column was ordered to support the infantry. Before Paul could put his plan into operation, Canby arrived on the scene and forbade it. He knew that the nature of the terrain would render such an attack almost suicidal. The cavalrymen's horses were weak and jaded, and they would have bogged down in the muddy ditches, allowing well-concealed Texan sharpshooters to pick off the riders. An infantry charge might have met with more success, but only at a heavy cost. At any rate, Canby's objective for the moment had been accomplished, for the bosques in the front and rear of the town were cleared and occupied by his forces.

When Sibley learned of Green's condition, he ordered Colonel Scurry to set out immediately to bolster the Fifth with the whole disposable force. Only a guard for the camp and train remained behind. The ford was nearly eight hundred yards wide and averaged about four feet deep. Holding their guns in their right hands and their cartridge boxes in their left, Scurry's men waded the icy waters of the Río Grande. Around nine o'clock Green's troops were heartened by the shouts of their comrades as they emerged from the river.[6]

Sibley, with part of his staff, followed shortly to assume immediate command. He had just crossed the river when a group of officers which had preceded him several hundred yards, galloped back to inform him that a large body of enemy cavalry (Paul's column) was approaching. Finding himself completely cut off, the General was forced to recross the river under enemy fire. Once again the Confederate commander did not lead his troops in battle.

The Federals had gone twenty-four hours—some as long as thirty-six hours—without eating. To allow his troops to obtain food and rest, Canby discontinued his attack for the time being. Though the men slept and ate, they still remained in line of battle. Near noon some hungry Coloradoans, "seeing no likelihood of getting any secesh to eat, . . . knocked over a dozen of their beeves."[7] The meat was broiled over the coals of their fires and made a fine meal.

During the lull, Canby sent out scouting parties to reconnoiter the approaches to Peralta. On the basis of their reports, he planned his next attack. About two o'clock in the afternoon a high wind sprang up, forcing a change in Canby's plans. As is typical of wind storms in New Mexico, the air became a solid cloud of sand and dust. It was difficult to breathe, much harder to see. Realizing that further operations were impossible, Canby abandoned his advanced positions about three o'clock and ordered his men to fall back to the shelter of their camp. The Federals had been on the battle line just beyond rifle range of the enemy for six hours. So ended the skirmish of Peralta.

Canby gave his losses as one killed and three wounded. Other accounts, particularly the records of the Colorado adjutant general's office, mention four deaths among the Colorado volunteers alone. In one instance during the skirmish, Colonel Chivington and one of his captains barely escaped being hit by a cannon ball. The missile, after skipping along the ground toward them, bounded a few inches over their heads, fatally striking two soldiers walking nearby. In addition to the losses sustained in the capture of the wagon train, the Confederates reported two men wounded.

About eight o'clock that night, with the wind still blowing furiously, the Confederates crossed to the west bank of the Río Grande. Green was forced to abandon three of his wagons in the river, for the teams were too weak to get them across. The mules were unhitched and later used to help pull the rest of the army's transportation. At four o'clock in the morning the last of the troops came into Los Lunas wet, cold, and sleepy. At daylight, after leaving behind a few sick and wounded soldiers without attendants or medicines, and almost without food, the Army of New Mexico quietly resumed its march down the river.[8]

Canby incurred a great deal of ill feeling for allowing the Texans to escape so easily. One Union soldier cynically remarked that the skirmish of Peralta was the "most harmless battle on record, putting one in mind of two gamblers colleagued to *do* a greeny, betting and bluffing together with perfect recklessness to bait him, but suddenly finding their judgment when he put his foot into it . . . As Sibley waved his farewell from the opposite bank he seemed to say, 'Thank you, gentlemen, for your hostile intentions. Doubtless they are sincere, but Canby and I understand each other.'"[9]

Such criticism was most unfair, for Canby had good reasons for not attacking more vigorously. Had he launched a full-scale assault against the entrenched Texans, his losses would have been heavy—and Canby considered an "honest man's life worth ten"[10] of the enemy. Aside from casualties, what would have resulted? Victory would probably have meant the capture of the entire Confederate army. That might have been glorious, to be sure, but it would not have been practical. The territory was stripped of provisions of all kinds, and even the Union troops were on short rations. If the Texans were captured, Canby would not only have to use the bulk of his army to guard them, but he would also have to feed them. This he was in no position to do. His only alternative was to let the Confederates slip away, and then follow closely behind to make certain they were evacuating the country and would not pillage villages on the way.

Since leaving Carnuel Pass, Canby knew that Sibley was abandoning New Mexico. He probably intended the skirmish at Peralta to be no more than a threat to hasten the enemy's departure. His course of action elicited a great deal of discontent within his own army, and the Unionists of the territory never forgave him. In retrospect, Canby's decision was undoubtedly a wise one.

The Texans' abandonment of their strong position at Peralta was ample evidence that they did not care to engage the Federals again. Since it was obvious that they were getting out of the country as fast as possible, Canby sent Colonel Roberts and his departmental staff officers to Santa Fé and Fort Union to make arrangements for future operations. These officers, plus the small force of volunteers accompanying them, did not weaken Canby's effective strength to any degree. Roberts set out from Peralta with his command and the staff on April 16. He reoccupied Albuquerque with a small garrison, and continued on to Santa Fé, arriving there on the evening of April 20. Northern New Mexico was once again in the hands of the Union.

Canby realized that the cavalry and draft animals of both his and the enemy's army were so weak and jaded that neither a retreat nor a pursuit could be carried out with any degree of speed. Before setting out, he divided his command into three divisions: Paul headed the first column, Chivington the second, and, with the exception of Graydon's Spy Company, all the cavalry was in charge of Captain Morris. Though he was certain the Texans had abandoned Peralta, Canby left nothing to chance. Cautiously he circled the town before entering. As his men observed the natural strength of the Confederates' former position, they were convinced Canby had exercised sound judgment in not storming the town the day before.

The wind continued to blow fiercely as the Union army started down the east bank of the river in pursuit of the enemy. In his official report Canby maintained that the reason he did not ford the river was that the road on the east bank was shorter than the one the Confederates were following. He reported that if he had not already overtaken the enemy before, he intended to cross to the west bank at some spot such as La Joya, a point opposite Polvadera, Sabino, or a point across from Fort Craig. Canby, of course, had no intention of overtaking the Confederates and engaging in another battle.

During the remainder of the day, the road ran over some heavily-turfed ground, but in other areas it was nothing but drifting sand or alkali-crusted wastes. On passing below Los Lunas, the men saw the smoking remains of several of Sibley's wagons. After a march of about twelve miles, Canby's troops encamped. They were now about five miles behind the Confederates.

Many still did not understand Canby's reasons for not overtaking and capturing the enemy. As one remarked, "Sixty miles per day to catch the traitors and ten to let them go. Of course it is all right. We do not want to take any unfair advantage of them. We would be chivalrous, like them. God grant they may never get the same advantage of us."[11]

The next day Canby's troops had been on the road but a short while when they sighted the Texans plodding slowly along about three or four miles ahead on the opposite bank. The Federals moved closer until only the wide river intervened to separate the belligerents. Aside from the pickets who skirmished throughout most of the day, the two armies proceeded peacefully along virtually side by side. The road on the Federal side passed through poor country which, except for a few scattered areas, was practically desert. Sandbanks up to fifteen feet high were common.

That afternoon the Confederates, on reaching the point where the Río Puerco drains into the Río Grande, halted and went into camp. The Federals continued on to La Joya, a point slightly ahead. Both camps were in full view of one another, causing a Texan to comment that "The sight of both campfires at night was both grand and awful."[12]

Canby's men made their camp in a barren area of deep, loose sand. Shortly after dusk the wind began to rise again, blowing furiously throughout the night and filling and covering everything with sand. "Men who had grown gray in the Service swore they never spent a worse night. Eating, drinking, talking, seeing or sleeping were alike impossible. Tents were prostrated and buried."[13] Too busy cursing the unpardonable stupidity of locating a camp in a sandbank, the men gave little thought to the Texans across the river.

On the other side of the Río Grande Sibley was pondering his next move. He feared a clash with the Union forces would be inevitable if he continued following the river route. His original plan had been to retreat down the Río Grande well ahead of Canby to attack and destroy Fort Craig as a parting gesture. Green's inability to cross over at Albuquerque had thwarted this, for the subsequent delay had enabled Canby to catch up at Peralta. About seventy miles below on the west bank of the river lay Fort Craig. Surely the garrison would contest his passage. While he was thus engaged, Canby's army could cross over to join the attack. Certain disaster would be the only outcome.

To add to Sibley's troubles, the road over which he had been traveling was very poor. Heavy sand had made it difficult for the weary draft animals to pull the wagons and artillery. All along the route forage and grass had been scarce, and the animals were suffering more than ever as a result. With his mules too weak to pull both the wagons and the caissons, it was obvious that he would have to abandon one or the other. At this trying and critical moment the General called a council of war to determine what course to pursue.

At the council someone suggested that the army, being too crippled to proceed any further, should surrender to the Federals. Green, Scurry, and a number of others objected vociferously. Scurry reputedly said, "By G——d, I will take the 1st [Fourth] regiment through or die in the attempt."[14] Because of such determined opposition, the surrender proposal was discarded. To avoid another encounter with the enemy, Fort Craig would have to be bypassed. Green, Scurry, and several other officers suggested that they leave the river road and make a detour around the mountains to the west and strike the Río Grande again below the fort. This would be a difficult and hazardous route involving passage through a mountainous, trackless waste nearly devoid of water. But regardless of the drawbacks, the council decided it was the only alternative. Since Captain Bethel Coopwood was familiar with the country, he was given the responsibility of guiding the army.

Lack of a road, the rugged nature of the terrain, and the broken-down condition of the draft animals required that all wagons which could possibly be dispensed with be abandoned. Some even suggested that the artillery also be destroyed. Scurry pledged, however, that his regiment would bring the six guns captured at Valverde over every obstacle, no matter how formidable.

This detour, Sibley mused, would have several advantages. It would mystify the Federals as to his intentions, and prevent another engagement with them. As it turned out, Canby was truly surprised by the detour, but certainly not mystified. This course of action, however, did prevent another major clash between the belligerents. According to Sibley this new route was not much longer than the river road, and was far more advantageous in regard to grass and a firmer road. Apparently he did not take into consideration the known scarcity of water. Indeed, there might be more grass for the animals, but the advantage of a firmer road is somewhat questionable. But then again, a mountainside is far firmer than a river valley!

After his troops had finished supper, Sibley ordered every man to wear what he could and burn the rest. Above all everyone was to carry his gun and ammunition, and to pack seven days' rations. Thirty-eight wagons were abandoned, most of the commissary provisions being packed on the backs of the mules. After dark, with the wind blowing furiously, the Army of New Mexico struck out for the mountains. Nearly everyone drove a pack mule or a broken-down horse. The infantry led the advance, followed by the few remaining wagons and artillery, with the cavalry bringing up the rear.

When the Federals gazed across the Río Grande on the morning of April 18, nothing but an abandoned camp met their eyes. Graydon's Spy Company crossed over to discover that, with the exception of some sick and disabled soldiers, the Confederates had departed, leaving thirty-eight partially loaded wagons. Graydon observed that the Texans had taken an old trail through the mountains which passed twenty miles west of Fort Craig and came out on the river about thirty miles below. After Canby secured the abandoned property and provided for the unfortunates left behind, he set out for Polvadera, fifteen miles away.

Colonel Canby was usually at the head of his column, attended by his staff and escorted by a few cavalrymen. "Tall and straight, coarsely dressed in citizen's clothes, his countenance hard and weatherbeaten, his chin covered with a heavy grizzly beard of two weeks' growth, a cigar in his mouth which he never lights— using a pipe when he wishes to smoke—he certainly has an air of superiority, largely the gift of nature, though undoubtedly strengthened by long habits of command."[15] Patient, prudent, and cautious, Canby exhibited not only foresight and sound judgment, but also great moral and physical courage. He was a regular army officer, and many of the Confederates he was now fighting had been his comrades only a short twelve months before. Undoubtedly this influenced his feelings, but it did not deter him from what he believed to be his duty.

The Federals arrived at a point across the river from Polvadera in the afternoon and made camp. The wagon train did not get in until late that night, since the draft animals were exceedingly jaded. Canby remained in camp the following day to rest his stock and to make certain that the Confederates were actually retreating behind the mountains and not attempting a feint. He also learned that a supply train from Fort Union was not far behind, and he wanted to wait until he was sure it would arrive safely.

While at the camp opposite Polvadera, William Pelham, the former surveyor general of the territory, came in, along with thirty Texans, to surrender. Because he was a civilian, Pelham was made a political prisoner and was not eligible for exchange. The others, after taking the oath of allegiance, were paroled. They left immediately afterward, presumably for Texas, where, according to numerous letters found in the abandoned wagons, the young Texan ladies "would fain wear Yankee ears for necklaces."[16] One disgruntled Federal cynically noted that these oaths meant nothing, and that the parolees would be met again whenever there was another engagement.

On learning that the supply train from Fort Union was proceeding safely, and assured that Sibley's men were retreating behind the mountains, Canby set out again. After a march of three miles, he crossed the Río Grande to the west bank at the ford opposite Lemitar. Not long after the men had encamped, about two miles below the ford, the commissary train arrived. The soldiers eagerly anticipated the new supplies, for they were thoroughly tired of rotten bacon, bread without soda, and a complete lack of salt, coffee, and sugar.

Graydon, whom Canby had sent out to reconnoiter the area of Sibley's retreat, reported that the enemy had buried all his artillery, except two pieces, had burned all but fifteen wagons, and was apparently going through the mountains to Mesilla by way of Cook's Springs. The Texans were suffering immeasurably, and it is significant that even a Colorado volunteer who bitterly hated them felt disposed to express his sympathy for them in their misery:

> Poor fellows! The climate and Uncle Sam's boys have sadly wasted them. They are now flying through the mountains with a little more than a third of the number with which they first assaulted us at Fort Craig. Many, very many, "softly lie and sweetly sleep low in the ground." Let their faults be buried with them. They are our brothers, erring it may be, still nature will exact a passing tear for the brave dead. And doubt not there are who will both love and honor their memory if we cannot. Any cause that men sustain to death becomes sacred, at least to them. Surely we can afford to pay tribute to the courage and nobleness that prefers death to even *fancied* enthralment.[17]

When Canby passed through Socorro, seventy-five Confederate stragglers and convalescents at the hospital were taken prisoner. After pledging the oath of allegiance the parolees were permitted to return to the Mesilla Valley and Texas. On April 22 Canby reached Fort Craig. With the enemy in full flight, his men looked forward to a few days of rest and relaxation.

Although Canby dispatched Graydon and advanced pickets southward to keep an eye on the enemy, he halted his southward movement at Fort Craig. His broken-down cavalry and draft animals were sorely in need of a rest, and he was still seriously short of supplies. To have continued down the valley in this condition, and perhaps engage in another battle, would have been dangerous, if not fatal. In the Mesilla Valley the Confederates had fresh troops under the command of Colonel Steele, and undoubtedly that officer had been busy gathering matériel to resupply Sibley's approaching forces.

Several days after Canby's arrival at Fort Craig, a reconnaissance party reported that the Confederates had come out on the river below and were still retreating southward. Dead stock, broken wagons, and camp refuse of every description marked the Texans' trail, for they were leaving behind everything that slowed them down—even their sick and wounded. Canby instructed

"Paddy" Graydon to bring in the abandoned unfortunates immediately, and to gather up all property of value.

The Texans still held prisoners about thirty officers and men. On April 26 Canby dispatched Captain Lewis with an escort under a flag of truce to overtake the Texans and propose an exchange. He was also to ask the Confederates to send back one or more surgeons, for Canby simply did not have enough medical personnel to look after both his sick and wounded and those the enemy had left behind. Lewis was unable to catch up with the fleeing Texans; so he returned to Fort Craig without accomplishing his mission.

With all danger from the enemy now removed, Canby departed for departmental headquarters in Santa Fé to expedite the gathering of supplies. Though it would involve a great deal of difficulty, he hoped to stockpile enough war matériel at Peralta and at Fort Craig to enable him to move against the Texans in the Mesilla Valley by June 1. Leaving Colonel Chivington in charge of the Southern Military District with headquarters at Fort Craig, Canby arrived in the capital on the night of May 3. The next day he issued the following congratulatory proclamation to his army:

HDQRS. DEPARTMENT OF NEW MEXICO
Santa Fe, N. Mex., May 4, 1862.
GENERAL ORDERS
NO. 41

The colonel commanding desires to express his grateful appreciation of the conduct and services of the troops in this department, tested as they have been in the past four months by two general battles, many skirmishes, and much toilsome and laborious service.

Daring and energetic in action, patient and reliant when policy dictated a different course; enduring with equal constancy and fortitude privations of food, of clothing, and of rest; forced marches; snow-storms of the mountains and the sandstorms of the plains, they have driven a superior force of the enemy into the mountains, forced him to abandon his trains, his supplies, and his plunder; to leave his sick and wounded by the wayside without care, and often without food, and finally to abandon a country which he has entered to "conquer and occupy," leaving behind in dead and wounded and in sick and prisoners one-half his original force.

These results have not been attained without serious losses, and the laurels won at Valverde and Apache Canon, hallowed by the blood of many brave and noble men, will ever be a bond of union and friendship between those who have struggled together to free New Mexico from the domination of an arrogant and rapacious invader.

By order of Col. E. R. S. Canby:
GURDEN CHAPIN,
Capt. Seventh Infantry and
Acting Assistant Adjutant-General.

From his executive offices in Santa Fé, Governor Connelly later added, "This is the second invasion our Territory has suffered from Texans, both of which have proved equally disastrous, and it is to be hoped we will never witness another."[19]

After nightfall of April 17, the Army of New Mexico, undaunted by the howling sandstorm, left the Río Grande and marched off in a southwesterly direction toward the Magdalena Mountains. Not until two o'clock in the morning did the men stop to rest among the cedars on the foothills. The next day, after an eight-mile march, the Texans reached the Río Salado and encamped for the night. Though the water here was very brackish, it was refreshingly welcome, nevertheless, to the thirsty men and animals.

The following morning, while still at the Río Salado, the Confederates realized that the rough and nearly impassable route they were following would necessitate the abandoning of more wagons and equipment. In an effort to prevent the Federals from capturing the matériel, they buried three howitzers (only the six pieces captured at Valverde now remained) and seventy-eight shells, destroyed six one-hundred-pound barrels of powder and burned nineteen wagons, ten ambulances, six caissons, and three carriages. After all encumbrances had been reduced to a few wagons belonging principally to brigade headquarters, the army set out southward over mountain, valley, and plain. Farther down the trail the Texans blew up another caisson, burned three more wagons, and destroyed some hospital supplies. What had started out to be a relatively orderly retreat had now become a veritable flight.

In the mornings when the Army of New Mexico would first set out, the column would be about a mile long. Toward the end of the day, however, it would stretch for at least ten miles. Picket duty was especially heavy for those who were still mounted. Since grass was scarce, the men turned their horses loose at night so they could roam about to find enough to eat. In the mornings the troopers would often have to walk long distances to round up their mounts before going on duty. Many soldiers were sick, and just barely able to move along. Baked bread in a frying pan and meat from a broken-down draft animal formed the basic diet. With supplies so short, Sibley sent orders ahead to Colonel Steele in the Mesilla Valley to bring all available provisions to meet the army when it came out on the Río Grande.

After proceeding down the western side of the Magdalena Mountains, the Confederates entered the San Mateo Mountains. Passage through this range proved to be the most difficult part of the detour since it involved moving in and out of a number of deep gorges and over high hills. On several occasions progress was held up while the troops of the Fourth Regiment attached long ropes to the artillery and wagons, and by a combination of pulling and pushing managed to drag them through a canyon or up a precipice.

About nine o'clock in the morning of April 24 the army reached the Alamosa River.[20] After quenching their thirst and eating breakfast, the exhausted troops lay down to rest for the remainder of the day. Only when evening came did they finally get the wagons and artillery up a steep hill and into camp. That night Colonel Steele, whose main force was encamped about six miles downstream, arrived with the heartening information that the Río Grande could easily be reached the next day, and that a large commissary train was on the way from Mesilla. The Colonel also brought with him the mail, which had been accumulating while the army had been away to the north. It was a night of rejoicing as the men sat around their campfires reading letters from home and loved ones.

Early the next morning the troops reached Steele's camp, where they rested briefly before moving on. Steele's men carried four full days' rations with them, and these they divided to the last mouthful with their hungry comrades. That afternoon as "the broken down 'foot pad' [infantryman] hove in sight of the Rio Grande and its fertile valley, he was led to exclaim 'how beautiful.'"[21] "Indeed, the thrilling spectacle of seeing the river again was indescribable. It was April 25, and for nine days the Confederates had struggled through the tortuous mountains. About ten miles below Alamosa the Army of New Mexico encamped. It was a pathetic sight to behold the weary, footsore, sick, half-starved men: "Some washing, some sleeping, some caring for the sick, and some dying, while but a few were cooking the ribs of some work oxen."[22]

Though the suffering had been intense, the detour had achieved its purposes — there had been no clash with the Federals, Fort Craig had been bypassed, and the Texans were now safely below the enemy. That the detour of over one hundred miles had been costly there could be no doubt. Abandoned equipment of all sorts marked the trail from beginning to end. At least sixty or seventy horses and mules had died from the rigors of the march. Near the Magdalena Mountains three partially buried bodies, and in another place the bones of a man's arm half eaten by wolves, attested to the tragic aspects of the retreat. A year later a Union officer passed over the trail and "not infrequently found a piece of a gun-carriage, or part of a harness, or some piece of camp or garrison equipage, with occasionally a white, dry skeleton of a man."[23]

While resting after their near-disastrous retreat, the Texans would have been cynically amused had they known of the following resolution passed by their government in Richmond:

Resolved by the Congress of the Confederate States of America, That the Thanks of Congress are hereby tendered to Brigadier General H. H. Sibley, and to the officers and men under his command, for the complete and brilliant victories achieved over our enemies in New Mexico.

Approved, April 16, 1862.[24]

On April 26 the Confederates set off down the Río Grande Valley. The next day, when about seven miles north of Fort Thorn, they met Steele's commissary train. What a joy it was, noted one soldier, to "get a little pickle & pork once more to eat with our bread baked in a frying pan."[25] When the troops reached San Diego on the evening of April 29, they began crossing to the east bank under Colonel Green's direction. Rafts were built to ferry over the ammunition, the howitzers, and the few remaining wagons containing the sick and the brigade's archives. The artillery, marching in advance that morning, had reached the ford considerably ahead of the infantry. Throughout the retreat, the gunners had kept their pieces loaded. Lest the charges get wet in the crossing, they attempted to pull them out. But they were stuck fast, so the cannoneers cleared the howitzers by firing them. As the six guns boomed out, their thunderous roar echoed throughout the valley. Most of the infantrymen, thinking that the Federals were attacking, reached an immediate decision: they would rather fight twenty Yankees apiece than try another of Coopwood's detours! Fortunately, the men soon learned the reason for the cannon blasts. With their anxieties relieved, and their bellicose feelings suppressed, calm prevailed among them once again.

The following morning, April 30, with his command safely across the river, Sibley left for Fort Bliss to set up his headquarters. He was accompanied by Colonel Reily (who had come up with Steele), and by Judge Baird and his family. Colonel Green, left in immediate command, marched as far as Robledo that day.

Since no part of the Mesilla Valley could support the whole army, it was necessary to quarter parts of it in the various villages which dotted the region. The Seventh Regiment went into quarters at its former camp above Doña Ana. Green left the unmounted men of his regiment at Las Cruces, and continued down the valley about three miles to encamp for the night. Under cover of darkness, someone— probably an irate Mexican—cut the bank of a nearby aqueduct and flooded the whole camp. After drying out somewhat in the morning, Green proceeded to Fort Fillmore, where, because of better grass, he quartered his mounted troops. The Fourth continued on to its old camp at Willow Bar. After a general muster on May 1, this regiment moved south into Texas—six companies were quartered in El Paso, while the other four encamped about a mile below.

While the bulk of the army remained idle, Colonel Steele's "fresh" troops of the Seventh Regiment, while maintaining a constant picket vigilance, conducted at least one raid against the Federals to the north.[26] Since the Confederates were in great need of horses, Lieutenant Bowman[27] set out with a party to capture the mounts belonging to the Union outpost at Paraje, about eight miles below Fort Craig.

In command at Paraje was Captain Joseph G. Tilford, U.S. Third Cavalry, with a force of twenty men. Some time prior to Bowman's raid, Tilford reported that a Confederate Lieutenant Taylor[28] with a small party had come into his post under a white flag. The Captain did not disclose the nature of Taylor's business, but it most likely dealt with prisoner exchange. Tilford later came to believe that Taylor and his men were actually spies who had come to observe the strength of his detachment and to note that his horses were herded day and night on the river bottom some distance from camp. If Tilford's assumption was correct, Taylor had accordingly informed his superiors of the situation, and Bowman's raid was the result. Meanwhile the Union garrison had been increased to forty-five men, and instead of leaving his horses out after dark to graze, Tilford now ordered them brought in.

On the night of May 20 Bowman and his troops cautiously approached Paraje and the area where the horses had formerly been herded. No doubt they were sorely disappointed to discover that the animals were not at their reported location. Instead of attacking the outpost, Bowman drew up the bulk of his command under a bluff on the river, and then dispatched one of his men to demand a surrender. About dawn a Union guard brought the Confederate, who was carrying a white flag, to Captain Tilford's quarters. Bowman's failure to storm the town was an error, for the Federal commander was still in bed—neither he nor his men being aware of the Confederates' arrival.

Upon being awakened by the guard and informed that a Texan was waiting to see him, Tilford lost no time in shaking the sleep from his head. While in the act of dressing, he quietly sent word to his command to prepare for immediate action. The Confederate was then ushered in. After hearing Bowman's ultimatum, Tilford informed the messenger that compliance depended altogether on Bowman's ability to enforce it. As soon as the Texan had left, Tilford set about stationing his men in defensive positions preparatory to the expected enemy assault.

Bowman, however, considered it inexpedient to attack. After a few straggling shots at long range, the Confederates withdrew southward down the Jornada del Muerto. Because he believed the enemy to number about a hundred men, and because of the jaded condition of his horses, Tilford did not set out in pursuit. He also feared that had he followed the retreating enemy, a larger force might have been lying in wait to ambush him. At any rate, Tilford saw no more of the Texans, and what was the last "skirmish" between the Confederates and the Federals in New Mexico came to an end.[29]

10

The End of the Campaign

THOUGH THE EXACT NUMBER OF CONFEDERATE CASUALTIES RESULTING FROM THE campaign is not known, the toll was, nonetheless, very heavy. At least eighty had been killed outright on the several battlefields, while some of the over two hundred wounded later died of their wounds. Diseases such as smallpox and, particularly, pneumonia carried many to the grave. The three hospitals left behind in Santa Fé, Albuquerque, and Socorro were filled with sick and wounded, and all along the line of retreat the Confederates had abandoned those too ill to continue. Over 100 Texans had been captured at Apache Canyon and Peralta. In addition, the Federals had taken a number of stragglers. According to Canby's official report of May 12, 1862, about 240 Confederate prisoners had been paroled and allowed to leave the territory, while another 240 remained. Of the latter, about two-thirds consisted of sick, wounded, and hospital attendants. The Colonel estimated that by the time the rest of the stragglers and deserters had been collected, the total number of prisoners would swell to 500. It is probably not an exaggeration to estimate that, either because of battle or disease, around 500 Confederates had lost their lives during the course of the campaign. If such was the case, Sibley's casualties amounted to 1,000 men. Consequently, of his invading force of nearly 2,500 men, only about 1,500 formed the army which straggled back to the Mesilla Valley at the close of the disastrous venture to capture New Mexico.[1] Of the large train which had accompanied the army, only seven wagons remained. With the exception of the six guns captured at Valverde, all the artillery had been buried, captured, or destroyed. To say the least, the campaign had left the Army of New Mexico in a shattered condition.

After establishing temporary headquarters at Fort Bliss, Sibley wrote the adjutant general a brief, but full account of his campaign. Far less exuberant than he once had been, Sibley reluctantly expressed the conviction, "determined by some experience, that, except for its political geographical position, the Territory of New Mexico . . . [was] not worth a quarter of the blood and treasure expended in its conquest."[2] This, of course, was not startling, since most Confederate expansionists from the first had viewed New Mexico solely as a means to an end, namely a stepping stone toward a port on the Pacific.

Sibley maintained that lack of supplies alone had necessitated his evacuation of New Mexico. He had found, as expected, that the land could not be relied upon for food or other goods. But, unexpectedly, he had failed to capture great stockpiles of Federal war matériel. Rather than admit he had underestimated the ability of his opponent, Sibley blamed lack of specie for his failure to obtain adequate supplies. Since Captain William H. Harrison, the brigade paymaster and quartermaster, had never left San Antonio, the General pointed out that he had had to wage his entire campaign "without a dollar" in the quartermaster's department. Hard money was virtually nonexistent, and one thousand dollars was all he could raise for the use of his hospitals and secret service.[3] Sibley noted that adequate supplies could have been purchased in Mexico, but since the merchants there refused to accept anything but specie, the Army of New Mexico consequently from the beginning had been hindered by lack of war matériel of all kinds.

In summing up his operations, Sibley toned down the true condition of his army. Undoubtedly he was reluctant to give a thoroughly accurate picture lest he suffer loss of prestige in Richmond or, worse still, be severely censured and reduced in rank. According to the General, his army was now comfortably garrisoned in the small towns from Doña Ana to Fort Bliss. Though his brigade had reached Fort Bliss that winter blanketless and in rags, he boasted that his men were now well clad and well supplied. In fact, he went so far as to assert that his forces were at present the best armed in the country! But even if the army were in such good condition, and even if the Texans had beaten the enemy in "every encounter," the General could not speak encouragingly for the future. His men, having suffered intensely during the campaign, naturally manifested a "dogged, irreconcilable detestation" of New Mexico and her people. The troops were eagerly awaiting only the time when they would take up the line of march for San Antonio. Sibley believed that the prevailing discontent among his men backed up by the distinguished valor they had displayed on every field, entitled them to marked consideration. These factors, combined with the scarcity of supplies in the area, and the rapid depreciation of Confederate currency, made it clear to the General that without waiting for orders, it might be necessary for his army to commence moving back to San Antonio. At that base of supply, he could re-mount and re-equip his forces, and recruit new men to fill the thinned ranks of his regiments.

Adding further credence to the necessity of returning to San Antonio was Captain Sherod Hunter's report that a large Union army had set out from Fort Yuma, California, apparently bound for the Río Grande. Just before he had launched his invasion from Fort Thorn, Sibley had sent Captain Hunter and his independent company of Arizona volunteers to take post at Tucson to secure western Arizona for the Confederacy. Hunter reached his objective on February 28, and within a short time had pickets out only eighty miles from California. On learning that a sizable enemy army was moving into Arizona, he abandoned Tucson on May 4. Although by the time Hunter's men had arrived in the Mesilla Valley Sibley had already determined to evacuate the country, news of the coming of a Union force from California certainly did nothing to bolster the spirit of the weary and demoralized Army of New Mexico.

On April 15 (the same day as the skirmish of Peralta) Lieutenant Henry Holmes, in command of eight scouts, was attacked by a Union reconnaissance force at Picacho Pass, about forty miles west of Tucson. The Federals lost three killed and three wounded. Three Confederates were taken prisoner (according to Hunter's muster roll), while Holmes and the others made good their escape. The skirmish of Picacho has the distinction of being the westernmost battle of the war.

When Sibley had been retreating down the Río Grande, the Confederacy had been suffering reverses elsewhere. The month of April witnessed the bloody battle of Shiloh and the fall of New Orleans. Even with these great disasters attracting his attention, General Paul O. Hébert, commander of the Department of Texas, had not forgotten the New Mexican campaign. When he received Sibley's urgent pleas for reinforcements, he ordered two regiments of cavalry which had been intended for service in Little Rock to march to his support. But communications were slow, and Hébert had not received notice that Sibley had already evacuated New Mexico.

In faraway Virginia, McClellan had begun his Peninsular campaign and was pressing upon Richmond. On the very day of the opening of the Battle of Seven Pines, May 31, 1862, Robert E. Lee, general in chief under the President, informed Hébert that Jefferson Davis had received reports of Sibley's destitute and critical condition and had approved his sending the two regiments of reinforcements. Lee advised Hébert to send at once all the supplies he could for Sibley's use. In this matter, he suggested that the departmental commander call upon the governor of Texas for assistance.

Not long after the victory of Valverde, Sibley sent Captain Thomas P. Ochiltree, his chatty aide-de-camp, to Richmond to report personally the progress of the New Mexican campaign and to expedite the sending of reinforcements. After hearing Ochiltree's report, President Davis considered Sibley's handling of the campaign thus far as most praiseworthy, and with pleasure informed the Captain that reinforcements were already on the way. The President suggested that when Ochiltree returned to his command, he should tell Sibley about the state of affairs in the east. This, Davis believed, would explain why the Army of New

Mexico had not been more quickly reinforced and supplied. Though the President knew that the enemy in New Mexico was superior in numbers and supplies, he expressed the fond hope that Sibley's military ability and astuteness, coupled with the valor of his troops, would more than offset any such disparity. Of course, Davis had not yet learned of the disastrous results of the far western venture, and it must have been highly embarrassing to Sibley when Ochiltree later delivered the President's congratulatory communication.

The first news of reinforcements came to Sibley through unofficial channels. During the latter part of May the week's mail brought information from several reliable persons that the government intended to send Sibley one or more regiments. In fact, Colonel X. B. Debray was supposedly already en route. Hamilton Bee, commander of the Western District of Texas, reportedly had announced that New Mexico and Arizona were to be held at all costs. All this was exceedingly distressing, for neither Sibley nor his men were desirous of engaging in another New Mexican campaign!

In a determined effort to forestall the sending of reinforcements and thus the renewal of the campaign, Sibley hastily wrote Bee a far more accurate account of the condition of his army than he had presented in his report to the adjutant general. Sibley pointed out that he had evacuated New Mexico because his provisions, forage, and ammunition had been completely exhausted. He warned that any force sent to operate in New Mexico could not expect to rely upon the country for supplies. In the vicinity of the Mesilla Valley and Fort Bliss, Sibley found himself but little better off. Having confiscated all spare supplies in the Mesilla Valley, he now ordered his foragers to secure all available provisions and transportation from the villages below Fort Bliss. Sibley's troops were in desperate straits, and were presently subsisting on a limited supply of poor meat and bread. Such luxury items as coffee and sugar were virtually nonexistent. With clothing stocks gone, the men were clad in rags—many were almost naked. Only about a hundred rounds of ammunition remained for the heavy guns. The army's sick and wounded were suffering from lack of medicines and other necessities. To be sure, with specie, supplies could have been purchased on the Mexican side of the river. In the area now held by Sibley's men, Confederate currency was selling at the rate of twenty cents on the dollar, and large amounts could have been bought for less had there been any purchasers.

Sibley lamented that he had sent report after report to his superiors during the recent campaign, but had not received a single line of acknowledgment or encouragement. In the absence of all official communication, he had been forced to rely entirely upon his own judgment. Since he now believed that the safety of his army depended upon its moving to a base of supply, he informed Bee that he had already given the order for the bulk of his forces to withdraw to San

Antonio. As far as Sibley was concerned, the New Mexican campaign was at an end. This view was shared by the rank and file as well. As one officer expressed it: "We are all tired of this country, we are all anxious to return to the sunny land of Texas, to behold for a short time the faces of the loved ones at home, and then renewed and invigorated we can meet the invaders of our soil, consoled by the reflection that we are 'striking for our altars and our fires' and not throwing our lives away in endeavoring to obtain possession of a country which is not worth the life of one good man, of the many who have breathed their last upon its arid sands."[4]

From Fort Bliss on May 14, 1862, Sibley addressed a valedictory proclamation to his men:

Soldiers of the Army of New Mexico: — It is with unfeigned pride and pleasure that I find myself occupying a position which devolves upon me the duty of congratulating the Army of New Mexico upon the successes which have crowned their arms in the many encounters with the enemy during the short but brilliant campaign which has just terminated.

Called from your homes almost at a moment's warning, cheerfully leaving friends, families and private affairs, in many cases solely dependent upon your presence and personal attention, scarcely prepared for a month's campaign, in the immediate defence of your own firesides, you have made a march, many of you over a thousand miles, before ever reaching the field of active operations.

The boasted valor of Texans has been fully vindicated. Val Verde, Glorietta, Albuquerque, Peralto, and last, though not least, your successful and almost unprecedented evacuation, through mountain passes and over a trackless waste of a hundred miles through a famishing country, will be duly chronicled, and form one of the brightest pages in the history of the Second American Revolution.

That I should be proud of you — that every participant in the campaign should be proud of himself — who can doubt?

During the short period of inaction which you are now enjoying, your General indulges the hope that you will constantly bear in mind that at any moment you may be recalled into activity.

God and an indulgent Providence have guided us in our councils and watched our ways: let us be thankful to Him for our successes, and to Him let us not forget to offer a prayer for our noble dead.

H. H. Sibley, Brig. Gen. Commanding.[5]

The evacuation began on or about May 20, when Major Pyron, in command of the battalion of the Second Regiment Mounted Rifles, left Fort Bliss for San Antonio. The men of the Second had been in this theater of operations longer than any of the others, having come out with Lieutenant Colonel Baylor in June and July, 1861. Another reason for their leaving first was that since they had originally entered the Confederate army for a period of twelve months only, their enlistments were due to expire on May 23. On the morning of June 5 Colonel Hardeman[6] called Companies A, B, D, E, G, I, and K of the Fourth into line preparatory to leaving. In addressing his men, the Colonel warned that their rations were short and that the going would be difficult. He hoped, however, that a supply train from San Antonio would meet them at Fort Lancaster. At the conclusion of his remarks, the seven companies marched off on the long road to San Antonio. The following day Major Hampton set out with the other three companies. Green's Fifth Regiment, scattered in parties of fifteen to twenty along the road between Doña Ana and El Paso, was preparing to take up the line of march shortly. By the morning of June 10, General Sibley and his staff were ready to leave. Though the bulk of the Confederate forces were evacuating, Sibley ordered Colonel William Steele, who was then at Doña Ana, to remain behind with his "fresh" force of about four hundred men to hold the Territory of Arizona.[7] Undoubtedly Sibley meant this to be a rear-guard holding operation. Surely he could not have seriously entertained the thought that Steele could have held the territory for long against Canby's impending invasion from the north. With the withdrawal of the greater part of the army, all hope for the conquest of New Mexico and the West, temporarily at least, came to an end.

Though Sibley's men had endured a great deal during the New Mexican campaign, their suffering was far from over. Lack of adequate transportation and food, as well as the rundown condition of most of the men, would make the long journey back to San Antonio a most difficult one. The ordeal which the first division of the dismounted Fourth Regiment experienced was typical of the others. When this unit set out, it was the month of June, and the weather was oppressively hot. One eyewitness reported that the sickness occasioned by the first few days' march was truly painful to behold. It was not an unusual sight to see some men "giving out" along the road after a march of only a few miles. Because of the spring thaws, the valley of the Río Grande was completely flooded. "The roads were impassable, the mail stations washed away, wheat fields destroyed, San Elizario . . . [had] become an island, and the sand hills were the only refuge for the traveller on his journey."[8] From Fort Bliss to Fort Quitman great swarms of gnats strove to intensify the miseries of the march. Travel through gnats and sand beds proved so trying that the exhausted men rested at Fort Quitman for a day. Eagle Springs, thirty-six miles away, was the next watering place. Lieutenant John H. Barnes (promoted from sergeant), in command of a small party, proceeded ahead to make certain that the springs were cleaned out and ready for use when the main body arrived.[9]

At daylight the division wearily plodded along from Fort Quitman and proceeded up Eagle Canyon. There was no orderly marching in line—it was every man for himself, and "the wagons take the hindmost." The advance members of the "foot pads" arrived at Eagle Springs about two o'clock that afternoon. After filling the water barrels and preparing two days' rations of beef and unsalted bread, the men resumed their march at sundown. At daybreak, twenty-two miles later, the command reached Van Horn's Wells. The wells here were similar to the ones at Eagle Springs, but the Indians had filled them in with dirt and sheep carcasses. Lieutenant Barnes had not attempted to clean them out. The next water was at Dead Man's Hole about thirty-eight miles away. Great, indeed, was the disappointment as the troops thirstily resumed their march.

The road to Dead Man's Hole ran through a relatively flat "boundless prairie." The weather continued to be extremely torrid as the unmerciful sun bore down upon the command. The teams were "fast caving," and the weary soldiers were strung out for miles. Many gave completely out and threw themselves down by the side of the road to die. Most kept surging onward, with tongues so swollen they could scarcely articulate a word. More crazed than rational, they looked like frantic mad men. As the sun was setting, the reeling troops could clearly see the foothills at whose base lay Dead Man's Hole. What a heartening sight, for it seemed just a short distance away. But the clear air of the West is deceiving, and the command was still fourteen miles from the spring. The men kept up the march for another six miles when, to their great joy and relief, Lieutenant Barnes arrived from Dead Man's Hole with a water-laden wagon! As each quenched his thirst, he would go back and lie down in the road. This was the only place the men could find to rest, for the area outside the roadbed was covered with sagebrush, cat's-claw, and cactus. At Dead Man's Hole the division rested for a day before continuing on to Barrel Springs. On arrival at Fort Davis, part of the command's supplies was met, and the soldiers hungrily feasted upon fat beef. There was plenty of wood at the fort, so the men kneaded unbolted flour, wound the dough around their iron ramrods, and baked it over the camp fires. After resting for a day and a night, the division resumed its march.

A woman riding on the stage from El Paso noted, as she passed by the various detachments of the Fourth Regiment, that "The men were suffering terribly from the effects of heat; very many of them are a-foot, and scarcely able to travel from blistered feet. They were subsisting on bread and water, both officers and men; many of them were sick, many ragged, and all hungry; but we did not see a gloomy face—not one! They were all cheerful, for their faces were turned homewards. 'We are going home!'"[10] She maintained that two-thirds of the suffering endured by the soldiers was due to the merchants of El Paso del Norte, Mexico, who would not accept Confederate currency for their foodstuffs and other merchandise.

The weather continued to be hot, and the barren, cactus-covered terrain was exceedingly dry and dusty. With dogged determination, the men trudged along from Fort Davis through the mountain passes and across the and plains to Fort Stockton. From here they moved eastward to the Pecos River, where, for several days, they followed along the course of that deep and muddy stream. Leaving the Pecos with its hordes of gnats and mosquitoes, the men passed by Fort Lancaster and then proceeded with great difficulty to get their wagons up the long, steep grade of that "hill of hills" near the fort. At the crest, many felt obliged to "bid a 'lasting farewell' to the Pecos & the innumerable hordes of gnats that infest its surroundings."[11] The next water was secured at Howard Spring, and from there the command pushed on toward Beaver Lake, which was forty-five miles away at the head of Devils River. Undoubtedly the most momentous event of the long march occurred twenty-two miles northwest of Beaver Lake. Here at daylight on July 3 the thirsty, haggard men met a supply train of six wagons which had come to their relief. Friends and relatives had sent barrels of water, clothing, soap, combs, fresh corn meal, sugar, salt, bacon, coffee, tobacco, and numerous other luxuries. "The boys were in no way disposed to be selfish or close-fisted with what they had received, but divided freely and to the last, with those of their companions whose friends had forgotten them in their hour of need, or had not yet had the time necessary to meet them."[12]

A number of officers had left Fort Bliss before their commands in order to make preparations for the arrival of their men. Colonel Reily, for example, addressed an appeal for aid to the citizens of eleven counties. After briefly pointing out the hardships his men had endured, he requested that each county immediately take steps to prepare clothing and supplies, and to select and establish a healthy and comfortable location where each company could rendezvous until recruited and ordered again into service. He pleaded that his troops needed transportation to reach their homes, and he asked that horses and wagons be sent as far on the road as possible to meet these returning heroes. The Colonel was confident that his appeal would not be in vain and that immediate action would be taken to "greet not only with warm hearts, but with substantial aid the survivors of the soldiers of a Regiment whose valor and patriotism have added lustre to the stars of that flag under which they fought and conquered."[13] One result of these appeals was the train of six wagons which met the destitute command northwest of Beaver Lake.

From Beaver Lake on, all went well. At D'Hanis many friends and relatives came to meet the returning veterans. Straggling back on foot in a broken and disorganized manner, the weary, destitute survivors of the far-western campaign were home again after an absence of nine months. For a while, at least, the hardships encountered in New Mexico were forgotten.

From early July until the latter part of August, the various detachments of the Army of New Mexico began arriving in San Antonio. On July 10, the Valverde Battery[14] came into town and was honored with an eleven-gun salute. During the middle of July, General Sibley and his staff, though apparently having traveled most of the way with the Fifth Regiment, proceeded ahead to San Antonio to the welcoming boom of cannon. Green's regiment left Fort Bliss around June 19, and reached town during the first week of August. The first battalion of the Seventh was reportedly due in from the West within a few days. All soldiers received sixty-day furloughs, though they were still subject to call at a moment's notice. While enjoying the pleasures and comforts of home, the men were under orders to remount and reoutfit themselves. As the San Antonio *Herald* of July 19, 1862, commented, "The men have seen hard times, but they are nothing daunted." Though the campaign in New Mexico might have come to a close, the war was far from over for the Sibley Brigade.

Confederate public opinion concerning the New Mexican campaign was confined almost exclusively to the state of Texas. For while Sibley's small army was engaged in distant New Mexico, the attention of the rest of the nation was held by the spectacle of far larger armies clashing in great bloody conflicts close at home. Among those who were aware of Sibley's efforts in the Southwest, and concerned about them, opinions were often widely divergent—not especially as to the conduct of the campaign, but as to the sagacity of having attempted the conquest of New Mexico in the first place.

The bulk of the rank and file of the Sibley Brigade were highly disgusted, and felt that they had been led on a wild-goose chase. Most believed that even if they had been successful in taking the territory, the results would have been nil, for as far as they were concerned, New Mexico was totally devoid of any value whatsoever. Almost to a man they had come to detest the area most vehemently. As one participant disgustedly commented: "The Territory of New Mexico is utterly worthless. It never will be the abode of civilized man ... The naturalist is the only character that could be benefited by travelling" there.[15] And what had the New Mexican campaign accomplished? Another soldier caustically commented that "We have brought down 6 pieces of cannon, the Valverde trophy, and fed ourselves for over 2 months on Yankee provisions; that is all the good we have done for our country, and if you balance that against the loss the farming interest on the Rio Grande has sustained, the odds will be considerably against us."[16] This prevailing opinion among the troops was not surprising—in fact, it was to be expected. After all, few soldiers took into account the important over-all aspects of the campaign and the importance it might have held if victory had been achieved. Homesick, and in a relatively desolate region, their viewpoints were products of bitter personal experiences.

On the other hand, what was the attitude of those who tried to view the New Mexican campaign from the standpoint of national perspective? The editor of the Austin *State Gazette* opined that Sibley and his men had been "chasing a shadow" in a barren wilderness. Although performing great deeds of valor, even defeating the enemy in two pitched battles, they had been "compelled to abandon the country from the sheer want of something to eat." What a fruitless sacrifice of gallant Texans! The editor, though apparently completely oblivious to any advantages which would accrue from possessing the Southwest, did display a true grasp of the military situation. He minced no words in condemning President Davis' policy of trying to "defend the Confederacy by posting a few thousand men at every assailable point." To him the only way to bring the war to a successful conclusion was for the Confederacy to concentrate its armies and then deliver knock-out blows against those of the enemy. Erroneously, he assumed that that was to be Davis' new policy. As such, he hoped that "the brave remnant now toiling their way back [from New Mexico], fighting against those worst of enemies hunger and thirst, yet [will] have the opportunity of meeting and conquering . . . [the enemy] somewhere within the bounds of civilization, where the soil is not sand, and water the essence of bitterness, towns hovels in mud, the comforts fleas and rattlesnakes, and the people cayotes [sic]."[17] Once the concentrated armed might of the South had defeated the main enemy armies then, the editor implied, if New Mexico was important enough to become a part of the Confederacy, it could be obtained at the peace conference. In retrospect, it seems unfortunate for the Confederacy that Davis did not heed the advice of this editorial from faraway Texas.

An article in the Houston *Telegraph* took a somewhat different attitude toward the campaign. Its author, too, noted that New Mexico had been conquered and "relinquished," not because the Texans had been defeated, but because the army had failed to find adequate provisions. He praised Sibley by saying that his plan of conquest was "well calculated." Unfortunately, the many unforeseen delays Sibley had experienced in the organization of his army and his getting it into field had given the enemy ample notice to be prepared to meet him. Under the circumstances, Sibley and his men had done all that it was possible for them to do. But, mused the author, "The expedition has proved in no sense a failure because it reached there too late to capture the forts, . . . [for] it has 'sloshed about' where it pleased and captured everything else it wanted." Though admitting that, except as a boundary, New Mexico was not worth having, he patriotically maintained that "all the officers and men have done nobly, and have upheld well the glorious name of Texas, as well as added lustre to its character in the field and in the march."[18] In other words, Sibley's western venture might have been a failure as far as its objective of capturing New Mexico was concerned, but the distinguished bravery displayed by the Texas troops during the campaign was adequate compensation! Unfortunately, to win the war, bravery alone would not suffice.

Most of those composing the militant "manifest destiny" school feared that if the Confederacy failed to occupy New Mexico, or at least hold Arizona to the war's end, the South might be denied those territories at the peace conference. This would be a crippling blow to those who dreamed of a Confederacy stretching from coast to coast. This view was clearly stated in another article in the Houston *Telegraph* berating those who criticized the "extravagance of sending an army a thousand miles to conquer a country not worth having." New Mexico, according to the author, was invaluable, because it would serve as an area for the extension of slavery and as a stepping stone to the Pacific coast. To win independence without New Mexico would leave the South surrounded by a cordon of free territory which, in effect, would "let slavery sting itself to death." It was to prevent this that President Davis approved Sibley's New Mexican plan of campaign. The writer presumed that neither Davis nor Sibley expected a Confederate army to be welcomed with open arms by the native New Mexicans. But that was irrelevant, for New Mexico had to be conquered or "our liberties would be but half won with our independence acknowledged. Nor is this all. The conquest of New Mexico opens the way to the portion of the Pacific coast that affiliates with us in sentiment. It is the entering wedge to the breaking off from the United States of all that coast we desire. It also is the opening scene for our manifest destiny."[19]

Colonel William Steele, who had been ordered to stay behind with his force of four hundred men to hold the Territory of Arizona, found himself in a highly unenviable position. He had formerly been at Doña Ana as Sibley's rear guard, but he now moved his headquarters to Fort Fillmore. From a purely military standpoint, his condition was critical. He had less than thirty days' supply of food, his ammunition was low, and his transportation facilities were inadequate. If something was not done soon, his men would be faced with starvation. Steele had been sick for several days, and though scarcely able to be about, he wrote Sibley asking that some of the supplies which Green and Hardeman had taken with them be left on the road for the use of his men. Obviously, Steele was planning to evacuate, rather than try to hold Arizona. To compensate Green and Hardeman, he suggested that supplies be sent from San Antonio to meet them on the way. Though the country would soon be producing flour and cornmeal, Steele knew that he would not be staying in the Mesilla Valley long enough for the crops to be harvested.

Of great concern to Steele also was the native Mexican population of the valley. After Sibley had left with the bulk of the army, the Mexicans correctly reasoned that Confederate tenure was "frail and uncertain." As such they were unwilling to sell anything for Confederate currency. Since Steele had no specie, he was compelled to authorize his men to seize needed supplies from the natives and force them to take scrip as payment. Food, wagons, and draft animals were the main items requisitioned. These foraging operations, which were even more thorough than Sibley's had been, aroused greater ill feeling. The Mexicans, having little interest in the present war between the states, were concerned solely with their own welfare. When the Texans began seizing their goods, they naturally attempted to defend their property. In many instances they offered armed resistance. In the various skirmishes which took place, one captain and several men of the Seventh Regiment were killed. It is, indeed, not difficult to understand the attitude of the Mexicans. While it had been Sibley's policy to treat the natives with kindness and justice, many of the soldiers from the beginning had acted otherwise. Since the days of the Revolution, Texans in general had held Mexicans in low regard. When the whole brigade was stationed in the valley, the natives had been powerless to resist. Against Steele's small force, however, they were able to express in deeds their hatred of the "Tejanos."

Steele was also troubled by the attitude of his own men. They were completely disgusted with the campaign and were anxious to return to Texas as had the other units of the army. So strong was this feeling that, on several occasions, the soldiers had been on the point of open mutiny. Unless they were speedily marched back to San Antonio, Steele feared his men would take matters into their own hands.

The day after Canby—now promoted to the rank of brigadier general—returned to departmental headquarters in Santa Fé, he learned through newspapers that five regiments of volunteers from the east had been ordered to his support. It is interesting to note that Canby first learned of this military development through the medium of the popular press rather than through official channels. In this respect, he and Sibley shared somewhat similar experiences. Canby immediately wrote the adjutant general that if these five regiments were to be used only for the defense of New Mexico and the reoccupation of Arizona, such a large force would not now be necessary. In his opinion, two regiments, in addition to his own troops, would be more than adequate for these purposes. In further support of this contention, he pointed out that the difficulty of obtaining supplies of all kinds in the territory made it imperative that no greater force should be sent to his aid than was absolutely necessary. If the high command had any plan, Canby cautioned, to use New Mexico as a base of operations to move against any part of the South, it should be discarded. Since all the supplies for such operations would have to be brought from the east—no reliance at all could be placed upon the resources of New Mexico, Arizona, or even Chihuahua—it would be totally impracticable from the logistical standpoint.

At Santa Fé Canby set about perfecting his plan to send a force to drive the remaining Texans from the Mesilla Valley and Arizona. He had hoped to launch an early offensive, but several factors caused delay: supplies from the east had been slow in arriving, local flour contractors had had difficulty in meeting his army's needs, and, finally, the flooding Río Grande had inundated long stretches of the valley roads, making any sort of military movement impossible until the waters subsided. Meanwhile the General discharged incompetent officers and inefficient men of the New Mexican volunteers, hoping as a result to have at least one serviceable native regiment.[20] Near the latter part of June he had been able at last to concentrate sixteen companies of infantry, eight of cavalry, and two batteries at Fort Craig. He designated Colonel Chivington, now the commander of the Southern Military District, to lead this army of two thousand men southward to retake Arizona for the Union.

Canby had planned his Arizona offensive without any knowledge of developments in the Department of the Pacific. In fact, the first news that he received of any army on its way to his relief from that quarter came indirectly from Colonel Chivington early in June. A Mexican who had come into Fort Craig reported that troops from California were moving through western Arizona. About a week later the native's story was confirmed by five men who arrived from Pinos Altos. Canby was still not convinced, and on June 16, he wrote Chivington that such "information is certainly very circumstantial, and seems probable, but I cannot think that any large force would have been sent from California without being advised of it."[21] The General reasoned that the reported troops were undoubtedly a detachment sent out from Fort Yuma to Tucson solely for reconnaissance purposes.

On June 20, however, Canby received a telegraphic dispatch confirming the coming of the California Column. In light of this new development, Canby instructed Chivington to send part of his command—one thousand men if practicable—southward to Santa Barbara, where he was to open communication with Carleton and to hold himself in readiness to support the Californians if they were advancing eastward from Tucson. Chivington was advised not to move into the Mesilla Valley—unless it was absolutely necessary for the bolstering of Carleton's column—until Canby could send adequate supplies there for the subsistence of his men.

Meanwhile Carleton's California Column had temporarily halted at Tucson in order to pacify the town, make needed repairs on the wagons and other equipment, secure supplies from Sonora, Mexico, and allow the men to rest up before setting out in force for the Río Grande. On the evening of June 15 Carleton dispatched a messenger to make contact with Canby's forces. At dusk five days later, the rider reached Picacho, several miles above Mesilla, completely exhausted and in a half-delirious state after a narrow escape from the Apaches. It was an irony of fate that after such a harrowing adventure he was captured by a party of Texans. For a third time Carleton had failed in his efforts to contact Canby. Worse still, all the messenger's dispatches fell into the hands of the enemy. A perusal of these documents, which enumerated the strength of the California Column and its intended movement, convinced Colonel Steele that his stay in the Mesilla Valley would be very short.

On June 21 Lieutenant Colonel Edward E. Eyre set out from Tucson for the Río Grande in command of two cavalry companies consisting of 143 men. Eight days later at Cow Springs, this advance guard of the Column met a party of scouts sent out by Chivington with dispatches for Carleton. This was the first formal contact between the two Union armies. After a day's rest at the springs, Eyre continued his march, reaching the river near Santa Barbara on July 4. Immediately after making camp, the Union flag was raised amid the loud cheers of his assembled command. It was Independence Day, and this was the first time that the "stars and stripes" had floated over the area below Fort Craig since the occupation of the territory by the Confederates. The following day Eyre moved three miles down the river to Fort Thorn.

The Río Grande was at flood stage and almost the entire bottom between Fort Craig and Mesilla was under water. It was impossible to approach Mesilla from the west bank, for the river had washed a new channel on that side of town. Shortly after reaching the Río Grande, Eyre sent a detachment eighteen miles southward to the San Diego ford to see if the river could be crossed. The scouts reported that, though at present it would be impossible, if the flood level continued to fall at its present rate, perhaps it could be forded in about a week. On the basis of this information, Eyre decided to remain at Fort Thorn for the time being to give his men and animals a needed rest. In addition, he preferred to await the reinforcements from Fort Craig which he had earlier asked for while at Cow Springs.

On July 8 Captain George W. Howland, in command of a hundred cavalrymen, arrived from Fort Craig and reported to Eyre for duty. The Colonel noted that this group's horses were in such a shockingly jaded condition that in the event he should make a mounted charge against the enemy, he would have to do it with his Californians alone.

Eyre was eager to move against Steele's Texans just as soon as the river fell sufficiently. But two days after Howland's arrival, a dispatch from Colonel Chivington upset, at least as far as the near future was concerned, any anticipations he might have had for achieving laurels on the battlefield. The commander of the Southern Military District informed him that Canby did not favor an advance from Fort Thorn until the arrival of a much larger body of troops. Meantime, Eyre was instructed to learn all he could concerning the enemy's strength, position, and plans.

Since Canby considered the California Column adequate to pacify and reoccupy all of Arizona, he discarded his former offensive plan. After taking the precaution of leaving a large force at Fort Craig to support Carleton if necessary, he shifted a thousand men to Fort Union to guard the supply line from the east.

Colonel Steele feared that with the coming of the seasonal rains Canby would soon be able to march across the Jornada del Muerto to invade the Mesilla Valley. He had learned from spies that the Federals had been reinforced by 500 more volunteers from Colorado, as well as by 250 soldiers and six rifled cannon which had accompanied the paymaster from Kansas. Not counting these additions, and even after leaving sufficient garrisons behind, Steele was certain that Canby would be capable of placing a three-thousand-man army in the field against him. From the captured dispatches, the Confederate commander also knew that the California Column consisted of fourteen hundred[22] men and would shortly set out from Tucson. With two armies poised to close in upon him, Steele lost no time in making preparations to evacuate the Territory of Arizona.

Since the actions of the Texans—particularly the foraging operations—had caused such great feelings of bitterness on the part of the Mexican population, Steele was afraid they might take their wrath out on the Americans who were remaining behind. All those who had sided with the Confederacy had either left with Sibley or were preparing to leave with Steele. The Americans who were staying, some of whom had families, had taken no part in the struggle between the Confederacy and the Union. But to insure their safety, the Texas commander entered into a covenant with the principal Mexicans of Mesilla, who bound themselves to protect them. The consideration was the release of a certain Domingo Cebeno who was Steele's prisoner "under circumstances which would ordinarily cost him his life." Before leaving the area, the Colonel addressed a letter to the Federal commanding officer informing him of the arrangement. "For the sake of humanity," Steele hoped that the Union officer would "inquire into the manner" in which the agreement had been kept.[23]

Confederate government in the Territory of Arizona naturally received a death blow with Steele's decision to leave. Sibley's abortive campaign in the north had already been reflected in the court record: "in consideration of the disturbed condition of the County," the regular session of the court which had been scheduled for May, 1862, was adjourned until the following June. On June 2, 1862, Charles A. Hoppin wrote the final sentence in the records of the Confederate judiciary of Arizona:

The Honl. J. Peter Deus having filed his notice of Resignation of the Judge-ship of the Court, this court is adjourned to the next Regular July term 1862 for the Probate Business and to September term 1862 for the Trial of Civil Cases.[24]

Governor Baylor was not present to see the collapse of his creation, for he had earlier journeyed to Richmond on official business.[25] On the same day that How-land's squadron united with Eyre's command, July 8, 1862, Colonel Steele gath-ered together his forces and marched from Fort Fillmore to Fort Bliss. With his evacuation the Confederate Territory of Arizona ceased to exist.

At Fort Bliss Colonel Steele made hasty arrangements to leave for San Antonio. All public property at the post which was too bulky to haul or not worth transport-ing, was ordered to be sold for specie or for food. Though there was a large amount of material which could not be disposed of—items such as horse and mule shoes, cannon ammunition, tents, etc.—the sale resulted in $830 in specie. This was turned over to Dr. M. A. Southworth for the use of the military hospital in El Paso. Credit to a larger amount was also left with parties in Mexico.[26]

With very limited means of transportation, with an insufficient supply of breadstuff and beef, and with his troops in many instances almost naked, Steele was ready to leave for San Antonio by July 12. Accompanying the force were the remaining Americans in and around El Paso who had not already left with Sibley. When Steele abandoned Fort Bliss, the northwestern frontier of the state of Texas and its line of military posts was left exposed to the oncoming Federal forces. Confederate military operations in extreme West Texas, Arizona, and New Mexico had come to an end.[27]

If Trevanion T. Teel's postwar statement is correct, Sibley looked upon the taking of New Mexico as merely a means to an end, the real goal being the con-quest of California. If this was the case—and many Unionists staunchly believed that it was—then the New Mexican campaign takes on added significance. In supposition that Sibley had succeeded in New Mexico, what would have been his chances of success in capturing California?

To have conquered New Mexico would have meant the fall of Fort Union and Canby's subsequent capitulation at Fort Craig. Undoubtedly before Canby and his subordinate at Fort Union surrendered their posts, they would have de-stroyed the bulk of their war matériel to have kept it from falling into the hands of the Confederates. Sibley's condition, then, would have been just as critical as before. Consequently, in order to have properly supplied his haggard army—especially in regard to ordnance—he would have had to receive supplies from Texas, or else be forced to evacuate New Mexico. It is to be remembered that Texas had been unable to supply Sibley adequately in the first place!

But supposing that Sibley had captured a large amount of supplies from both Fort Union and Fort Craig, how long would he have been able to hold his conquest? The evidence indicates that his tenure would have been short at best, for two Union armies were preparing to converge on him. To be sure, Sibley was to receive reinforcements in the form of two regiments, and, perhaps, additional men could have been recruited from Utah and Colorado. But would this have been enough? Part of the volunteer force raised in California was on the way to attack from the west. Composed of "green" troops, not great in number, the California Column might have suffered defeat at Sibley's hands. The road to California would then have been open, but it was a long road through a vast desert. By the time Sibley would have arrived in the vicinity of Fort Yuma, the bulk of the Union forces of California would have concentrated to challenge his further advance. Could Sibley have counted upon a revolt of Confederate sympathizers in southern California? This seems unlikely, for that minority element had already been quieted and thoroughly overawed by the might of Union troops. But even if Sibley had conquered the California Column, his attention would not have been turned toward California, but toward the northern part of New Mexico. While the Confederates were preparing to advance upon Fort Union, a force of five thousand men was being outfitted at Fort Riley, Kansas, for service in New Mexico. There can be little doubt that Sibley would have been overwhelmed by this Federal army. And even if he had been successful, the Union would have renewed its efforts with even greater vigor—not because the Federals considered New Mexico so valuable, but because they feared Confederate designs on California and northern Mexico. The South, and Texas in particular, were extremely limited as to the number of men and supplies they could send to Sibley. In comparison, the Union was well manned and generously supplied.

If the capture of New Mexico by the Confederates would have rendered the conquest of California probable, then the New Mexican campaign of 1862 should be viewed as one of the most important military operations of the war. But for the reasons already advanced, Confederate success in New Mexico would have been of such an ephemeral nature that California would not have been seriously endangered. A much more meaningful evaluation of this situation indicates that had Sibley been successful in conquering New Mexico, a much greater part of the war would have been fought on far-western soil.

The New Mexican campaign was a gallant, but essentially impractical, effort to accomplish a great objective with woefully inadequate resources. Though the evidence is overwhelming that Sibley's plan for the West had no chance of success, nevertheless, like the whole Confederate adventure, it might have succeeded!

Appendix

The muster rolls of the various units which comprised the Army of New Mexico are now housed in the National Archives. Because of time and wear many are partially mutilated and faded. All the names, of course, were written in longhand, and, though the script on many is quite legible, several are exceedingly poor. Even when the writing is relatively clear, it is often difficult to determine whether a "u" is an "n," and "a" an "o," an "m" a "w," and so on. In at least two instances the way in which the company clerk recorded a name was at variance with the way the soldier spelled it. The first name of Lieutenant Ellsberry R. Lane is written "Elsbury" on the company roll (Company B, Fourth Regiment), even though, as mustering officer of the Fourth Regiment, his signature appears on seven rolls as "Ellsberry R. Lane." Private Ebenezer Hanna of Company C, Fifth Regiment, is recorded as "A. Hannor." His nickname was "Abe," which accounts for the "A.," but the "Hannor" probably resulted from the way he pronounced his name to the recording clerk. In these two cases, and in a few others, the names have been corrected. Undoubtedly many soldiers were illiterate and the clerks wrote their names the way they thought they should be spelled. Wherever first names have been abbreviated—and if it is apparent what the abbreviation stood for—the names have been written out in full, e.g., "James" for "Jas.," "John" for "Jno.," and "Joseph" for "Jos." In all cases of uncertainty in regard to spelling, rank, or age, a question mark follows immediately after the item in doubt. Where no age is given, or if the age is illegible, a dash is employed. If only one numeral is illegible, a dash is placed either before or after the legible numeral, whichever is applicable. Because of the factors enumerated, it is impossible to determine accuracy of spelling for some names in this compilation.

The commissioned and noncommissioned officers are listed by rank in their respective groups. Beneath them are the buglers, musicians, blacksmiths, and farriers (in those companies which had them). The privates are arranged in alphabetical order, although on the original rolls they were alphabetized only in a general way. Following the name of each soldier is his rank and age. In the case of privates the age follows immediately after the name.

Wherever possible the disposition of a casualty is indicated in parentheses following a soldier's age. The names of the killed and wounded were derived from official reports, casualty lists published in newspapers, privately-kept journals and diaries, and the casualty lists found in the appendix of Noel, *A Campaign from Santa Fe to the Mississippi*. Very few names of those who died of disease or who were captured are available. Noel has a list of those who died of disease in the brigade down through 1864, but he does not state specifically which deaths occurred during the course of the New Mexican campaign.

After the rolls were completed, recruits continued to join the ranks of the various companies. Consequently, when the newspapers published casualty lists names not found on the rolls often appeared. In such cases these have been listed separately under the heading, "Casualties Not on the Muster Roll." In instances where Noel has a soldier listed as either killed or wounded, but no other reference is found, it is specifically noted that this is "according to Noel."

At best these casualty notations are fragmentary. For example, in Company A, Fifth Regiment, eight individuals are listed as killed (or mortally wounded) and twenty-two as wounded. The San Antonio *Herald* of August 9, 1862, however, observed that when this unit returned to San Antonio after the campaign, only about twenty-five men were eligible for duty. The rest had either been killed in battle, had died from wounds or disease, had been left behind in hospitals, or had been paroled (thirty-four had been taken prisoner at the skirmish of Apache Canyon).

The original rolls include such additional information—not given here—as the date and place of enrollment of each soldier, the name of the enrolling officer, the period of enrollment (all were for "the war"), the number of miles to the place of rendezvous, and the appraised value of each soldier's horse, horse equipment, and arms.

THE ARMY OF NEW MEXICO

STAFF
(As of December, 1861)

Brigadier General Henry Hopkins Sibley, Commanding Officer, 45

Major Alexander M. Jackson, Assistant Adjutant General, —

Major Richard T. Brownrigg, Chief of Commissary, 29

Major Willis L. Robards, Chief of Ordnance (slightly wounded at Valverde), —

Captain William H. Harrison, Paymaster and Chief Quartermaster, —

Captain Joseph E. Dwyer, Inspector General, —

Lieutenant Thomas P. Ochiltree, Aide-de-Camp, 21

Dr. E. N. Covey, Chief Surgeon and Medical Director, —

FIRST TEXAS CAVALRY BRIGADE
(The Sibley Brigade)

FOURTH REGIMENT
Texas Mounted Volunteers (Cavalry)

FIELD AND STAFF
(As of September, 1861)

James Reily, Colonel, —

William R. Scurry, Lieutenant Colonel, 40 (promoted to colonel March 28, 1862)

Henry W. Raguet, Major, — (wounded at Valverde; killed at Glorieta)

Ellsberry R. Lane, Adjutant, 22 (wounded at Glorieta)

Henry E. Loebnitz, Assistant Quartermaster and Assistant Commissary, 29

John B. McMahon, Sergeant Major, 45

Arthur Middleton, Quartermaster Sergeant, 28

M. A. Southworth, Surgeon, —

L. M. Taylor, First Assistant Surgeon, —

J. F. Matchett, Second Assistant Surgeon, — (resigned while in New Mexico)

L. H. Jones, Chaplain, — (wounded at Johnson's Ranch)

Howitzer Battery (four guns):

John Reily, Lieutenant Commanding, —

Charles M. Raguet, Second Lieutenant, 27

COMPANY A
(As of August 28, 1861)
Mustered in Caldwell and Guadalupe Counties

William P. Hardeman, Captain, 44 (slightly wounded at Valverde; promoted to lieutenant colonel March 28, 1862)

Lenford Stephenson, First Lieutenant, 30 (later promoted to captain)

Joseph C. Roberts, Second Lieutenant, 26 (wounded at Valverde)

Norval D. Cartwright, Second Lieutenant, 26 (wounded at Valverde)

Robert P. Hunter, First Sergeant, 26 (wounded at Valverde)

John H. Barnes, Second Sergeant, 30 (later promoted to lieutenant)

Benjamin E. Frasier, Third Sergeant, 20

Nathaniel Hysaw, Fourth Sergeant, 25

John H. McNutt, First Corporal, 33

Joseph Francis, Second Corporal, 35 (wounded at Valverde)

Thomas H. Huff, Third Corporal, 25

James A. McAlester, Fourth Corporal, 39

Charles P. Wright, First Bugler, 22

Byron T. Hamilton, Second Bugler, 22

Henry C. Goldenberger, Farrier, 22

Peter M. Curtis, Blacksmith, 33

PRIVATES:
1. Abernathy, Jesse, 29
2. Allen, Burrwell C., 17 (died near Dead Man's Hole on return)

3. Beaty, John M., 19
4. Brown, Willis, 18
5. Clyett, Hugh L., 24
6. Duncan, John F., 22
7. Duncan, Robert J., 32
8. (Illegible), 18
9. Eustace, Thomas A., 19
10. Fentress, Thomas H., 20
11. Fergerson, Austin O., 22
12. Fergerson, William A., 23
    (wounded at Valverde)
13. Fleming, Robert F., 25
14. Forth, Casper E., 25
15. Foster, John C., 20
16. Franks, Mathew, 34
17. Gillaspy, Asbury F., 28
18. Gollahar, Granderson D., 18
19. Grady, James C., 19
20. Green, Thomas E., 29
21. Greenwood, Thomas C., 18
22. Hall, William P. R., 20
23. Hampton, John P., 24
24. Hines, Joseph G., 29
25. Hunter, Samuel, 38
26. Hysaw, Benjamin L., 23
27. Jeffrey, Jesse, 19
28. Jones, Henry, 33
29. Kese, John A., 18
30. Kimble, Charles C., 26
31. Kirk, James, 22
32. Lacy, Thomas, 26
33. Lockwood, Harvey N., 30
34. Loftis, Andrew, 20
35. Loftis, Archibald T., 24
36. Maney, Henry, 31 (wounded at
    Valverde)
37. Maney, Samuel B., 26 (was a
    physician; promoted to replace
    Matchett; in charge of hospital at
    Santa Fé and taken prisoner there)
38. McCoy, Green, 21
39. McCracken, Green H., 20
40. McDonel, John, 20
41. McLane, John, 23
42. Nicholson, Granville M., 20
43. Nixon, James K., 18
44. Nixon, Jesse H., 18

45. Parchman, James M., 27
46. Patten, William C., 26
47. Patterson, William A., 23
48. Pierce, John B., 18
49. Pierman, Sterling, 19
50. Praiter, James B., 23
51. Raymer, George F., 25
52. Rogers, Martin, 22
53. Smith, Robert J., 19
54. Smith, William C., 18
55. Sowell, Asa J. L., 18
56. Sowell, James A., 20
57. Stewart, McNeal, 18
58. Stricklin, George W., 18
59. Teale, Ferdinand, 30
60. Tedford, James, 21
61. Tiney, Jacob, 20
62. Turner, George W., 18
63. Watts, Thomas, 24
64. Webb, George W., 18
65. Wells, Leroy W., 19
66. White, George W., 23 (wounded at
    Valverde)
67. Whitley, Hiram, 24
68. Wiley, Daniel L., 20 (wounded at
    Valverde)
69. Wiley, William S., 23
70. Wood, Alexander N., 18
71. Woodall, William H., 24
72. Young, Benjamin F., 31

Casualties Not on Muster Roll
1. Cook, J. W. (wounded at Valverde)
2. Hison, B. F. A. (wounded at
   Valverde)
3. Lott, J. (wounded at Valverde)
4. McRight, R. (wounded at Valverde)

COMPANY B—*"Davis Rifles"*
(As of August 27, 1861)
Mustered in De Witt County

Andrew J. Scarborough, Captain, 34
James B. Holland, First Lieutenant, 34
Jonathan Nix, Second Lieutenant, 37
    (slightly wounded at Valverde)
Ellsberry R. Lane, Second Lieutenant,
    22 (transferred to regimental staff)

Marmeduke B. Grigg, First Sergeant, 25
William D. Atkinson, Second Sergeant, 27
David C. O'Steen, Third Sergeant, 25
James M. Hall, Fourth Sergeant, 20
Rees Ridout, First Corporal, 26
Alexander R. Cudd, Second Corporal, 28
Burwell Blanton, Third Corporal, 20
John H. Atkinson, Fourth Corporal, 20
Richard B. C. Miller, First Bugler, 28
Job Clifton, Second Bugler, 23
Benjamin F. McDonald, Farrier, 29
James C. Stroud, Blacksmith, 28 (wounded at Valverde and at Glorieta)

PRIVATES:

1. Allen, Morris H., 30
2. Barow, Isum, 18
3. Barow, William L., 30
4. Beazley, John C., 25
5. Bishop, Oliver, 43
6. Booth, Gabriel H., 21
7. Brooks, Arthur T., 33 (mortally wounded at Valverde)
8. Buchanan, John M., 24
9. Bunton, Joseph L., 18 (wounded at Valverde)
10. Burge, William W., 31
11. Byars, James M., 33 (wounded at Glorieta)
12. Byers, William H., 20
13. Clark, John, 20
14. Copenhaber, Mathew, 26
15. Covey, John, 42
16. Crawford, Pleasant, 24 (wounded at Glorieta)
17. Dauckerty, Daniel, 26
18. Doyle, Thomas B., 40
19. Everett, Thomas I., 19
20. Foley, Everett C., 28 (killed at Glorieta)
21. Freeman, John R., 20
22. Gibbs, Stephen J., 27
23. Gilmer, Peachy R., 30
24. Goodson, Andrew J., 18
25. Hanks, Andrew J., 18
26. Hargrove, Bunyon, 18
27. Harris, Benjamin, 21
28. Harris, Thompson, 33 (wounded at Valverde; killed at Glorieta, according to Noel)
29. Hart, John E., 23 (promoted to sergeant of howitzer battery)
30. Henderson, Ivel H., 23
31. Hermes, Edward, 39
32. Hester, James H., 25
33. Holland, John M., 18
34. Holland, Robert A., 22
35. Holmes, John, 36
36. Houston, James A., 18
37. Houston, Robert, 19
38. Hudson, Marion L., 20
39. Joslin, Bazilee L., 23
40. Joslin, Silus B., 26
41. Keylich, Max G., 20
42. Maulding, Pres, 40
43. McCord, James, 20 (killed at Glorieta)
44. McDonald, Barney O., 35
45. McDonald, Felix W., 23
46. McDonald, James P., 26
47. McMahon, Jacob S., 18
48. McMahon, John B., 45 (transferred to regimental staff)
49. Miller, William H., 18
50. Moore, Lewis W., 22
51. Murray, Francis W., 22
52. Porter, John W., 24
53. Potts, Eugene F., 18
54. Quirle, Thomas J., 18
55. Rhode, Hugs, 20
56. Sawey, Roland, 30
57. Shaws, John, 24
58. Stell, Leonard H., 25
59. Tally, Fredrick, 18
60. Talley, Jacob R., 19 (mortally wounded at Valverde, according to Noel)
61. Terry, Jonathan A., 23
62. Thames, Christian, 21
63. Vanderheider, Henry, 21
64. Wiley, Alexander H., 28
65. Wiley, James, 18
66. Williams, Jeremiah, 18 (wounded at Valverde)

67. Williams, William C., 23

Casualties Not on Muster Roll
1. Hendricks, M. (wounded at Valverde)
2. Nixon, Thomas (killed at Valverde)
3. Standifer, E. R. (killed at Glorieta)

COMPANY C—"Victoria Volunteers"
(As of September 11, 1861)
Mustered in Victoria County

George James Hampton, Captain, 34 (wounded at Valverde; promoted to major March 28, 1862)
Charls Caroll Linn, First Lieutenant, 24
Henry Edmund Loebnitz, Second Lieutenant, 29 (transferred to regimental staff)
Ferdinand A. Fenner, Second Lieutenant, 24
Ludwig van (or von) Roeder, First Sergeant, 24
James Francis Coffee, Second Sergeant, 32
W. F. Davis, Third Sergeant, 22
Charls Alexander Woodapple (?), Fourth Sergeant, 34
Albert G. Field, First Corporal, 24 (promoted to sergeant; wounded at Valverde)
L. J. Bartlett, Second Corporal, 22 (wounded at Glorieta)
Albert Glock, Third Corporal, 23
J. J. Hall, Fourth Corporal, 21

PRIVATES:
1. Armstrong, James H., 21
2. Arnica, W., 21
3. Baker, George B., 23
4. Brown, Sam, 28 (wounded at Glorieta)
5. Calender, C. B., 22
6. Carey, Martin V., 21
7. Clark, Thomas M., 22
8. Dietzel, Edwin, 21
9. Egg, Gideon, 22
10. Elliot, Henry, 20
11. Ferguson, A. P., 27
12. Field, S. S., 18
13. Field, Thomas M., 18
14. Freitag, John, 25
15. Garnett, H., 19
16. Goldman, A., 24
17. Green, S., 31
18. Hahn, Charles, 20
19. Hamilton, C. H., 31
20. Hanna, Ebenezer, 18 (killed at Glorieta)
21. Harssolt, George, 24
22. Hensoldt, Armin, 22
23. Henson, J. F., 20 (killed at Glorieta)
24. Hiller, Michel, 23
25. Hughes, James, 29
26. Hughes, L. F. V., 23
27. Hyatt, Sam R., 22
28. James, W. B., 21
29. Jenke, Julius, 24
30. Jones, B. A., 20
31. Keenan, Owen, 35
32. Kleberg, Otto, 19 (wounded at Valverde)
33. Kneiber, F. D., 27
34. Krudler, C. F., 44
35. Kuykendall, John, 25
36. Laly, Patrick, 32
37. Lang, Charles, 27 (?)
38. Licktenstein, Morris, 23
39. Lozano, Elias, 19
40. Lytle, N. B., 18
41. May, L., 23
42. McNeill, J. A., 18
43. Meyer, P., 20
44. Mobley, William H., 30 (wounded at Valverde)
45. Montgomery, Alexander, 18 (killed at Glorieta)
46. Moody, F. M., 22
47. Moody, G. H., 19
48. Moonch (?), Andrew, 26
49. Onderdonk, W. H., 21 (wounded at Valverde)
50. Owens, John W., 28
51. Percel, R. C., 22
52. Peticolas, A. B., 22
53. Posey, T. J., 18

54. Powell, E., 45
55. Ragland, H., 19
56. Reeves, Johnson, 24
57. Roesch, Charles, 26
58. Rolley, Thomas, 24
59. Rootts, T. R., 26
60. Rose, V. P., 18
61. Roth, F., 31
62. Sager, P., 18
63. Schmidt, John, 26
64. Schmidt, S., 21 (wounded at Valverde)
65. Schultz, Theodor, 19
66. Seidel, Herrman, 19
67. Ship, Morris, 21
68. Tichoepe, Luis, 25
69. Tippett, Robert D., 18
70. Trautwein, William, 23
71. Trell, Henry, 30
72. Unger, Henry, 30
73. Wahlstab, William, 23
74. Warburton, J. A., 24
75. Wheeler, J. O., 18
76. White, Ben N., 18 (wounded at Glorieta)
77. Whitley, Wiley James, 22
78. Williams, J. T., 23
79. Woolfe, A. S., 18

Casualties Not on Muster Roll
1. Berkowitz, L. (wounded at Valverde)
2. Crook, J. (wounded at Valverde)

COMPANY D
(As of September 16, 1861)
Mustered in Milam County

Charles M. Lesueur, Captain, 36
Abner B. Parrott, First Lieutenant, 47
Henry G. Carter, Second Lieutenant, 24
Peter M. Kolb, Second Lieutenant, 34 (wounded at Valverde)
Moritz Maedgen, First Sergeant, 31
John Anders, Second Sergeant, 38
Daniel Huffman, Third Sergeant, 54
James Gilleland, Fourth Sergeant, 22
Joseph E. Pike, First Corporal, 28
Charles W. Hamilton, Second Corporal, 26

Elias R. Boles, Third Corporal, 19
Samuel Hill, Fourth Corporal, 19 (wounded at Glorieta)
Thomas P. Norman, Musician, 22
Braxton Robinson, Musician, 18
Josiah Blackman, Farrier, 46
William L. Lutner, Blacksmith, 28

PRIVATES:
1. Aplin, John, 25
2. Bates, Isaac V., 26
3. Brown, Nicholas G., 19
4. (Illegible)
5. Carr, Robert, 20
6. Carter, Elbert, 24 (wounded at Glorieta)
7. Carter, Thomas, 20
8. Christian, Andrew C., 21
9. Clinchey, Joseph P., 44 (mortally wounded at Glorieta)
10. Coker, William, 25
11. Cook, James F., 30
12. Cravy, Marion J., 25
13. Dotson, Noah, 34
14. Farmer, William M., 28 (wounded at Glorieta)
15. Flores, Jesús, 25 (wounded at Glorieta)
16. Gilleland, Daniel, 25 (killed at Valverde)
17. Gilmore, William H., 21
18. Graves, Thomas H., 19
19. Hillyard, Landon B., 21
20. Huffman, Alex, 21 (wounded at Valverde)
21. Huffman, Wiseman D., 19 (wounded at Valverde)
22. Hughs, John D., 31
23. Hughs, William, 37
24. Jones, Andrew J., 29
25. Jones, David M., 23
26. Jones, Richard A., 19
27. Kenly, James, 32
28. Kirtland, Dorrance, 24
29. Kolb, Hugh W., 20
30. Lehman, John M., 33
31. Locklin, James, 18
32. Loveless, Peyton, 29

33. Maedgen, Gustavus A., 26
34. McDaniel, Robert, 18
35. McDougle, James, 18
36. Mitchell, William H., 33
37. Norman, John N., 21
38. Partin, Hugh L., 21
39. Philips, Alexander, 20
40. Philips, Wilson, 23
41. Rister, William, 19
42. Robinson, David N., 18
43. Robinson, Dewitt C., 33
44. Saddle, John H., 26
45. Scott, William, 21
46. Slicker, Wesly, 24
47. Stephenson, Wollum, 18
48. Stevens, James R., 30 (killed at Glorieta)
49. Stokes, John G., 25 (wounded at Glorieta)
50. Stokes, Robert, 23
51. Stone, Burton R., 22 (killed at Glorieta)
52. Strader, John M., 21
53. Stramler, Stanford A., 21
54. Taylor, Benjamin F., 23
55. Thomas, John R., 18
56. Vining, Edmund C., 30
57. Whittington, Bryant, 22
58. Whittington, George, 19
59. Wilson, Charles B., 22
60. Wood, Leander, 18

Casualties Not on Muster Roll
1. Slaughter, E. S. (mortally wounded at Valverde, according to Noel)
2. Slaughter, E. R. (killed at Glorieta)
3. Straughn, W. M. (killed at Glorieta)

COMPANY E
(As of September 24, 1861)
Mustered in Milam County

Charles Buckholts, Captain, 37 (killed at Glorieta)
James M. Noble, First Lieutenant, 36
Joseph H. Long, Second Lieutenant, 26
F. A. Hill, Second Lieutenant, 36
Rufus J. Trotter, First Sergeant, 22

M. F. Carlock, Second Sergeant, 30
J. H. Alley, Third Sergeant, 30
Eli Hardcastle, Fourth Sergeant, 39
H. Anderson, First Corporal, 43
J. Moreau, Second Corporal, 31
W. J. S. Wilson, Third Corporal, 21
B. J. Mark, Fourth Corporal, 38

PRIVATES:
1. Able, Joseph G. H., 24 (killed at Glorieta)
2. Allen, J. H., 28
3. Bailey, James, 20
4. Bailey, Winfred, 20
5. Bigham, A. J., 19
6. Blunt, A. L., 24
7. (Illegible), 25
8. Carr, Crocket, 19
9. Carr, Thomas M., 20
10. Cave, Wayne, 22
11. Chaudoin, N. G., 28
12. Chaudoin, P. W., 18
13. Cloud, F. M., 20
14. Cotton, J. S. L., 20 (killed at Glorieta)
15. Currie (?), N. C., 25
16. Donaldson, John F., 23
17. Donaldson, Thomas J., 22
18. Doss, J. M., 28
19. Eckman, Daniel, 25
20. Favors, Hartwell, 21
21. Favors, John W., 18
22. Fisher, T. B., 18
23. Fowler, T. B., 18
24. French, C. E., 27
25. Goodnight, E., 30
26. Granthan, Y. W., 22 (wounded at Valverde)
27. Henderson, David, 19
28. James, David, 33
29. Jones, J. H., 36
30. Logan, Mat., 18
31. Long, A. J., 22 (mortally wounded at Valverde)
32. Long, J. E., 21
33. Luce, Z. (?), 23
34. Mercer, J. L., 26
35. Monroe, Daniel, 18

36. Moore, David P., 23
37. Moore, M. C., 18
38. Moreau, N., 26
39. Narin (?), William, 56
40. Newsom, William, 18
41. Olive, T. J., 19
42. Oliver, M. D., 22
43. Perkins, G. (or Z.), 24
44. Posey, Mathew, 19
45. Price, W. M., 19
46. Ritchie, J. S., 22
47. Ritchie, S. T., 19
48. Rogers, J. M., 24
49. Sage, C. C., 20
50. Saxton, Asa, 19
51. Schoonover, Eli, 41
52. Sides, J. H. D., 29
53. Sides, P. L., 23
54. Smith, Henry, 22
55. Springer, W. J., 19
56. Trotter, Harvey, 45
57. Vancleve, E. S., 23
58. Wade, J. S., 19
59. Weems (?), J. A., 18
60. West, B. C., 34
61. Williams, John, 23
62. Williams, R. T., 31
63. Woodrich, Peter F., 20
64. Wooster, George E., 25
65. (Illegible)

Casualties Not on Muster Roll
1. Alder, R. A. (killed at Glorieta)
2. Young, J. J. (wounded at Glorieta)

COMPANY F
(As of September 25, 1861)
Mustered in Polk County

James Murray Crosson, Captain, 37
David R. McCormick, First Lieutenant, 41 (killed at Valverde)
Byron L. Taylor, Second Lieutenant, 25
William T. Carrington, Second Lieutenant, 28
Marcellus Winston, First Sergeant, 22
John M. Larkin, Second Sergeant, 31
James A. Manning, Third Sergeant, 36
Shockley H. Adams, Fourth Sergeant, 30

Martin A. Jones, First Corporal, 34
Robert N. Green, Second Corporal, 32
James Patrick, Third Corporal, 18
John T. Poe, Fourth Corporal, 25 (wounded at Glorieta)

PRIVATES:
1. Adams, Edwin B., 18 (promoted to ordnance sergeant; wounded at Glorieta)
2. Allen, Oscar E., 20
3. Allen, William O., 22
4. Andress, William H., 20
5. Barron, James A., 27
6. Bentley, Reuben P., 23 (killed at Glorieta)
7. Bonner, Joseph F., 27
8. Carrington, Edward I., 18
9. Clark, John, 20
10. Cook, John B., 22 (wounded at Valverde)
11. Cook, Peter J., 23
12. Copeland, John S., 20
13. David, Joshua A., 28
14. Dial, Napoleon, 19 (wounded at Valverde)
15. Efner, Jerome B., 27
16. Faircloth (?), William H., 21
17. Gill, James A., 35 (wounded at Valverde)
18. Goodwin, John, 21
19. Graham, William T., 26
20. Harbison, John, 22 (wounded at Glorieta)
21. Harbison, Thomas, 37
22. Haynes, Evans P., 20
23. Hilliard, James A., 26
24. Hindman, Smith, 35
25. Holston, William H., 25
26. Hooker, Leander, 26
27. Hooker, Leroy, 23
28. Hughes, Daniel L., 26
29. Hughes, John, 23
30. Jarvey, Gustavus A., 21
31. Jones, Harman, 20
32. Jossey, Travis, 28
33. Knight, Kindred K., 17
34. Lewis, William P., 20

35. Manry, William H. H., 20
36. Marler, Jackson J., 21
37. Martin, John R., 20 (killed at Glorieta)
38. Marsh, Dillard, 20
39. Marshall, King, 20
40. Matthews, Augustus L., 28 (wounded at Glorieta)
41. Matthews, William F., 26 (wounded at Valverde and at Glorieta)
42. McCaghren, Dolphus D., 18
43. McCormick, Samuel, 24
44. McCormick, Willie, 21 (killed at Glorieta)
45. McDaniel, Henry, 34
46. McGee, William J., 20
47. Middleton, Arthur, 28 (transferred to regimental staff)
48. Parsons, William T., 19 (killed at Glorieta)
49. Peters, Joseph F., 36
50. Pierrot, Eugene, 37
51. Ratliff, Robert, 20
52. Scott, Lucius M., 27
53. Smith, Matthew T., 30
54. Sykes, William L., 19
55. Tanner, George W., 25
56. Thomason, Isaac I., 27
57. Thomason, John I., 20
58. Tyler, Brinkly H., 24
59. Tyler, Moses B., 19
60. Voss, Fields M., 27
61. Williams, H., 22
62. Williams, John W., 20
63. Wright, Henry C., 21

Casualty Not on Muster Roll
1. Dunham, S. H. (mortally wounded at Valverde, according to Noel)

COMPANY G**

The first page of this muster roll is completely illegible.
(As of September 24, 1861)
Mustered in Austin County

Colonel Reily stated that Captain Heuvel was a native of Belgium. If this is correct, the "v. d." probably stood for "van der." Marinus v. d. Heuvel,**** Captain, — (killed at Valverde)

Paul Vogelsary, First Lieutenant, —

Julius Giesecke, Second Lieutenant, — (promoted to captain after Valverde)

Albert Schlick, Second Lieutenant, —

PRIVATES:
25. Foch, Christian, 29
26. Hilgert, Dr. Henry, 32
27. Lampe, Albert, 27
28. May, Charles, 26
29. Melcherr, Ernst, 20 (wounded at Valverde)
30. Meusing (?), Gustav, 25
31. Meyer, Ernst, 33
32. Muller, Joseph, 30
33. Neumann, J., 21
34. Reuter (?), John, 23
35. Rickers (?), A., 24
36. Schaler (?), T. (?), 26
37. Schandorn, Joseph, 28
38. Scharenberg, Henry, 23
39. Schmidt, Christoph, 26
40. Schultz, Aug., 23
41. Slahmer, Joseph, 20 (wounded at Valverde)
42. Spis, Henry, 18
43. Spis, John, 23
44. Sternenberg, Julius, 21 (wounded at Valverde)
45. Sternenberg, Otto, 23
46. Stoltze, Charles, 20
47. (Illegible), Otto, 24
48. (Illegible)
49. Trenckmann, (?), 28
50. Vandermenth (?), John, 23
51. Voelkel, John, 19
52. Voelkel, William, 19
53. Wallers, Edward, 19
54. West, Thomas, 35
55. Wildner, F., 25
56. Wildner, Joseph, 21
57. Willerick, Julius, 20
58. Winkler, John, 25
59. Yavisch, H., 18

1. Amthar, A. (wounded at Glorieta)
2. Becher, H. (wounded at Valverde)
3. Buhl, A. (killed at Glorieta)
4. Frenkman, H. (wounded at Valverde—may be Trenckmann on muster roll)
5. Gadky, H. (killed at Valverde)
6. Gise, H. (wounded at Glorieta)
7. Gollmer, Charles (killed at Glorieta)
8. Konff, W. (wounded at Valverde)
9. Rhodius, C. (wounded at Valverde)
10. Schaefer, T. (killed at Glorieta)
11. Schilock, R. (wounded at Valverde)
12. Schroder, Sergeant A. (mortally wounded at Glorieta)
13. Spierf, H. (wounded at Valverde)

COMPANY H

(As of September 29, 1861)
Mustered in Nacogdoches County

John F. F. Doherty, Captain, 41
William H. Harris, First Lieutenant, 24
Francis M. Rainbolt, Second Lieutenant, 26
Giles B. Crain, Second Lieutenant, 22
Albert A. Nelson, First Sergeant, 47 (wounded at Glorieta)
John H. McKnight, Second Sergeant, 29 (killed at Glorieta)
William H. Yarborough, Third Sergeant, 24
Jesse Lee, Fourth Sergeant, 30
William H. Jones, First Corporal, 39
Thomas J. Hill, Second Corporal, 22
William Poe, Third Corporal, 23
William L. Eddins, Fourth Corporal, 33
Robert B. Johnson, Bugler, 22

PRIVATES:

1. Acrey, Abner, 21
2. Alexander, William L., 28 (promoted to captain of this company before campaign)
3. Allen, Andrew B., 20
4. Anderson, James M., 18
5. Boone, James R., 24
6. Boykin, Henry B., 22
7. Boykin, Thomas J., 24
8. Brewer, William M., 22
9. Brulan (?), Rufus G., —
10. Burns, John R., 38
11. (Illegible)
12. Casey, Rufus M., 24
13. Castles, James R., 18 (wounded at Valverde)
14. Cessna, J. Green K., 23
15. Coats, Napoleon B., 23 (wounded at Valverde)
16. Coon, Edwin F., 22
17. Cooper, James G., 32
18. Dees, Andrew, 34
19. Eddins, Andrew B., 31
20. Finley, Charles R., 30
21. Garrett, Charles R., 25
22. Graham, Edward S., 18
23. Graham, John G., 24
24. Griffith, Alfred, 33
25. Hardwick, William L., 25 (wounded at Valverde)
26. Henson, William H., 18
27. Hotchkiss, Atanacio, 18
28. Johnson, John W., 22
29. Jones, Jesse W., 18 (mortally wounded at Glorieta)
30. McIntosh, John W., 19
31. McQuistian, William S., 28
32. Millard, John J., 19
33. Moore, Henry H., 24
34. Moore, Rufus C., 22
35. Morgan, William H., 18
36. Norvell, John E., 18
37. Orton, Richard D., 2–
38. Pitts, Thomas T., 28 (wounded at Valverde)
39. Raguet, Charles M., 27 (promoted to lieutenant; second in command of howitzer battery)
40. Rainbolt, Walter S., 22
41. Richardson, Samuel T., —
42. Rogers, Joseph C., 18 (wounded at Glorieta)

43. Rusk, Benjamin L., 33
44. Rusk, Cicero, 26
45. Russell, Marion, 25
46. Russell, Moses W., 28 (mortally wounded at Valverde)
47. Scogin, James I., 32
48. Scogin, Toliver S., 19
49. Scogin, William J., 35
50. Sharp, Joseph H., 18
51. Starr, James F., 18 (wounded at Valverde)
52. Stone, Samuel H., 23
53. Strode, James A., 19
54. Sutphen, David S., 23
55. Sutphen, George W., 21
56. Tindall, Elisha J., 23 (mortally wounded at Valverde)
57. Tindall, William, 19
58. Wade, Henry H., 18
59. Walton, J. K. T., — (killed at Valverde)
60. Weatherly, Edward M., 26
61. Weatherly, Hiel, 2–
62. Weaver, James A., 18
63. Whitaker, Madison F., 19
64. White, Devreaux C., 25
65. White, John T., 19
66. White, Hardy Nelson, 18 (wounded at Valverde)
67. Williams, James T., 25 (killed at Valverde)
68. Williamson, John, 3–
69. Wisener, Richard P., 17
70. Wisener, William M., 18

COMPANY I
(As of September 29, 1861)
Mustered in Houston and Madison Counties

D. A. Nunn, Captain, 25
James M. Odell, First Lieutenant, 30 (later promoted to captain of this company; wounded at Glorieta)
William E. Moore, Second Lieutenant, 25
J. P. Stephenson, Second Lieutenant, 27 (wounded at Valverde)

John Collins, First Sergeant, 23
John Rice, Second Sergeant, 23
R. M. Almar, Third Sergeant, 22 (wounded at Valverde)
W. J. Jones, Fourth Sergeant, 23 (promoted to first lieutenant; wounded at Glorieta)
G. C. Blackburn, First Corporal, 40
Jerre Odell, Second Corporal, 35 (died in Socorro of wounds received at Valverde)
G. W. D. Hail, Third Corporal, 28
E. H. Bilbo, Fourth Corporal, 26
Samuel Sauls, First Bugler, 30
W. E. Bradley, Second Bugler, 28
James McManus, Blacksmith, 37 (killed at Glorieta)

PRIVATES:
1. Armstrong, H., 20
2. Armstrong, James, 20
3. Arnold, Thomas, 21
4. Arnold, William, 19
5. Atmar, J. Y., 30
6. (Illegible), L. H., —
7. Bailey, L. N., 24
8. Barker, Henry, 22
9. Blakeway, William, 22
10. Bland, B. F., 19
11. Brown, James, 21
12. Brundrill, J. N., 28
13. Burnes, Lafayette, 26
14. Collard, S. J., 20
15. Creasy, J. A., 27
16. Cruce, J. K., 21
17. Davenport, Thomas, 21
18. Dawson, A. J., 23 (wounded at Valverde)
19. Dickerson, W. B., 25
20. Dickerson, W. D., 28
21. Durm, L. E., 19
22. Edwards, W. H., 28
23. Elem, A. D., 25
24. Farris, E. P., 19
25. Freeman, G. W., 23
26. Furlo, A. M., 21
27. Furlo, R. N., 20
28. Gayle, J. H., 27

29. Glenn, Charles, 21
30. Gosset, G. M., 24
31. Gosset, Zebedee, 19 (died in Socorro of wounds received at Valverde)
32. Graham, J. M., 36
33. Hadlett (?), J. N., 19
34. Haeldor (?), Cawel (?), 26
35. Harrington, Lacy, 25
36. Harrison, W. W., 23
37. Hartgraves, B. G., 29
38. Hartgraves, J. D., 18
39. Hendley, William, 18
40. Hoffman, Andrew, 17
41. Hopkins, F. J., 26 (killed at Glorieta)
42. Houffman, J. J., 19
43. Houffman, M., 26
44. Jones, A. J., 24
45. Jones, J. F., 18
46. Kerr, Robert, 24
47. Larue, T. D., 18
48. Lee, William, 20
49. Little, J. M., 29
50. Lynch, M., 35
51. Maning, J. M., 18
52. Marsh, A. B., 24 (wounded at Glorieta)
53. McAnelly, W. R., 21
54. McCoy, William, 24
55. McDonald, J. M., 18
56. Monday, W. A., 18
57. Moore, W. L., 23
58. Mott, J. C., 30
59. Mulder, J. K., 19
60. Murchison, W. J., 23
61. Ousley, R. C., 22
62. Pesskin (?), D. E., 29
63. Pickering, John, 26
64. Pierson, J. A., 19
65. Poestridge, L. J., 18
66. Sanders, B. B., 22
67. Shaver, Jasper, 18
68. Shivers, J., 18 (wounded at Glorieta)
69. Smotherman (?), A. B., 2–
70. Stewart, A. J., 26
71. Stubblefield, W. M., 26
72. Thomas, J. W., 45 (wounded at Glorieta)
73. (Illegible)
74. Walker, G. W., 21 (wounded at Glorieta)
75. Warner, C. W., 21
76. White, J., 23
77. White, W. A., 24
78. Williams, Y. R., 23
79. Wilson, T. D., 21 (promoted to sergeant; killed at Glorieta)
80. Windham, J. L., 23
81. Wright, L. A., 22 (mortally wounded at Glorieta)
82. Woodson, G. W., 24

Casualties Not on Muster Roll
1. Campbell, John (wounded at Valverde)
2. Rhodes, J. (wounded at Valverde)
3. Sharp, J. A. (wounded at Valverde)

COMPANY K
(As of October 4, 1861)
Mustered in Cherokee County

William W. Foard, Captain, 39
Edward L. Robb, First Lieutenant, 25 (wounded at Glorieta)
Clinton S. Henry, Second Lieutenant, 26
Wiley J. Thompson, Second Lieutenant, 23
Albert F. Wilson, First Sergeant, 27
Thomas West, Second Sergeant, 38
J. J. Fuller, Third Sergeant, 33
J. M. Vining, Fourth Sergeant, 19 (killed at Valverde)
J. M. Walters, Fifth Sergeant, 30
J. H. Griffin, First Corporal, 23
J. D. Thompson, Second Corporal, 19
Thomas B. Robb, Third Corporal, 20
J. E. Mathews, Fourth Corporal, 21
T. B. Nash, Bugler, 24
M. D. L. Mucklesry, Blacksmith, 19

PRIVATES:
1. Abbott, Britt, 20
2. Alexander, T. J., 18

3. Armstrong, T. E., 25
4. Atkinson, C. S., 29
5. Burton, B. (?), 18
6. Burton, M. L., 25
7. Campbell, J. N., 24
8. Coleman, J. N., 21
9. Cooper, David, 30
10. Cooper, T. C., 19
11. Davis, J. W., 21
12. Findlay, David, 18
13. Findlay, S. B., 24
14. Fish, A. L., 27
15. Haaron (?), A. G., 18
16. Hardin, Griffin, 25
17. Harry, C. M., 21
18. Hatchett, E. A., 29
19. Hill, B. F., 22
20. Hillyer, J. T., 24
21. Hogg, J. T., 27
22. Hoyt, E. D., 21
23. Jasper, W. B., 24
24. Jones, William, 25
25. King, R. F., 28
26. Kuykendall, M. S., 23
27. Legg, H. L., 23
28. Linard, Thomas E., 33
29. Maddux, L. H., 22
30. Manning, E. D., 22
31. McHenry, J. G., 19
32. McTyre, J. H., 23
33. Millikin, James, 25
34. O'Quinn, J. J., 20
35. Porter, G. G., 20
36. Powell, J. W., 18
37. Price, M., 19
38. Ramsey, W. J. L., 26
39. Red, C. S., 19
40. Rodes, John, 17 (died in Socorro of wounds received at Valverde)
41. Ruby, E. L., 21
42. Ruby, J. W., 27
43. Selman, W. E., 18
44. Selman, W. W., 21
45. Sharp, J. A., 24 (wounded at Valverde)
46. Stephens, S. D., 24
47. Stewart, J. B., 23
48. Teer, William, 24 (wounded at Glorieta)

49. Teer, N. J., 21
50. Veitch, J. L., 27
51. Veitch, J. W., 24
52. Walker, M. B., 21
53. Walker, M. D. L., 27
54. Wallace, J. E., 20
55. Walters, Mack, 23
56. Walters, W. C., 18
57. Warren, Calvin, —
58. Wilkins, N. N., 25
59. Williams, J. C., 22
60. Williams, T. E., 18 (wounded at Glorieta)
61. Wolff, P. H., 18

FIFTH REGIMENT
Texas Mounted Volunteers (Cavalry)

FIELD AND STAFF
(As of September, 1861)

Thomas "Tom" Green, Colonel, 47 (slightly wounded at Valverde)
Henry C. McNeill, Lieutenant Colonel, 24
Samuel A. Lockridge, Major, 33 (killed at Valverde)
Joseph D. Sayers, Adjutant, 19 (promoted to captain May 3, 1862)
M. B. Wyatt, Assistant Quartermaster, 27
J. H. Beck, Jr., Assistant Commissary, 23
Charles B. Sheppard, Sergeant Major, 18 (promoted to lieutenant May 3, 1862)
W. Lott Davidson, Quartermaster Sergeant, 23
F. Bracht, Surgeon, —
John M. Bronough, First Assistant Surgeon, —
J. R. McPhaill, Second Assistant Surgeon, —
R. W. Pierce, Chaplain, —
Howitzer Battery (four guns):
William S. Wood Lieutenant Commanding, 27
Philip Fulcrod, Second Lieutenant, —

COMPANY A

(As of August 29, 1861)

Mustered in Colorado County

John S. Shropshire, Captain, 28
(promoted to major February 21,
1862; killed at Glorieta)

Thomas G. Wright, First Lieutenant, 30

David A. Hubbard, Second Lieutenant,
28 (died in Socorro of wounds
received at Valverde)

Pleasant J. Oakes, Second Lieutenant, 24

William S. Land, First Sergeant, 33

Lovard T. Tooke, Second Sergeant, 20

George O. Sloneker, Third Sergeant, 29
(severely wounded at Valverde)

George H. Little, Fourth Sergeant, 20

John D. Campbell, First Corporal, 19

Tredell R. Taylor, Second Corporal, 20

John T. Harwell, Third Corporal, 20

Sylvinus N. Kellogg, Fourth Corporal,
36

Edward Marsden, First Bugler, 27

Samuel O. Wilson, Second Bugler, 36

Manly C. Knowlton, Farrier, 33
(severely wounded at Valverde)

Andrew Galilee, Blacksmith, 23

PRIVATES:

1. Adams, Edwin T., 28
2. Allen, John O., 19
3. Barker, Augustus L., 27 (severely
   wounded at Valverde)
4. Beckwith, Henry, 24
5. (Illegible), Sebastian, 29 (May be S.
   Clapp—severely wounded at
   Valverde)
6. (Illegible), Michael,—
7. (Illegible), Peter L., 21 (May be
   P. L. Clapp—wounded at Valverde)
8. (Illegible), 23
9. Campbell, John P., 27 (slightly
   wounded at Valverde)
10. Carson, James, 20
11. Carter, Ashley B., 25
12. Carter, Robert H., 28 (mortally
    wounded at Valverde)
13. Crebbs, William C., 22
14. David, John Henry, 22 (died in
    Socorro of wounds received at
    Valverde)
15. David, William L., 23
16. De Graffenreid, William G., 36
17. Dick, Jacob J., 25
18. Donald, Holman B., 25 (slightly
    wounded at Valverde)
19. Friar, John H., 23
20. Gilbert, James H., 25
21. Gillespie, Thomas B., 20 (severely
    wounded at Valverde)
22. Goode, Thomas F., 20
23. Griffits, Abraham A., 32
24. Guinn, George R., 18
25. Halyard, Alphonse B., 19
26. Harbert, Andrew J., 19
27. Henderson, Samuel, 24 (slightly
    wounded at Valverde)
28. Henderson, Thomas, 22
29. Henderson, William, 24
30. Hume, Peyton G., 23
31. Kahn, Henry, 20
32. Knowles, Edmond R., 33
33. Knowles, John Q., 30 (severely
    wounded at Valverde)
34. Landrum, John T., 18
35. Landrum, William F., 21
36. Martin, George, 19 (wounded at
    Valverde)
37. Mathews, E. T., 20
38. McLeary, James H., 18 (wounded
    at Valverde)
39. Mitchell, Albert G., 27 (severely
    wounded at Valverde)
40. Montgomery, John D., 18 (slightly
    wounded at Valverde)
41. Murphy, Thomas G., 23
42. Newsom, John L., 24
43. Nias, Henry, 26
44. Norman, Adolphus G., 24
45. Obenchain, John T., 22
46. O'Neill, William, 21
47. Pankey, Martin, 21 (mortally
    wounded at Valverde)
48. Schly, Fredrick W., 25
49. Schroeder, Charles, 19
50. Schubert, August, 20 (slightly
    wounded at Valverde)

51. Seymour, George W., 23 (wounded at Glorieta)
52. Shaw, William, 19
53. Silvey, Peter G., 21
54. Skelton, William, 19
55. Slick, Thomas, 18
56. Slater, Benjamin F., 25
57. Smith, James A., 19
58. Smith, Joshua S., 22
59. Smith, Josiah E., 23 (killed at Valverde)
60. Taylor, David H., 22 (wounded at Glorieta)
61. Terrell, Samuel, 18
62. Waddill, George G. G., 19
63. Walter, George H., 24
64. Weller, Cyrus O., 19
65. Wells, Stephen M., 28
66. Wenfree, John B., 23
67. Wheeler, Benjamin, 45

Casualties Not on Muster Roll
1. Caldwell, J. E. (wounded at Valverde)
2. Grorr, A. D. (severely wounded at Valverde)
3. Jones, S. E. (mortally wounded at Glorieta, according to Noel)
4. McDonald, H. (wounded at Valverde, according to Noel)
5. Putnam, Sandford (died in Socorro of wounds received at Valverde)
6. Roberts, W. G. (slightly wounded at Valverde)
7. Slotts, J. I. (severely wounded at Valverde)

COMPANY B (Lancers)
(As of September 2, 1861)
Mustered in Falls County

Willis L. Lang, Captain, 31 (died in Socorro of wounds received at Valverde)
Demetrius M. Bass, First Lieutenant, 26 (died in Socorro of wounds received at Valverde)

John J. Scott, Second Lieutenant, 28
John J. Coleman, Second Lieutenant, 25
Isaac N. Price, First Sergeant, 27
James A. Forbes, Second Sergeant, 23 (severely wounded at Valverde)
Charles B. Mattock, Third Sergeant, 28 (resigned October 1, 1861)
John P. Conly, Fourth Sergeant, 19
Benjamin G. Greely, First Corporal, 22 (killed at Glorieta)
George H. Perkins, Second Corporal, 21
Alfred M. Shelton, Third Corporal, 25
William Moore, Fourth Corporal, 43
William T. Price, First Bugler, 18
James H. Shelton, Second Bugler, 24 (resigned October 31, 1861)
Silas Ivans, Farrier, 22 (killed at Valverde)
Silas Chambers, Blacksmith, 26

PRIVATES:
1. Barton, James A., 19
2. Bell, William A., 23 (mortally wounded at Valverde)
3. Bolton, Evan, 28
4. Brown, John A., 18
5. Brown, Robert T., 22
6. Calk, James A., 19
7. Canarian, Adam, 21
8. Canty, Francis M., 24 (killed at Valverde)
9. Church, Madison M., 20
10. Coleman, Wade H., 23 (severely wounded at Valverde)
11. Curry, Joseph L., 23 (killed at Valverde)
12. Daugherty, John K., 31 (killed at Valverde)
13. Davis, Andrew J., 36 (severely wounded at Valverde)
14. Davis, William T., 21
15. Donaldson, Achilles B., 27
16. Duty, John H., 26
17. Elgin, Charles W., 21 (replaced Mattock as sergeant)
18. Ferguson, John M., 23 (killed at Valverde)
19. Francks, Henry Clay, 18

20. Frazzell, Albert, 21
21. Galz (?), William H., 22
22. Garrett, Robert J., 20
23. Hardwicke, George J., 36
24. Harris, John, 22
25. Hersey, Albert J., 26
26. Irvin, William M., 29
27. Landrum, Samuel, 45
28. Lea, Thomas N., 19 (slightly wounded at Valverde)
29. Logan, Thomas G., 25
30. Long, Emil, 22
31. Marlin, Isaac, 30 (killed at Valverde)
32. McCarrell, William, 42
33. Morriss, Aaron P., 18
34. Murray, John, 23 (died September 29, 1861)
35. Nash, John B., 36
36. Nations, Andrew J., 32 (appointed fifth sergeant October 12, 1861; wounded at Glorieta)
37. Nations, Daniel J., 25
38. Nations, John T., 24
39. Oakes, Francis M., 18
40. Parker, John P., 22 (severely wounded at Valverde)
41. Persons, Henry J., 22 (mortally wounded at Valverde)
42. Pierson, Hilary, 20 (slightly wounded at Valverde)
43. Polster, George, 24 (severely wounded at Valverde)
44. Rolfe, Calvin H., 44
45. Shelton, Edmond, 25 (slightly wounded at Valverde)
46. Smith, James Henry, 31
47. Smith, Joel E., 24
48. Snyder, William, 23
49. Sowders, John A., 18 (severely wounded at Valverde)
50. Steele, Frank R., 21
51. Stone, Daniel H., 21
52. Strong, John, 21
53. Thompson, George, 23
54. Underwood, Joseph, 22
55. Wadzock, Albert L., 21
56. Wheat, Thomas G., 21
57. Wilder, James A., 29
58. Wilson, Hiram, 29
59. Wood, Robert C., 32
60. Wright, James, 21
61. Wright, (?), 38

Casualty Not on Muster Roll
1. Mitchell, R. H. (killed at Valverde)

COMPANY C
(As of August 31, 1861)
Mustered in Grimes County

Denman W. Shannon, Captain, 25 (captured at Glorieta; promoted to major March 28, 1862)
William A. Shannon, First Lieutenant, 33
J. P. Clough, Second Lieutenant, 25 (slightly wounded at Glorieta)
J. C. Naylor, Second Lieutenant, 23
John T. Stover, First Sergeant, 26
J. H. James, Second Sergeant, 21
Silas Johnson, Third Sergeant, 21 (died in Socorro of wounds received at Valverde)
J. M. Cosgrove, Fourth Sergeant, 25
John C. Naile, First Corporal, 21 (died of pneumonia in Albuquerque)
J. K. Grissett, Second Corporal, 23 (mortally wounded at Glorieta)
William R. Evans, Third Corporal, 24
S. M. White, Fourth Corporal, 23

PRIVATES:
1. Aspinwall (?), C. A., 25
2. Barker, Henry, 21
3. Beall, C. B., 30
4. Beurdash (?), Adam, 18
5. Bigler, C. D., 32
6. Bingle, Nicolas, 38 (severely wounded at Glorieta)** A name which has been scratched off the muster roll. Possibly this man was transferred to help man the battery commanded by Lieutenant William S. Woods.
7. Bowie, James J., 30
8. Breland, Robert, 25

9. Brown, Thomas J., 21
10. Byars, T. J., 20
11. Caffield, Pat, 23
12. Camp, Frank, 22
13. Camp, Moses, 22
14. (Illegible), 19
15. Catlett, R. P., 26 (mortally wounded at Glorieta)
16. Chappman, William, 38
17. Cheesborough, J. B.,* 30
18. Coats (?), Joseph, 22
19. Cum——(?), Ira,* 20
20. Davis, V. W.,* 24
21. Davis, William, 18
22. Dean, Robert,* 19
23. Dimerett, Lewis, 22
24. Donaghan, Thomas, 22
25. Dowd, Pat, 24 (wounded at Glorieta)
26. Dubos, M. T., 20 (wounded at Glorieta)
27. Duncan, Martin M., 20
28. Dupree, J. L.,* 20
29. Dupree, Sam, 20 (died in Santa Fé as Sibley was evacuating)
30. Ellis, John, 40 (died in Mesilla after retreat)
31. (Illegible), S. B., 18
32. Flynt, G. W., 20
33. Frankland, T. H., 21
34. Frazers, C. H.,* 25
35. Fream, D., 18
36. Fulson, S. R., 23
37. Gary, J. M., 25
38. Giessel, Herman, 27
39. Gilroy, George, 28
40. Gray, E. L., 26
41. Green, William,* 20
42. Gressitt, H. H.,* 19
43. Harrison, Montgomery, 30
44. Henry, John,* 32
45. Herrick, W. D., 27
46. Hickey, Robert, 23
47. Hix, C. T., 30
48. Howell, Allen N., 26
49. Howell, W. R., 20
50. Humphries, William, 30
51. Johnson, T. V., 18 (slightly wounded at Valverde)
52. Jones, R. H., 21
53. Karnole (?), Henry, 21
54. Kellum, Ed., 35
55. Kirby, John A. J., 22
56. Lawles, H. D., 20 (slightly wounded at Glorieta)
57. Lawles, Lucius,* 22
58. Lawton (?), Sam, 22
59. Masters, John, 19
60. Mayers, Davis, 23
61. Mayes, James H., 18
62. Maywald, Henry, 18
63. McDowels (?), W. D., 23
64. McNair, A. C., 23
65. Medley, M. G.,* 23
66. Moody, John W., 38
67. Moore, J. D., 18 (slightly wounded at Valverde)
68. Nash, James S., 23
69. Nichols, J. B., 21
70. Niles, H. H., 27
71. Noland, P., 23
72. Nott, G. W., 18
73. Odom, James, 22
74. O'Neill, Edward, 30
75. Oram, William, 18
76. Pearson, J., 25
77. Perry, William, 18
78. Pitleck (?), A. A., 26
79. Powers, John P., 37
80. Prist, Charles W., 23
81. Raymond, John, 32
82. Reicherzer, Adolph, 20
83. Sapp, P. W., 19 (slightly wounded at Glorieta)
84. Smith, Thomas, 22
85. Spencer, C. W.,* 41
86. Stewart, William, 25
87. Stuckey, S., 20
88. Sullock, John H., 21
89. Taylor, Charles S., 18
90. Taylor, William, 20
91. Terry, Thomas S., 21
92. Thomas, L., 28
93. Van Block, William, 29
94. White, Thomas, 18
95. Whitley, Moses, 36
96. Wiggans, C. C., 22

97. Williams, W., 25
98. Wood, W. S., 27
99. (Illegible), W. H., 21
100. (Illegible), 23

COMPANY D

(As of September 3, 1861)
Mustered in DeWitt, Victoria, Karnes, and Gonzales Counties

Daniel Henry Ragsdale, Captain, 25
Jacob George Marshall, First
    Lieutenant, 30
J. H. Beck, Jr., Second Lieutenant, 23
    (transferred to regimental staff)
Felix Roan, Second Lieutenant, 24
    (captured at Glorieta)
J. K. T. Walton, First Sergeant, 20
Gustavus H. Schmeltzer, Second
    Sergeant, 31 (wounded at Glorieta)
C. A. Napier, Third Sergeant, 18
Graves Sharp, Fourth Sergeant, 23
Napoleon Odom, First Corporal, 18
A. C. White, Second Corporal, 25
R. T. Ham, Third Corporal, 18
B. F. McCann, Fourth Corporal, 21
Joseph Little, Musician, 21
G. W. Rivers, Musician, 30
William S. Tyson, Farrier, 23 (killed at
    Valverde)
Charles White, Blacksmith, 38

PRIVATES:

1. Baily, Thomas Jefferson, 18
2. Bampass (?), John, 24
3. Bell, L. L., 19
4. Bell, M. Davis, 18
5. Bell, W. B., 24
6. Berry, William T., 27
7. Brown, David, 30 (wounded at
    Valverde)
8. Brown, Henry, 18 (killed at
    Glorieta)
9. Byars, Joseph Jeremiah, 20
10. (Illegible)
11. Cattle, L. C., 20
12. Cooper, G. W., 19
13. Davenport, W. L., 19
14. Dominic(?), Charles, 20
15. Enríquez, José M., 23
16. Felder, J., 20
17. Finte (?), John, 28
18. Ford, John T., 30
19. Friar, Jac. H., 19
20. Frochlich, William, 18
21. Gay, Gilbert, 41
22. Graves, J. T., 26
23. Halemudd (?), G., 18
24. Hanne, August, 18
25. Harrison, H. C., 18
26. Hart, John, 19
27. Hinkley, George C., 35
28. Korpile, Jacob, 19
29. Krempkan, Louis, 30
30. Lad, James, 24 (wounded at
    Valverde)
31. Langford, B. F., 25
32. Loe, George A., 18
33. Lorenz, J. A., 21 (wounded at
    Valverde)
34. Mann, W. H. H., 20
35. Mayes, A., 19
36. McKinney, James, 29
37. Meadows, John, 25
38. Meckel (?), William, 23
39. Miller, Frank, 18
40. Odom, John, 28
41. Odom, William C., 21
42. Pfeuffer, Daniel, 22
43. Philippe, (?), Jr., 22
44. Prithen, A. W., 23
45. Reed, Dan, 31
46. Reed, Henry, 21
47. Reinlander, John, 28
48. Richard, C. W., 28
49. Rider, T. M., 28
50. Schoemert, A., 26
51. Sharp, T. H., 22
52. Shelton, Peter, 18
53. Stiles (?), Riley, 25
54. Trimble, F. M., 20
55. Tschoepa (?), R., 18
56. Varga, Paul, 19
57. Webber, Jacob, 21
58. West, Herrman, 23

59. Wright, Sam, 18
60. Yokum, Sam H., 23 (died in Socorro of wounds received at Valverde)

Casualty Not on Muster Roll
1. Sherwood, H. T. (wounded at Glorieta)

COMPANY E
(As of September 4, 1861)
Mustered in Washington County

H. A. McPhaill, Captain, 31
W. G. Wilkins, First Lieutenant, 24 (wounded at Valverde)
J. P. Pressly, Second Lieutenant, 28
Adolph Testard, Second Lieutenant, 32
M. B. Wyatt, First Sergeant, 27 (promoted to lieutenant; transferred to regimental staff)
Lester Clark, Second Sergeant, 22
W. A. Rumple, Third Sergeant, 25
J. D. Hardin, Fourth Sergeant, 22
J. C. Jennings, First Corporal, 30
J. M. Rainwater, Second Corporal, 20
John B. Wilkins, Third Corporal, 19 (wounded at Valverde)
N. B. Terry, Fourth Corporal, 21
Christoph Durke (?), Musician, 19
F. Riebe, Musician, 19

PRIVATES:
1. Allcorn, T. J., 21
2. Allmon, B. F., 23
3. Andrews, Joseph C., 25
4. Applewhite, J. W., 21
5. Boykin, J. L., 22 (mortally wounded at Valverde)
6. Barnhill, Pleasant H., 22
7. Chapple, W. C., 31
8. Cook, R. H., 21
9. Crosier, K. T., 25
10. Dahl, John, 34
11. Danhouse (?), F. W., 21
12. Danniehy, John, 35
13. Dawson, H. W., 21
14. Dookle, A., 22
15. Dorris, G. W., 18
16. Early, B. F., 18
17. Eldrid, J. F., 28
18. Estes, B. F., 26
19. Gary, C. D., 19
20. Gary, William, 31
21. Gaston, R. A., 26
22. Gaston, T. B., 20
23. Giesenschley, William, 18
24. Harmes, Fredrick, 24
25. Harris, R. O., 18
26. Henry, J. L., 19
27. Hensley, T. G., 18
28. Hewitt, L. R., 24
29. Hewitt, W. H., 21
30. Higgins, M. C., 30
31. Hill, T. B., 20
32. Hoffmann, John, 24
33. Hosea, T. J., 21
34. Hosea, W. H., 23
35. House, Samuel, 18
36. Howard, T. W., 31
37. Johnson, W. J., 20
38. King, Henry, 25
39. Knight, James P., 19
40. Lallier, V. A., 26
41. Lyons, J., 22
42. Lyons, William, 18
43. McLemore (?), A. I., 30
44. McNeil, Malcom, 21
45. McNeil, N. G., 23
46. McPhall, A. A., 22
47. Miles, J. A., 23
48. Mills, J. E., 18
49. Myrick, Ross, 27 (mortally wounded at Valverde)
50. Parrott, W. E., 18
51. Perry, B. T., 19
52. Petty, J. T., 18
53. Pfleghaug (?), August, 19
54. Pipkin, R. M., 22
55. Pompell, John, 18
56. Portis, R. S., 21
57. Punderson (?), August, 19
58. Rainwater, George M., 23
59. Rankin, John G., 20
60. Reed (?), J. F., 22
61. Robinson, A. J., 24
62. Robinson, John, 25

63. Robinson, John, 22
64. Roff, N. B., 22
65. Rosenberg, Lewis, 20 (died in Socorro of wounds received at Valverde)
66. Sanders, W. J., 21
67. Sheppard, Charles B., 18 (transferred to regimental staff September 5, 1861)
68. Simons, V. J., 21
69. Slade, W. C., 24
70. Sprain, Henry, 20
71. Stevens, R. A., 19
72. Stewart, J. W., 27
73. Stringer, John S., 30
74. Tyler, A. C., 20
75. Tyler, William L., 22
76. Tyson, J. H., 24 (wounded at Valverde)
77. Walker, T. J., 22
78. Watts, Frank, 22
79. Webush (?), George, 23
80. Welch, Barnet, 18
81. White, W. D., 22
82. Winter, C. F., 31
83. Wood, A. W., 18
84. Young, J. S., 25
85. Young, J. S., 21
86. Weiss, Nicolas, 30

COMPANY F

(As of September 5, 1861)
Mustered in Washington County

G. W. Campbell, Captain, 30
J. A. Shepherd, First Lieutenant, 20
B. B. Seat, Second Lieutenant, 28 (slightly wounded at Valverde)
Marion Brown, Second Lieutenant, 25
H. C. Curry, First Sergeant, 25
J. F. Webb, Second Sergeant, 27
N. Selars, Third Sergeant, 23
J. A. Levy, Fourth Sergeant, 30
W. S. Bishop, First Corporal, 30
M. P. Kerr, Second Corporal, 20
Wesley Givens, Third Corporal, 23
Albert Wilkerson, Fourth Corporal, 24

PRIVATES:
1. Armstrong, J. D., 22
2. Baker, Charles, 22
3. Boyd, Augustus, 19
4. Boyd, Sam, 18
5. Brown, D. M., 20
6. Brown, John L., 28
7. Brown, J. G., 22
8. Brown, J. M., 18
9. Brown, T. J., 18
10. Bullard, W. J., 29
11. Burton, W. C., 26
12. Carmean, W. B., 20
13. Carter, John C., 20
14. Carter, J. (?). P., 39
15. Castles, G. W., 20
16. Clarke, B. C., 31
17. Cleveland, J. M., 18
18. Cochran, F., 24 (wounded at Valverde)
19. Copeland, J., 23
20. Craig, Robert, 21
21. Craig, W. B., 23 (killed at Valverde)
22. Croft, William, 28 (mortally wounded at Valverde)
23. Demint, S. X., 25
24. Derrick, J. P. (?), 25
25. Dial, James, 25
26. Dial, John, 19
27. Edmondson, Charles W., 22
28. Fisher, H., 25
29. Fuquea, J. N., 19
30. Gamble, P. H., 18
31. Garland, Samuel, 21
32. Gaston, F. M., 24
33. Givens, James R., 20
34. Green, A. N., 22
35. Hasele, Walter, 21
36. Heck, Joseph, 19
37. Hensley, C. M., 18 (wounded at Valverde)
38. Hill, J. S., 18
39. Hill, R. J., 59
40. Hines, N. H., 19
41. Holbert, J. C., 18
42. Holt, James, 18
43. Johnson, H., 18

44. Jordel, Lewis, 20
45. Kathocar (?), D., 19 (wounded at Valverde)
46. Kerr, Augustus H., 20
47. Kerr, T. P., 21
48. Lacklam, T. J., 31
49. Lewis, J. M., 18
50. Lindsey, William H., 30
51. Linzziguen (?), C., 21
52. Linzziguen (?), George, 19
53. Mallman, William, 20
54. Maxwell, J., 27
55. McAneley, S., 18
56. McCulloch, M. T., 30
57. McMinn, F. M., 24 (slightly wounded at Valverde)
58. Meherge, W. A., 21
59. Messinger, William, 20
60. Morlock, T. J., 21
61. Myrick, D. J., 28
62. Newman, J. G., 21
63. Nunn, Samuel, 32
64. Pyner, W. J., 20
65. Shaw, Charles, 18
66. Spratt, (?). H., 25
67. Thomas, Lewis, 20
68. Thomas, William, 26
69. Tidwell, C. M., 23 (killed at Valverde)
70. Wakefield, John, 32
71. Webb, J. J., 19
72. Wetstone, T. M., 23
73. Whitner, H. T., 24
74. Wilkerson, J. H., 27
75. Winkler, Gustav, 21
76. York, M. Y., 18

Casualties Not on Muster Roll
1. Anderson, A. (slightly wounded at Valverde)
2. Lewis, Charles (mortally wounded at Valverde, according to Noel)
3. Wensley, C. M. (severely wounded at Valverde)

COMPANY G (Lancers)
(As of September 25, 1861)
Mustered in Austin County

Jerome B. McCown, Captain, 41
Steph S. Cannon, First Lieutenant, 26 (contracted smallpox on return to Mesilla Valley)
William M. Francis, Second Lieutenant, 22
Jerry W. Perrine, Second Lieutenant, 22 (wounded at Valverde)
Charles W. Gould, First Sergeant, 22
John H. Good, Second Sergeant, 27
Nicolas Hanes, Third Sergeant, 31
James H. Farr, Fourth Sergeant, 23 (wounded by Mexicans at Los Padillas; left at Peralta)** On April 13, 1862, Captain McCown sent ten of his men across the river to escort a civilian family which intended to accompany the Confederates as far as El Paso. While the escort was engaged in cooking supper that night near Los Padillas, the men were attacked by a band of Mexicans. The Texans lost two killed and one wounded.
William Farr, First Corporal, 26
A. Snow, Second Corporal, 27 (wounded at Valverde; left at Peralta to attend sick)
Thomas B. Woodruff, Third Corporal, 24
Allen Johns, Fourth Corporal, 33 (may be Allen V. Jones in official report, who was mortally wounded at Valverde)
W. H. Brown, Bugler, 28
James Tobin, Farrier, 21 (killed by Private Tom Harvey)
John P. Byrnes, Blacksmith, 24 (slightly wounded at Valverde)

PRIVATES:
1. Abbott, Pierce, 24
2. Arey, Edwin A., 34
3. Askew, James, 18
4. Benton, George, 28 (left sick at Peralta)
5. Boykin, John, 27
6. Brooks, Francis A., 23 (reported killed at Peralta)

7. Bullock, R. W., 21
8. Burns, Thomas H., 25
9. Cochrane, Thomas M., 19
10. Farr, William H., 50
11. Figley, Henry F., 21 (died in Socorro of wounds received at Valverde)
12. Fisher, Robert, 21
13. Fisher, William, 21
14. Fowler, Asa S., 21
15. Francis, Joseph W., 18
16. Goodram, Francis M., 30 (left sick at Peralta)
17. Graf, Christian H., 21 (killed by Mexicans at Los Padillas)
18. Guisecke, August, 21
19. Guisecke, Frank, 23
20. Harrison, Albert, 23
21. Harvey, Thomas N., 36 (executed on January 11, 1862 at Fort Bliss for killing James Tobin)
22. Henson, John J., 18 (left at Peralta to attend sick)
23. Henson, Joseph N., 19 (left sick at Peralta)
24. Himes, J. P., 19 (killed by Mexicans at Los Padillas)*
25. Hutcherson, William L., 21 (left sick at Peralta)
26. Hutchins, John, 39
27. Kay, James A., 18
28. King, Thomas B., 26
29. Lamoth, T., 18
30. Laurence, James, 21
31. Leach, E. D., 18
32. Lilly, Richard, —
33. McBride, Steph, 30
34. McKay, Marcus, 42
35. Miller, Andrew B., 20 (left sick at Peralta)
36. Mills, Lafayette, 17
37. Nichols, Thomas, 30
38. Pearson, William B. T., 21
39. Punchard (?), L. H., 23
40. Richey, James A., 27 (died at El Paso, February 14, 1862)
41. Rose, J. W., —
42. Russell, F. B., 28
43. Scales, J. H., 18
44. Schassa, Conrad, 22
45. Skinner, John E., 19
46. Smith, G. A., 26
47. Smith, J. B., 23
48. Thompson, J. H., 19
49. Truell (?), Peter, 26
50. Van Ness, William, 31 (contracted smallpox after return to Mesilla Valley)
51. Ward, David G., 25
52. Whitesides, J. J., 23
53. Winissen (?), William H., 23
54. Worsham, M. L., 18
55. Wrister, Hugh, 36 (slightly wounded at Valverde; left at hospital in Socorro)
56. Zeidler, Ernst, 26

COMPANY H
(As of October 11, 1861)
Mustered in Travis County

Redden S. Pridgen, Captain, 37
William W. Apperson, First Lieutenant, 33
Dennis Corwin, Second Lieutenant, 27
James A. Clinton, Second Lieutenant, 30 (died while training at Camp Manassas)
T. W. Dailey, First Sergeant, 35
William J. Good, Second Sergeant, 19 (severely wounded at Valverde)
Z. C. Wilson, Third Sergeant, 23
Ed. T. Burrows, Fourth Sergeant, 19 (mortally wounded at Glorieta)
William Chaffin, First Corporal, 32
Allan J. Ballard, Second Corporal, 21
Thomas R. Ovenbaun, Third Corporal, 33 (slightly wounded at Valverde)
John Reynolds, Fourth Corporal, 21
Harvey McClinton, (?), 25 (killed at Valverde)

PRIVATES:
1. Adams, J. D., 16
2. Adams, William J., 23
3. Atkison, James, 19

4. Beazley, John R., 18
5. Bird, Cornelius, 25 (severely wounded at Valverde; later captured and paroled)
6. Bodenhemer (?), William W., 28
7. Brashears, James, 21
8. Brashears, William, 23
9. Cawen (?), R. C., 28
10. Chadwick, Elijah, 28
11. Chadwick, John, 18 (left sick at Santa Fé)
12. Copeland, N. A., 24
13. Cox, Isaac H., 18
14. Crist, Elria, 23
15. Dailey, William A., 29
16. Darrell (?), Franklin, 26
17. Devane, B. B., 32
18. Edens, B. F., 16
19. Evans, Peter, 25
20. Fleming, George, 21
21. Gault, Robert, 21
22. Gearney (?), John, 38
23. Green, James B., 19 (died of pneumonia near Doña Ana on return)
24. Hager, Simon C., 20 (slightly wounded at Valverde)
25. Harris, Austin G., 25
26. Harris, Berry, 20
27. Higley (?), Simon C., 20 (slightly wounded at Valverde)
28. Horn, R. H., 16
29. Jones, H. Warren, 21 (died of pneumonia at Fort Thorn before campaign)
30. Jones, William, 18
31. Kating, John, 22
32. Keen, S. E., 19
33. Kirk, John, 22
34. Land, Jerome, 22 (discharged at Fort Bliss for deafness)
35. Land, Thomas H., 24 (slightly wounded at Valverde)
36. Little, George W., 25
37. Little, Green B., 23
38. Lloyd, Richard, 19 (taken prisoner at Peralta; paroled)
39. Lloyd, William W., 21

40. Massey, Hiram, 18 (died of pneumonia at Fort Thorn before campaign)
41. McCauley (?), L., 25
42. (Illegible)
43. McElroy, John, 23
44. Miller, John J., 19
45. Mitchell, M. C., 29
46. Moore, W. C., 29
47. Moreland, Thomas H., 24
48. Neeley, O. D., 22
49. Norman, William, 30 (severely wounded at Valverde)
50. Parker, F. H., 25
51. Parker, Josiah, 17
52. Pate, William R., 18
53. Pettie, Calvin C., 27
54. Rapp, John M., 25 (taken prisoner at Albuquerque; paroled)
55. Sawens (?), Henry, 17
56. Settgarth (?), William, 22
57. Smith, Lucius W., 18 (mortally wounded at Valverde)
58. Stanley, John H., 31
59. Stell, Raphineas, 19
60. Taylor, J. W., 17
61. Thornburg, Felix H., 17 (taken prisoner at Peralta; paroled)
62. Vinson, Homer K., 34
63. Whiddan (?), Eli, 36
64. Whitley, G. W., 23
65. Whitley, J. D., 18
66. Wilson, James K., 22

Casualties Not on Muster Roll

1. Ainsworth, A. F. (wounded at Valverde)
2. Grooms, G. W. (slightly wounded at Valverde)
3. Marling, G. W. (slightly wounded at Valverde)
4. Walling, H. (mortally wounded at Valverde, according to Noel)

COMPANY I
(As of October 19, 1861)
Mustered in Fayette County

Ira G. Killough, Captain, 32

James A. Darby, First Lieutenant, 32 (captured near Peralta April 15, 1862)

E. Wilson Miller, Second Lieutenant, 24

Robert J. Robinson, Second Lieutenant, 30

James D. Williams, First Sergeant, 18

Livingston G. Young, Second Sergeant, 20

Franklin A. Howell, Third Sergeant, 22

Joseph A. Bell, Fourth Sergeant, 20

Jared E. Winburn, Fifth Sergeant, 22 (killed at Valverde)

Freeling H. McCollum, First Corporal, 18

Lewis J. Gaddis, Second Corporal, 35

Albert R. Allen, Third Corporal, 19

Samuel N. Lowell, Fourth Corporal, 22

PRIVATES:

1. Adams, Henry A., 49
2. Allen, W. (?), 18
3. Ansley, Frederick W., 30
4. Baggett, A. T., —
5. Brown, James, 23
6. Crow, James T., 22
7. Eastman, William B., 23
8. Ellis, James F., 21
9. Ezell, Christo. P., 24
10. Faires, Richard, 20
11. Faires, William A., 24
12. Hale, Edward B., 20
13. Haller, William F., 17
14. Harmen, Fritz, 22
15. Harrison, Luke A., 19 (severely wounded at Valverde)
16. Henry, Zac, 21
17. Herndon, John, 20
18. Hill, Isaac P., 18
19. Holmes, John, 46
20. Ingram, William H., 28
21. Keepene (?), James H., 18
22. Kemp, Wilson S., 24 (died of pneumonia February 12, 1862)
23. Lane, Crawford J., 21
24. Lane, John W., 33
25. Lawhorn, David W., 24

26. Matchins, Edward L., 27
27. Matchins, William, 31
28. McColluman (?), Cincinnattus J., 20
29. Moore, Benjamin A., 24
30. Moore, David D., 18 (died at Fort Bliss January 7, 1862)
31. Moore, Lafayette R., 21
32. Moore, Robert J., 19
33. Niskern, Aaron, 27
34. Quinn, John, 26
35. Read, William H., 22
36. Robinson, Thomas E., 21
37. Robinson, Vincent G., 22
38. Sawyers, Frank, 18
39. Sawyers, Robert F., 18
40. Schroeder, Antoine, 19
41. Sellers, Stephen S., 19
42. Shatte (?), John, 24
43. Smith, Henry J., 26 (killed at Valverde)
44. Smith, William H., 21
45. Sutton, Wesley, 40
46. (Illegible)
47. (Illegible)
48. (Illegible)
49. Townsend, Jack, 18
50. Vincent, Powell P., 20
51. Votaw (?), Landon J., 28
52. Wells, John J., 18
53. Wesson, Thomas S., 27
54. Willard, Stephen J., 18
55. Woodford, William, 21
56. Wool, William T., 19
57. Yarborough, Thomas S., 21

COMPANY K
(As of October 23, 1861)
Mustered in Parker County

Charles L. Jordan, Captain, 26

John W. Squyne, First Lieutenant, 32

Isaac Roach, Second Lieutenant, 27

James F. Cole, Second Lieutenant, 27

William T. (Illegible), First Sergeant, 36

James R. Dean, Second Sergeant, 21

De Kalb Fordson (?), Third Sergeant, 22

John Foster, Fourth Sergeant, 20

E. S. R. Patton, Fifth Sergeant, 57

Edwan A. Leach, First Corporal, 17
Samuel E. Layne, Second Corporal, 20
William M. Mulkin, Third Corporal, 19
Austin Fox, Fourth Corporal, 19
S. Bectfield (?), (?), 24
B——(Illegible) Washington, (?), 18
Gus D. Anderson, Blacksmith, 20

PRIVATES:

1. Baker, J. U. S., 30
2. Barns (?), Peter, 18
3. Brown, Eli P., 26
4. Bumgarner, William J., 22
5. Burrows, John Henry, 22
6. Cornett (?), Granville, 26
7. Cross, James M., 18
8. Crum (?), George, 35
9. Davis, Edward B., 21
10. Dean, Levi, 23
11. Edwards, C. C., 21
12. Fossdren (?), S., 21
13. Fox, John J., 26
14. Gilpin, J. K., 23
15. Hardin, Ambrose, 29
16. Hill, James C., 22
17. Hogsett (?), John Henry (?), 18 (wounded at Valverde)
18. Holly, Isaac C., 21
19. Jones, G. D., 23
20. Jones, James Cincinnatus, 20
21. Kent, Smith, 27 (?)
22. Kern, J. Mike, 22
23. Lambert, J. H., 24
24. Lancaster, Newton, 24
25. Lee, John, 19
26. Littlepage, James J., 27 (?) (wounded at Valverde)
27. Long, A. B., 22
28. Martin, E. B., 20 (mortally wounded at Valverde)
29. Massey, E. J., 24
30. McCowin (?), William, 23
31. Moore, James C., 19
32. Patillo, J. W. (?), 18
33. Rader, J. W. (?), 31
34. Radick, D. C., 23
35. Ribble, H. W., 18
36. Robinson, Albert M., 24
37. Shelby (?), M. V. D., 24
38. Sisk, H. S., 22 (wounded at Valverde)
39. Smith, Sam H., 19
40. Smothers, G. S., 17
41. Smothers, G. W., 19
42. Smothers, John, 18
43. Stradley, J. H., 21
44. Watson, John M., 25
45. White, John, 23
46. Wilkins, Sam N., 23
47. Wilson, John, 18

Casualty Not on Muster Roll
1. Shurley, W. U. S. (mortally wounded at Valverde, according to Noel; may be Shelby (?), M. V. D. on muster roll)

SEVENTH REGIMENT
Texas Mounted Volunteers (Cavalry)

FIELD AND STAFF
(As of November, 1861)

William Steele, Colonel, 41 (promoted to brigadier general April 4, 1862)
John Schuyler Sutton, Lieutenant Colonel, 40 (killed at Valverde)
Arthur P. Bagby, Major, 28 (promoted to lieutenant colonel April 4, 1862)
T. C. Howard, Adjutant,—
W. L. Ogden, Assistant Quartermaster,—
A. R. Lee, Assistant Commissary,—
J. M. Ferguson, Sergeant Major,—
George Cupples, Surgeon, 45
J. W. Cunningham, First Assistant Surgeon,—
T. B. Greenwood, Second Assistant Surgeon,—
No Chaplain

COMPANY A
(As of October 4, 1861)
Mustered in Parker County

Powhatan Jordan, Captain, 33 (promoted to major February 21, 1862)

Alfred S. Thurmond, First Lieutenant, 46 (promoted to captain after Valverde)

James C. Burke, Second Lieutenant, 37

Henry H. McGrew, Second Lieutenant, 24

J. Ash Dowden, First Sergeant, 28

Samuel Johnson, Second Sergeant, 21

Samuel Kinney, Third Sergeant, 19

Charles Bostwick, Fourth Sergeant, 30

James C. George, First Corporal, 29

(No name entered for Second Corporal)

Thomas J. Hill, Third Corporal, 19

William C. Frazier, Fourth Corporal, 26

E. J. Hobgood, Bugler, 40

Peter Edwards, Farrier, 27

F. H. Graham, Blacksmith, 25

PRIVATES:

1. Ballard, Charles, 22
2. Caffy, C. J., 24
3. Campbell, Ed. B., 21
4. Carruthers, George, 21
5. Clarkson, Robert D., 27
6. Cody, John W., 30
7. Crawford, J. C., 21
8. Crawford, M., 19
9. Crews, Thomas, 25
10. Crisp, James M., 30
11. Duke, Stephen, 18
12. Ferguson, James, 22
13. Gillespie, R. H., 18
14. Goodrich, H. R., 28
15. Graham, George (?), 27
16. Gunter, George C., 21
17. Harrison, B. L., 25
18. Harrison, Charles A., 25
19. Hayden, Selden, 30
20. Hews, E. N., 24
21. Hogan, James M., 22
22. Howe (?), Thomas B., 25
23. Huff, George, 19
24. Huff, Jerome, 18
25. Huff, R. F., 24
26. Hunteen, James, 23
27. Mason, Will, 42
28. Mayfield, George, 18

29. Millender, J. E., 19
30. Miller, George E., 25
31. Moore, William A., 19
32. Moreau, George W., 27
33. Neal, Arthur H., 19
34. Newsom, Frank J., 18
35. Patton, Charles A., 22
36. Romley, Peter F., 30
37. Scanthse (?), F. M., 20
38. Scott, Charles R., 18
39. Shannon, L. F.,—
40. Smith, Levi, 21
41. Sutter, Joshua,—
42. Tarver, Jack, 18
43. Thedford, E., 20
44. Thedford, D. G., 19
45. Williams, William H., 21
46. Young, Thomas G., 18

*COMPANY B***
This muster roll is extremely faded. This, plus the fact that the names are German, accounts for the number of doubtful spellings and possible errors. (As of October 8, 1861)
Mustered in Comal County

Gustav Hoffmann, Captain, 42 (promoted to major December 21, 1862)

S——(Illegible) Schwarzhoff, First Lieutenant, 45

Charles Conrads (?), Second Lieutenant, 39

H. Weichold (?), Second Lieutenant, 42

Herrmann Gelven, First Sergeant, 28

Stephen Harbach, Second Sergeant, 26 (killed at Glorieta)

Charles Hasenbeck, Third Sergeant, 40 (wounded at Glorieta)

Julius Platz (?), Fourth Sergeant, 21

Julius Eggeling (?), Fifth Sergeant, 44

Henry Sappel, First Corporal, 20

F. W. Philippe, Second Corporal, 25

Henry Jonas (?), Third Corporal, 21

Henry Schaefer, Fourth Corporal, 18

Fredrich Müller, First Bugler, 37

F. Schleicher, Second Bugler, 22

Ferdinand Blume, Blacksmith, 35

PRIVATES:

1. Aening (?), Otto, 20
2. Bratze (?), Fredrich, 18
3. (Part of roll missing)
4. (Part of roll missing)
5. Fenske, George, —
6. Gelven, Adolph, — (wounded at Valverde)
7. Gotthardt, G., —
8. Haas, W. P., 18
9. Habermann (?), August, — (killed at Glorieta)
10. Halm, Charles, 21
11. Harm (?), F., 18 (wounded at Valverde)
12. Hein, Ferdinand, 26
13. Heintz, Otto, 19
14. Hurtwig (?), Fredrich, 26
15. Kaubact (?), Fredrich, 24
16. Kimpel, Peter, 25
17. Kremer, John, 22
18. Levebee (?), William, 28
19. Linnartz, P. J., 22
20. Linnartz, Peter, 47
21. Lüders, Fredrich, 45
22. Marckesardt (?), John, 26
23. Meier, August, 26
24. Meier, Ch., 28
25. Mergenthal (?), John, 27
26. Mergenthal (?), William, 25
27. Moos, Kasper, 18 (one slightly wounded at Glorieta)
28. Moos, Robert, 26
29. Nitsche, Charles, 20 (killed at Valverde)
30. Panthermuhl, C., 23
31. Panthermuhl, J., 30
32. Penishorn (?), Jn., 20 (Spelled Penhom in newspaper; slightly wounded at Glorieta)
33. Ransom, James, 22
34. Rheinlander, Charles, 30
35. Salerm (?), Adolph, 20
36. Schiel, Robert, 21
37. Schiel, William, 19
38. Schmidt, William, 24
39. Schmith, Martin, 25
40. Schonemann (?), Charles, 21
41. Schuhl, Jacob, 22
42. Schulz, Fr., 20
43. Schumann, Fritz, 21
44. Schütz, Charles, 22
45. Simon, Sylvester, 20
46. Simon, William, 20
47. Smith, John, 22
48. Stratemann, Charles, 22
49. Waldschmidt, Phil, 22
50. Weber, Conrad, —
51. Weyel (?), Adolph, 21
52. Weyel (?), John, 23
53. Wicke, Christian, —
54. Wiedmer, Henry, 18
55. Willmann, Herrmann, 20
56. Worf, Peter, —

Casualty Not on Muster Roll

1. Reidel, Frank (mortally wounded at Glorieta)

COMPANY C—"Williamson Grays"
(As of October 24, 1861)
Mustered in Williamson County

H. M. Burrows, Captain, 39
John C. Robinson, First Lieutenant, 21
John F. Snyder, Second Lieutenant, 23
James F. Lewis, Second Lieutenant, 22
G. D. Lacy, Ordnance Sergeant, 29
Abe McMurdie, Quartermaster Sergeant, 23
Thomas Thomason, Sergeant, 20
W. J. Gunn, Sergeant, 18
G. W. Miller, Sergeant, 21
Thomas D. Holliday, Corporal, 26
H. B. Elliott, Corporal, 21
B. L. Werst, Corporal, 26
L. Forbion (?), Corporal, 18
O. E. Ward, Bugler, 18
John Graham, Bugler, 25

PRIVATES:

1. Allen, Travis, 22
2. Anderson, G. W., 18
3. Bower, W. H. C., 18
4. Branch, J. W., 19
5. Bratton, W. H., 25

6. Bridges, J. L., 21
7. Brooks, E., 18
8. Chick, R. M., 23
9. Clinton, J. H., 22
10. Clinton, T. J., 19
11. Cluck, Joseph J., 25
12. Collier, L. H., 25
13. Davis, John R., 18
14. Edwards, Leonard, 18
15. Elkins, H. D., 27
16. Ellington, George, 25
17. Hail, John, 20
18. Inman, Marion, 27
19. Iuvenall (?), Ben, 18
20. Iuvenall (?), Josiah, 20
21. Kirk, H. N., 18
22. Krampkan, O. M., 23
23. Lewis, Samuel, 21
24. McNutt, H. W., 22
25. Morrison, F. M., 21
26. Morrison, J. C., 20
27. Nowack, John, 22
28. Organ, Sterling, 25
29. Rodgers, Lafayette, 18
30. Seaward, T. H., 23
31. Sellers, Ben, 24
32. Sellers, W. F., 18
33. Snyder, S. E., 20
34. Soublett (?), J. G., 28
35. Standifer, D. T., 20
36. Thaxton, T. B., 18
37. Tucker, J. M., 18
38. Welch, Mike, 26
39. Willis, John, 18
40. Wolfpin (?), C. W., 18
41. Woodall, Thomas, 18

COMPANY D
(As of October 24, 1861)
Mustered in Angelina County

William H. Cleaver, Captain, 25
A. L. Hudiburgh, First Lieutenant, 43
H. A. Parton, Second Lieutenant, 28
G. W. Eaton, Second Lieutenant, 56
Charles Pate, Ordnance Sergeant, 57
M. Cushman, Quartermaster Sergeant, 23

John J. Spears (?), Sergeant, 29
Samuel Brown, Sergeant, 25
S. M. Tucker, Sergeant, 37
S. Hudiburgh, Corporal, 18
R. W. Thompson, Corporal, 25
A. Hutchinson, Corporal, 25
Samuel S. Page, Corporal, 27
W. C. Spears, Bugler, 22

PRIVATES:
1. Alexander, B. H., 41
2. Alexander, John, 19
3. Allen, W. P., 19
4. Baxter, (Illegible), 25
5. Brash — — (Illegible), 21
6. Bras — — (Illegible), 21
7. (Illegible)
8. Brewer, B. W., 40
9. (Illegible)
10. (Illegible), 39
11. (Illegible)
12. (Illegible), 22
13. Cour — — (Illegible), 19
14. Clay — — (Illegible), 23
15. Cole, T — —, 18
16. Collins, G. (?), 21
17. Daniels, E. R., 28
18. Davis, W. H., 26
19. Elliott, J., 22
20. Fairchild, A., 20
21. Finley, L., 19
22. Forrest, James, 21
23. Fuller, B. J., 26
24. Haley, Thomas, 22
25. Herron (?), J., 18
26. Herron (?), S. L., 18
27. Jones, C., 30
28. Jones, J., 18
29. Jones, J. C., 21
30. Jones, J. H., 40
31. Kirkwood, James, 26
32. Latta, A., 32
33. Lee, W. H., 25
34. Lindsay, W. G., 19
35. Marler, G. W., 25
36. Maulden, (?), 24
37. Maulden, G., 23
38. McInnis, J. G., 19

39. McInnis, S. P., 22
40. McMullen, E. (?), 18
41. Middleton, (?), 40
42. Moore, J. B., 30
43. Nelson, James, 31
44. Nemen, B. F., 22
45. Neyland, J. (?), 23
46. Oates, J. W., 20
47. Perkins, John, 23
48. Phillips, J. S., 18
49. Phillips, W. (?), 24
50. Pratt, W. D., 18
51. Renfro, J. D., 22
52. Rush, Charles A., 22
53. Scott, J. W., 53
54. Smith, W. H., 19
55. Spivey, G. M., 28
56. Standard, W. H., 22
57. Sterne, Sal, 29
58. Stringer, J. J., 23
59. Tubervil— —(Illegible), 23
60. Weeks, J. (?), 26
61. W— —(Illegible), 18

COMPANY E
(As of October 23, 1861)
Mustered in Trinity County

W. L. Kirksey, Captain, 32
G. F. Tullos, First Lieutenant, 26
C. T. Chandler, Second Lieutenant, 35
J. O. Hesless, Second Lieutenant, 36
W. T. Davis, Ordnance Sergeant, 32
D. T. Wagnon (?), Quartermaster
    Sergeant, 24
W. T. Morgan, Sergeant, 29
A. R. Faglie (?), Sergeant, 31
J. D. Turner, Sergeant, 28
G. M. Hill, Corporal, 21
H. H. Womack, Corporal, 19
F. S. Wagnon (?), Corporal, 19
J. A. Oaks, Corporal, 29
W. B. Mathis, Bugler, 31
J. P. Mangum, Bugler, 38

PRIVATES:
  1. Albrittan, (no first name listed), 18
  2. Bertram, W., 32
  3. Blackshear (?), J. M., 22
  4. Brown, J. M., 23
  5. Caswell, S. H., 22
  6. Chandler, C. I., 26
  7. Chapman, G. S., 23
  8. Clark, B., 35
  9. Davis, B. S., 23
10. Davis, T. A.,—
11. Dunlap (?), W. F., 18
12. Dun— —(Illegible), J. R.,—
13. Durham, J., 27
14. Elliott, W. M., 20
15. Evans, C., 27
16. Faglie, T. C., 25
17. Fain, R. L., 20
18. Farley, F. F., 25
19. Farley, J. A., 31
20. Finch, John, 35
21. Ford, J. H., 19
22. Handley, W. J., 22
23. Harris, F., 18
24. Hashaw, G. W., 35
25. Hilliard, J. M., 43
26. Hodges, J. H., 20
27. Hodges, W. C., 21
28. Hutto, W. J., 23
29. Jones, L. J., 33
30. Lancaster, George W., 24
31. Linam, W. J., 22
32. Madden, J. C., 33
33. McClendon, H. M., 23
34. McClendon, T. B., 21
35. Moore, A. H., 24
36. Moore, L., 22
37. Moore, J. P., 18
38. Moore, P. W., 20
39. Mullins, B. F., 23
40. Oglesby, J. C., 18
41. Pate, John, 46
42. Peterson, A. J., 22
43. Phipps, T. H., 18
44. Ricks, J. L., 24
45. Scott, P. D., 33
46. Sims, E., 27
47. Tennison, W. H., 19
48. Thornton, R. M., 30
49. Townsend, A., 20

50. Tullos, J. B., 20
51. Tullos, W. J., 23
52. Tyler, W. W., 25
53. Walse, F., 21
54. Wiley, W., 18
55. Wilson, John, 23
56. Wood, T., 19

COMPANY F
(As of October 26, 1861)
Mustered in Rusk County

J. F. Wiggins, Captain, 37
J. W. Gray, First Lieutenant, 41
   (wounded at Valverde)
A. P. Goldsberry, Second Lieutenant, 41
W. C. Wiggins, Second Lieutenant, 28
   (wounded at Valverde)
W. Wren, Ordnance Sergeant, 34
F. M. Elkins, Quartermaster Sergeant,
   30 (wounded at Valverde)
P. H. Johnson, Sergeant, 23
M. Mays, Sergeant, 20
S. D. Montgomery, Sergeant, 23
   (promoted to lieutenant; wounded
   at Valverde)
S. S. Hiller (?), Corporal, 44
A. W. Prather, Corporal, 24 (mortally
   wounded at Valverde)
A. E. Payne, Corporal, 26
Thomas Garrason, Corporal, 43 (died
   in Socorro of wounds received at
   Valverde)

PRIVATES:
1. Airheart, H. T., 18
2. Baker, J. C. C., 18
3. Baker, W. S., 21
4. Bates, L. C., 22
5. Bates, W. L., 22
6. Bradshaw, R. B., 18 (mortally
   wounded at Valverde)
7. Bradshaw, (?). T. F., 21
8. (Illegible)
9. Cook, C. W., 23
10. Cook (?), J. W., 2—
11. Crews, T. C., 18 (wounded at
   Valverde)

12. Crews, (?), 24
13. Dial, L. J., 23 (wounded at
   Valverde)
14. Dotson, James M., 21
15. Featherston, S. T., 28
16. Few, J. S., 20
17. Garrason, D. W., 19
18. Garrett, George D., 18
19. Garrett, William H., 19
20. Garrett, William T., 20
21. Gill, J. C., 22
22. Goldsberry, R., 18
23. Gordon, Charles A., 18
24. Graham, W. L., 25
25. Green, W. H., 18
26. Greenway, J. W., 25
27. Harman, James D., 20
28. Harris, James, 27 (died in Socorro
   of wounds received at Valverde)
29. Hays, J. O., 33
30. Heflin, M. H., 18
31. Heflin, R. A., 24 (wounded at
   Glorieta)
32. Hicks, C. M., 26
33. Higginbotham, Charles, 27
34. Higginbotham, O., 27
35. Higginbotham, William, 23
36. Hiller (?), Nathaniel, 32 (wounded
   at Glorieta)
37. Jay, C. P., 20
38. Johnson, John H., 18
39. Johnson, H. F., 18 (wounded at
   Glorieta)
40. Jones, James M., 18
41. Jones, W. H. H., 20 (wounded at
   Glorieta)
42. Keahey, D. B., 23
43. Kendrick, J. T., 28 (wounded at
   Valverde)
44. Knight, L. M., 18
45. Landrum, James Z., 18
46. Loftis, George W., 20
47. Loftis, N. L., 22
48. May, H. M., 22
49. Mays, Byrd, 24
50. McCrummon (?), D. H., 21
51. McDowell, T. R., 26

52. McMillen, W. F., 18
53. Moore, S. M., 22
54. Nelson, R. W., 25
55. Nelson, Samuel, 23
56. Newsom, W., 22
57. Preston, John R., 25
58. Pruitt, J. M., 20 (wounded at Valverde)
59. Quaid, B. W., 23 (wounded at Valverde)
60. Reagan, N. M., 22
61. Reynolds, A. J., 28
62. Richardson, E. E., 20
63. Richardson, J. H., 18 (?)
64. Richey, B. A., 23 (killed at Valverde)
65. Richey, R. E., 22
66. Roberts, W. G., 24
67. Row, John, —
68. Seay, R. T., 18
69. Sharp, D. (?)., 18 (wounded at Valverde)
70. Summers, J. M., 19
71. Tipton, J. C., 24
72. Wells, Michael, 23
73. Wells, W. W., 25
74. Whitley, S. R., 23
75. Windsor, Jacob, 33
76. Woodmand, P. D., 23

COMPANY G
(As of October 28, 1861)
Mustered in Walker County

H. W. Fisher, Captain, 34
William Hobday (?), First Lieutenant, —
H. H. Lee, Second Lieutenant, 35
John M. Scott, Second Lieutenant, 21
B. D. Sessums (?), Ordnance Sergeant, 25
James King, Quartermaster Sergeant, 36
W. T. Curling, Sergeant, 27
John Tankersley, Sergeant, 27
William Haskins, Sergeant, 27
Lewis Lee, Corporal, 23
A. W. Yates, Corporal, 25
J. B. Cunningham, Corporal, 23
E. F. Owens, Corporal, 31

PRIVATES:
1. Baird, A. M., 27 (?)
2. Barrett, W. R., 18
3. Beechum, E. Ray V., 20
4. Beechum, G. M., 18
5. Bets, M., 20
6. Brazier, W. H., 21
7. Bridges, E. J., 21
8. Burden, George, 20
9. Burk, L. Y., 21
10. Burk, Lee, 27
11. Burk, Nathan, 20
12. Caldwell, (?). J., 26
13. Carter, E., 28
14. Cates, B. F., 23
15. Chesher, James, 18
16. Clark, E. A., 39
17. Collard, F. R., 18
18. Cude, J. H., 22
19. Cunningham, W. A., 20
20. Drew, Samuel, 18
21. Elisor, H. S., 18
22. Elisor, N. T., 29
23. Hardy, H. F., 20
24. Hardy, W. S., 19
25. Haskins, A. C., 21
26. King, Alf., 24
27. King, Mike, 31
28. King, Nathan, 19
29. King, Robert, 27
30. King, Smalley (?), 21
31. Knight, Calvin, 25
32. Knight, John, 24
33. Jones, A. T., 18
34. Jones, T. A., 22
35. Lagrone, James, 28
36. Lee, C. W., 18
37. Lee, J. S., 24
38. Lindley, J. W., 18
39. Little, William, 20
40. Malone, B. S., 21
41. May, David, 26
42. McKibben, J. W., 20
43. Murrah, Newton, 24
44. O'Neil, J. R., 28
45. Palmer, W. R., 18
46. Parker, James, 33
47. Perry, C. W., 23

48. Powell, F. W., 20
49. Powell, T. J., 22
50. Purseley, John, 21
51. Robin, W., 26
52. Robinson, Jesse, 21
53. Sanders, John, 20
54. Seals, W. J., 18
55. Sessums, George, 21
56. Sessums, Peter, 22
57. Shephard, Robert, 20
58. Shoock, J. D., 18
59. Taylor, J. C., 25
60. Weatherby, T. J., 23
61. Wells, J., 28
62. Wells, John, 19
63. Wells, R. J., 18
64. Willet, John, 20
65. Williams, Daniel, 18
66. Williams, F. H., 23
67. Williams, J. A., 18
68. Williams, J. H., 18
69. Wintor (?), Sherman, 22

COMPANY H

(As of October 28, 1861)
Mustered in Houston County

Isaac Adair, Captain, 55 (mortally wounded at Glorieta)
Charles O. Haley, First Lieutenant, 41
B. B. Arrington, Second Lieutenant, 28
James M. Daniels, Second Lieutenant, 38
William Miller, Ordnance Sergeant, 45
W. S. M. Morris, Quartermaster Sergeant, 33
J. M. Davis, Sergeant, 30
J. M. Rabun (?), Sergeant, 27
J. M. Porter, Sergeant, 26
Henry McKenzie, Corporal, 19
R. J. George, Corporal, 32
Asa McKenzie, Corporal, 23
A. J. Saxon, Corporal, 22
G. N. Taylor, Bugler, 42 (killed at Glorieta)
Silas Lags (?), Bugler, 21

PRIVATES:

1. Allen, A. M., 34
2. Avery, T. G., 37
3. Booker, James, 18
4. Booker, William, 20 (killed at Glorieta)
5. Brian (?), William, 18
6. Bruton, Samuel, 23
7. Bruton, Silas, 21
8. Buson, John, 19
9. Calhun, G. M., 18
10. Caraway, B. N., 24
11. Carlton, W. A., 25
12. Cartwright, Thomas, 34
13. Castrin (?), C. C., 23
14. Cobb, Henry P., 25 (wounded at Glorieta)
15. Davis, W. W., 30
16. Dickey, D. H., 21
17. Dickey, J. P. T., 23
18. Dickey, M. A., 22
19. Dupree, S. J., 26
20. Fitzgerald, M., 21
21. Flores, V., 26
22. Gibson, J. H., 23
23. Hail, George, 22
24. Hail, James, 33
25. Hail, Peter, 18 (killed at Glorieta)
26. Harris, Hugh, 21
27. Harris, L. H., 24
28. Hart, J. J., 18
29. Hatton, N. J., 29
30. Hennis (?), George, 22
31. Herrod, W. S., 21
32. Herrod, William, 20
33. Hestor, A. P., 21
34. Hestor, J. H., 27
35. Hill, Edmond, 19
36. Johnson, J. H., 19
37. Johnson, Nathaniel, 35
38. Keneday, J. A., 49
39. Kenneday, J. H., 23
40. Kenneday, S. E., 52
41. Kirk, Patrick J., 18
42. Leatherwood, W. P., 37
43. Lough, Hugh, 32
44. Lusk, George, 18
45. Mahomey, John, 23
46. Mason, Oliver, 49
47. McGuire, J. T., 22
48. Murchison, John, 18

49. Murchison, John W., 23
50. Nail, A. B., 19
51. Owens, J. A., 18
52. Payne, P. B., 30
53. Peacock, George W., 21
54. Pool, J. H., 20
55. Powell, G. W., 21
56. Renfro, W. C., 24
57. Richards, H. R., 26
58. Sansome, William M., 21
59. Saxon, B. F., 27
60. Saxon, J. W., 20
61. Scarborough, William, 23
62. Scott, William W., 25
63. Shiflett, J. G. W., 23
64. Shiflett, W., 18
65. Stone, W. D., 28 (?)
66. Stovall, S. M., 22
67. Walker, George, 20
68. Walker, R. P., 18 (killed at Glorieta)
69. Walker, W. M., 22
70. White, J. D., 18
71. Whitley, N. B., 19
72. Wiggins, G., 19
73. Wiggins, John, 19

Casualties Not on Muster Roll
1. Cone, Robert (mortally wounded at Valverde, according to Noel)
2. Tucker, J. G. (mortally wounded at Valverde, according to Noel)

COMPANY I
(As of November 1, 1861)
Mustered in Anderson County

James W. Gardner, Captain, 41 (wounded at Valverde)
William B. Key, First Lieutenant, 33
John W. Taylor, Second Lieutenant, 32
Charles H. Mills, Second Lieutenant, 33 (killed at Glorieta)
Jacob W. Moore, Ordnance Sergeant, 46
Robert W. Willett, Quartermaster Sergeant, 36
C. C. Horn, Sergeant, 36
B. F. Broyles, Sergeant, 26
J. W. K. Bryan, Sergeant, 31
John W. Barnett, Corporal, 43

(wounded at Valverde)
N. A. Glenn, Corporal, 23
William Langston, Corporal, 19 (killed at Glorieta)
W. T. Miller, Corporal, 23
T. W. Brooks, Bugler, 47
S. J. Hill, Bugler, 21
Perry Holliman, Farrier, 27 (wounded at Valverde)

PRIVATES:
1. Alexander, J. H., 27 (wounded at Valverde)
2. Aspley (?), L. G., 35
3. Barnett, G. D., 18
4. Barnett, John, 18
5. Bishop, John, 24
6. Bowen, F., 18
7. Box (?), J. J., 18
8. Cohen, J. O., 34 (?)
9. Cone, Robert, 18 (wounded at Valverde)
10. Crist, W. H., 19
11. Davis, D. T., 18
12. Day, James E., 18
13. Deller, William P., 18
14. Dial, J. J., 19
15. Drinkard, Allen, 24
16. Duke, Albert, 18
17. Ferguson, J. J., 22
18. Ferguson, John F., 18
19. Fitzhugh, D. H., 23
20. Fowler, N. G., 18
21. Garner, H. F., 24
22. Garner, J. P., 22
23. Garner, William A., 20
24. Goanes (?), John M., 44
25. Goezorg (?), Lemuel, 36
26. Hamilton, R. D., 20
27. Haynes, John, 19
28. Hightower, A. G., 23
29. Hogue, John M., 19
30. Hudson, J. J., 22
31. Hudson, R., 19
32. Hunter, J. D. C., 18
33. Hunter, H. J., 24 (a surgeon; promoted to assistant surgeon March 10, 1862)

34. Jackson, T. E., 18
35. Jones, Jasper N., 19 (died in Socorro of wounds received at Valverde)
36. Kennedy, Thomas, 19 (wounded at Valverde)
37. Kyle, Henry, 18
38. Lyles, Joseph H., 22 (wounded at Valverde)
39. Malone, William H., 19
40. Mason, M. L., 27
41. McKenzie, L. C., 24
42. McMorris, B. F., 22
43. Mead, William M., 27
44. Miller, J. T., 19
45. Murdock (?), J. A. W., 18
46. Oldham, P. J., 20
47. Pace, C. D., 18
48. Palmer, Levi, 20
49. Parker, J. M., 32
50. Rainey, John B., 22
51. Robertson, J. A., 22
52. Robertson, J. M., 30
53. Robinson, John D., 28
54. Robison, W. L., 25
55. Rodgers, J. V., 23
56. Roundtree, R. D., 21
57. Seigler, William P., 18
58. Self, James E., 24
59. Shelton, Thomas W., 30
60. Shelton, (Illegible)
61. Small, D. R., 18
62. Smith, James C., –4
63. Starr, D. P., 28
64. Stuart (?), Oliver, 25
65. Swearingen, Zach, 31
66. Talley, John T., 36
67. Taylor, F. B., 18
68. Tucker, J. B., 36 (wounded at Valverde)
69. Vaunoy, A. N., 23 (wounded at Valverde)
70. Watts, John W., 24
71. Williams, James A., 20
72. Wilson, James G., 21
73. Wilson, H. J., 27
74. Witcher, G. I., 18
75. Woolverton, James H., 22

76. Woolverton, William J., 20
77. Word, John J., 18
78. Yoe, (?). C., 20

COMPANY K
(As of November 15, 1861)
Mustered in Tarrant County

Thomas O. Moody, Captain, 40
L. G. A. Steele, First Lieutenant, 40
Isaac G. Bowman, Second Lieutenant, 41
J. P. Smith, Second Lieutenant, 29
J. C. Hancock, Ordnance Sergeant, 31
L. B. Chriswell, Quartermaster Sergeant, 45
N. S. Ewalt, Sergeant, 28
Nat Terry, Sergeant, 21
L. Wetmore, Sergeant, 33
William Turner, Corporal, 18
J. B. Haynil (?), Corporal, 30
John F. (Illegible), Corporal, 19
(Illegible), Corporal, 42

PRIVATES:
1. Baker, Alexander, 21
2. Beale, W. D., 33
3. Beale, William, 36
4. Belew, H., 18
5. Belostri, Lewis, 27
6. Bersey (?), J. (?)., 18
7. Burnett, L. D., 31
8. Burnett, M. B., 20
9. Byers, Thomas, 18
10. Campbell, (?). C., 27
11. Campbell, (Illegible)
12. Chriswell, C., 18
13. Chriswell, William, 18
14. Courson, Simeon, 18
15. Crocker, E. W., 24
16. Crocker, J. (?)., 20
17. Crocker, W. P., 27
18. Daggett, E. B., 22
19. Deane, Thomas, 18
20. Dewess (?), J. W., 23
21. Dobkins, W. C., 20
22. Fields, Joseph, 21
23. Findland, W., 24

24. Gibson, Daniel, 30
25. Gilmore, (?), 20
26. Greer, J. F., 18
27. Grimes, H. D., 24
28. Hancock, L., 18
29. Heist, H., 28
30. Heurdt (?), T. B., 22
31. House, P. M., 28
32. Hughes, William, 23
33. Jackson, James, 18
34. King, L. C., 25
35. Mack, P., 23
36. Manning, T., 18
37. Martin, James D., 20
38. Mayhall, T., 41
39. Mays, R. K., 19
40. McClure, Jesse, 25
41. Miller, Charles, 37
42. Miller, J. W., 23
43. Moore, J. D., 28
44. Morril, C. J., 21
45. Neace, J. R., 23
46. Panier, E., 31
47. Pate, B. L., 27
48. Penfold, J., 26
49. Pettigew, W. J., 20
50. Preston, J. R., 20
51. Preston, W. R., 22
52. Read, Reuben, 24
53. Rodgers, W. D., 28
54. Roland, F. D., 22
55. Ross, W. D., 35
56. Roy, A. H., 23
57. Sanderson, G. B., 19
58. Smith, Guilford, 23
59. Story (?), H. H., 20
60. Sullivan, Nathan, 30
61. Summor, J. B., 19
62. Teague, C. B., 21
63. Terry, W. J., 24
64. (Illegible), 23
65. Thomas, W. (?)., 19
66. Vickery, L. G., 32
67. White, B. F., 25
68. Wilson, Orlando, 30
69. Young, A. F., 26

BAYLOR'S COMMAND
Second Regiment Texas Mounted Rifles

John R. Baylor, Lieutenant Colonel
    Commanding, 39
Edwin Waller, Jr., Major, —

COMPANY A
(As of October 31, 1861)
Mustered in the Counties of Anderson,
Cherokee, Houston, and Nacogdoches**
According to a postwar statement of a
member of the company. The muster roll
lists Rusk, Cherokee County, as the place
where the company was sworn in.

Peter Hardeman, Captain, 30
John T. Aycock, First Lieutenant, 31
Marshall Glenn, Second Lieutenant, 24
Malcolm K. Hunter, Second
    Lieutenant, 23
Nat W. Hunter, First Sergeant, 21
Richard J. Johnson, Second Sergeant, 25
William M. Payne, Third Sergeant, 25
Charles A. Shanks, Fourth Sergeant, 28
William P. McHenry, First Corporal, 21
Nathaniel G. Witherspoon, Second
    Corporal, 21
Andrew Thompson, Third Corporal, 24
William H. Ezell, Fourth Corporal, 19
Benjamin F. Frymier, Bugler, 22

PRIVATES:
1. Alford, Albert N., 19
2. Armstrong, William A. D., 25
3. Arnold, Stephen J., 22
4. Beeson, Argyle, 22
5. Blackshear, Rufus K., 25
6. Bonner, J. H., 19
7. Bowers, John E., 19
8. Box, Frank S., 18
9. Box, Stephen W., 21
10. Broom, Augustus C., 18
11. Burton, John, 20
12. Bush, Elkanah, 26
13. Camp, Thomas L., 25
14. Cannon, Robert T., 25
15. Cessna, Waller G., 28
16. Coals, Claudius C., 21

17. Collins, Samuel, 17
18. Copeland, John M., 20
19. Cox, Leroy A., 43
20. Crooms, John W., 25
21. Cruce, Stephen, 25
22. Davenport, Thomas E., 22
23. Dean, Robert W., 24
24. Derden, Stephen M., 21
25. Dernnica (?), Thomas K., 19
26. Donahoo, James M., 20
27. Dorsey, William F., 20
28. Dossett, Felix E., 21
29. Duke, Napoleon B., 19
30. Edmiston, Frank, 19
31. Ford, Andrew W., 43
32. Graves, Peyton S., —
33. Graves, Peyton S., Jr., 19
34. Green, Samuel, 18
35. Hamilton, Campbell, 22
36. Hardaway, G. W., 20
37. Harris, Jerome B., 22
38. Harris, Junius B., 21
39. Hatchett, William W., 25
40. Heth, John W., 18
41. Hubert, Henry C., 25
42. Huntsman, Adam, 32
43. Hurt, Charles W., 18
44. Hyde, William F., 36
45. Jackson, Robert M., 19
46. Jones, Jesse R., 25
47. Joyce, William J., 32
48. King, James C., 19
49. King, William A., 21
50. King, William F., 23
51. Kirk, John C., 24
52. Kyle, James M., 20
53. Langston, James, 21
54. Lee, William F., 20
55. Lee, (no first name listed), 30
56. Lewis, Dabney W., 21
57. Logan, Abel C., 27
58. Logan, John S., 20
59. Long, Green H., 22
60. Looscan, Michael, 22
61. Macgill, William D., 23
62. Mallard, Mark M., 16
63. Margraves, John M., 24
64. Marlon, William F., 28

65. McClure, Robert, 20
66. McHenry, Thomas L., 26
67. McKellar, John, 44
68. Millican, Ira, 19
69. Moore, M. D., —
70. Moseley, William, 20
71. Mynatt, Hillsman S., 23
72. Ninnson, George T., 24
73. Ozment, John, 17
74. Perry, William H., 18
75. Prewitt, George T., 21
76. Quarles, Cara M., 17
77. Raines, Johnathan P., 19
78. Roscoe, Gabriel, 31
79. Rose, William B., 25
80. Sauks (?), John A., 31
81. Simpson, Thomas L., 18
82. Skelton, Pinck, 15
83. Sloan, Andrew J., 22
84. Spivey, John W., 31
85. Stribling, Thomas B., 24
86. Taylor, Charles I., 23
87. Taylor, Milam, 22
88. Tredwell, Egbert A., 26
89. Tucker, James William, 24
90. Vest, J. T., 24
91. Vinson, Henry H., 21
92. Webster, Albert, 25
93. Welch, William S., 25

COMPANY B
(As of May 23, 1861)
Mustered in Bexar County

Charles L. Pyron, Captain, 42
    (promoted to major)
William G. Jett, First Lieutenant, 40
David M. Poor, Second Lieutenant, 22
Thomas D. Reeves, Second Lieutenant,
    27
Sam B. Luckie, First Sergeant, 21
Franklin Cook, Second Sergeant, 25
Lorenzo Trevinia, Third Sergeant, 33
James Conly, Fourth Sergeant, 30
Thomas Bruce, First Corporal, 24
Lycurgus Small, Second Corporal, 26
Franklin Smith, Third Corporal, 21
Alex Pérez, Fourth Corporal, 26

John Day, Bugler, 35
Thomas Noland, Blacksmith, 35

PRIVATES:

1. Adams, Fitch S., 37
2. Baker, John C., 19
3. Barker, Sam J., 21
4. Beitle, Francis J., 22
5. Blanco, Santos, 27
6. Boyles, Noah, 18
7. Brown, Will J., 22 (probably transferred to Hunter's company; listed as Corporal William Brown on Hunter's roll)
8. Brownrigg, Junius, 37
9. Cárdenas, Juan, 18
10. Cárdenas, Rafael, 28
11. Carrabajal, Louis, 25
12. Carrillo, Joseph, 28
13. Carter, Henry A., 25
14. Cavillo, Pancho, 22
15. Chalderón, Ramón, 32
16. Cooper, George W., 36
17. Cortinas, José, 23
18. Dean, Jesse A., 23 (transferred to Hunter's company)
19. D——(illegible), William, 22
20. Duncan, Francis M., 38
21. Dunson, Erastus, 28
22. Durand, Macleto, 20
23. Dye, Benson A., 27
24. Flores, Pedro, 23
25. Flores, Salvador, 19
26. Garza, Estéban, 26
27. Garza, Jesús, 27
28. Gerloff, Andreas, 17
29. Guerrero, Félix, 30
30. Harris, Daniel A., 25
31. Hernández, José María, 28
32. Hernández, Mauricio, 31
33. Herrera, Francisco, 33
34. Hogan, Joseph L., 24
35. Howard, King L., 25
36. Hudson, Amos, 26 (transferred to Hunter's company)
37. Hutchinson, Will C., 26
38. Johnson, Charles S., 25
39. Kuhfus, Edward, 24

40. Lackly, James W., 23
41. Lamberd, Joshua K., 18
42. Lane, Wesley C., 21
43. Langley, Marion J., 22
44. Leal, Alfonso, 30
45. Martínez, Jesús, 28
46. McClelland, Joseph P., 20 (transferred to Hunter's company)
47. Menchaca, Bernaret, 25
48. Montes, Anchacio, 22
49. Murphy, James W., 23
50. Navarro, Sexton, 28
51. Newcomb, John G., 22
52. Ogden, John, 19
53. O'Grady, Robert J., 22
54. O'Neil, James R., 21 (transferred to Hunter's company)
55. Olivari, Paulo, 29
56. Pérez, (?), 23
57. Perryman, W. W., 19
58. Petmecky, Frank W., 27
59. Reitzer, Joseph, 24
60. Rivas, Andalacio, 28
61. Rivas, Frederico, 25
62. Robertson, Frank G., 20
63. Robinson, William, 28
64. Rodriques, José, 32
65. Rodriques, Miguel, 23
66. Rutledge, Jefferson J., 29
67. Rutledge, Will, 25
68. Sierra, Juan, 30
69. Stephanes, Henry F., 19
70. Thomas, Griffin T., 25
71. Tremble, Fred W., 21
72. Turner, Oliver J., 20

COMPANY D

(As of October 31, 1861)**
This company was actually formed months earlier. Troops were mustered periodically, and this is probably the second muster roll.
Mustered Principally from Lavaca County

James Walker, Captain, 45
John R. Pulliam, First Lieutenant, 20
William P. White, Second Lieutenant, 29

R. E. Mays, Second Lieutenant, 26
(killed by Indians, August 11, 1861)
James M. Francisco, First Sergeant, 22
J. B. Hawkins, Second Sergeant, 26
Hiram Brown, Third Sergeant, 22
John C. Brown, Fourth Sergeant, 20
B. F. Stell, Commissary Sergeant, 23
William H. Wheeler, First Corporal, 20
W. C. Jones, Second Corporal, 22
L. S. Jennings, Third Corporal, 24
James E. Harris, Fourth Corporal, 21
R. B. Nicholls, Bugler, 19

PRIVATES:

1. Allen, J. C., 41
2. Arnold, J. B., 45
3. Blackman, Carroll, 25
4. Bridgers, William L., 18
5. Brown, John C., 20 (killed by Indians August 11, 1861)
6. Buchanan, John, 18
7. Burke, Martin, 23
8. Byars, Joseph, 24
9. Campion, Ed. J., 18 (killed at Valverde)
10. Campion, Joseph, 23
11. Carroll, Thomas E., 25 (killed by Indians August 11, 1861)
12. Carroll, William G., 23
13. Cleghorn, John, 22 (severely wounded at Valverde)
14. Coffer, W. A., 19
15. Crowder, A. D., 25
16. Davis, D. H., —
17. Davis, S., —
18. DeBord, G. W., 18
19. DeBord, James, 23
20. DeBord, Jesse H., 19
21. Desper, Samuel K., 19 (killed by Indians August 11, 1861)
22. DeWolf, D., —
23. Drydan, Thomas H., 23
24. Embro, W. W., —
25. Emmanacker, Joseph, 25 (killed by Indians September 3, 1861)
26. Fatheree, James, 18
27. Fatheree, L. B., 22
28. Frazer, John W., 23
29. Freen, J. C., —
30. Glasscock, I. B., —
31. Graper, John H., 26
32. Hanks, Richard S., 22
33. Henderson, Henry, 22
34. Hume, William, 18
35. Jacobs, John, 25
36. Jetton, John C., 20
37. Jones, Camillus, 22
38. Jones, Cal., —
39. Kaufman, Louis, 21
40. Kelly, J. F., —
41. Koehler, Joseph, 25
42. Laughton, W. P., 21
43. Lee, B. F., 20
44. Lewis, Thomas, 19
45. Lockett, D. A., 30
46. Maclelendall, J., —
47. Major, A. C., 24
48. Mallick, L. P., 19
49. Mann, John F., 21
50. Martin, John O., 18
51. Martin, W. J., 21
52. May, John, 21
53. Mosse, Joseph V., 23 (killed by Indians September 3, 1861)
54. Newsom, W. L., —
55. Osgood, B. O., 19
56. Osgood, G. D., 30
57. Pater, J., —
58. Pemberton, Thomas G., 25 (killed by Indians September 3, 1861)
59. Perkins, Fred, 24 (killed by Indians August 11, 1861)
60. Ponton, Alexander, 18
61. Ponton, Joel, 19
62. Price, Thomas, 26
63. Priestly, E. L., 18
64. Sanders, Floyd A., —
65. Seeley, Thomas H., 18
66. Simpson, Jordan A., 18
67. Stephenson, Eli, —
68. Stroud, Irvin, 36
69. Tarkington, Ed., 20
70. Tate, Joel, 25
71. Thompson, E. S., 18
72. Thompson, W., —
73. Tittle, Archibald, 20

74. Tucker, Felix, 19
75. Turk, William H., 18
76. Turner, Fred, 23
77. Wafford, P. L., 19
78. Walker, C. W., 23
79. Walker, John S., 22 (killed by Indians August 11, 1861)
80. Waller, J., —
81. Willis, Manoah, 45
82. Young, D., —

COMPANY E
(As of May 23, 1861)
Mustered in Harris County

Isaac C. Stafford, Captain, 23
Richard B. Wilson, First Lieutenant, 25
William H. Lloyd, Second Lieutenant, 20
Benjamin W. Loveland, Second Lieutenant, 30
Leonidas M. Stacy, First Sergeant, 25
Peter S. Brown, Second Sergeant, 28
William H. Davis, Third Sergeant, 23
Albert I. Eldridge, Fourth Sergeant, 26
Joseph P. Ayers, First Corporal, 23
Joseph H. Byrd, Second Corporal, 22
William H. Voris, Third Corporal, 23
Julius W. Butler, Fourth Corporal, 23
David C. Miller, Surgeon, 27
Edward B. Reeves, Bugler, 26
Charles H. Langer, Farrier, 25
Butler Flemming, Blacksmith, 23

PRIVATES:
1. Angus, Alexander, 30
2. Barkley, William C., 25
3. Beacom, Robert, 26
4. Beavers, Thomas J., 21
5. Borgstread (?), William, 28
6. Bracken, James, 30
7. Christie, Joseph, 21
8. Church, William H., 18
9. Clark, William, 18
10. Cockburn, William, 29 (transferred to Hunter's company)
11. Cole, Lazerus, 24
12. Cope, James B., 24
13. Craig, (?). M., 20
14. Daniels, William J., 22
15. Dorsch, Lyons, 24
16. Dwyer, William, 25 (transferred to Hunter's company)
17. English, Thomas W., 24
18. Enlad, James, 23
19. Eulack, James, 25
20. Ervin, Daniel, 20
21. Fields, Charles, 22
22. Flowers, Benjamin C., 19
23. Gill, Patrick, 25 (transferred to Hunter's company)
24. Good, Robert, 18
25. Grubb, William, 23
26. Harkin, John A., 24
27. Henry, George, 24 (transferred to Hunter's company)
28. Henson, Thomas J., 24
29. Hermann, John, 20
30. Highsmith, William A., 22
31. Hill, John, 27
32. Hogan, Frank V., 21
33. Hogan, Shields, 18
34. Howard, Annesley, 20
35. Johnstone, John, 31
36. Kasse, Max W. C., 23
37. Keiff, John D., 24 (transferred to Hunter's company)
38. Kneippe, John, 20
39. Lambert, Antonio
40. Lamothe, Francis, 23
41. Maney, James, 24
42. Marshall, Edward O., 23
43. Marshall, John, 27
44. McCarty, James, 28 (transferred to Hunter's company)
45. McCracken, John, 21
46. McCracken, William H., 19
47. McDougal, Henry, 30 (transferred to Hunter's company)
48. McGarvey, James, 22
49. McGowan, John R., 18
50. Millett, Thomas H., 26
51. Moerer, Fred., 20
52. Moffot, Robert, 23
53. Moore, Thomas P., 22
54. Morris, Jonathan, 28
55. Nichols, Sam Houston, 19
56. Norton, George C., 22

57. Odlum, Edward, 19
58. Parkinson, Joseph, 21
59. Patillo, George F., 21
60. Pettit, William A., 21 (probably transferred to Hunter's company; listed as William H. Pettit on Hunter's roll)
61. Rader, Jeremiah D., 26 (probably transferred to Hunter's company; listed as Jerry Rader on Hunter's roll)
62. Rumley, Christian, 24
63. Sawyer, Albert B., 24
64. Schmidt, John, 23
65. Shaw, James R., 21
66. Sheckell, James O., 29
67. Simpson, William, 23
68. Skinner, Ira, 24
69. Stansberry, George T., 18
70. Stubblefield, George, 24
71. Tison, William D., 30
72. Usener, John D., 19
73. Voreager, John, 19
74. Whitley, Eli H., 23
75. Wilson, John, 26
76. Wood, George W., 23 (probably transferred to Hunter's company; listed as George Woods on Hunter's roll)
77. Young, William C., 18

INDEPENDENT VOLUNTEER COMPANIES ATTACHED TO BAYLOR'S COMMAND

LIGHT COMPANY B
First Regiment of Artillery (Texas Volunteers)
(As of May 1, 1861)**
This muster roll does not list the ages of the soldiers.
Probably Mustered Mainly from Bexar County

Trevanion T. Teel, Captain (slightly wounded at Valverde)
Jordan W. Bennett, First Lieutenant
Joseph McGuinness, First Sergeant (promoted to lieutenant)

Elijah W. Cook, Corporal
Samuel J. Bennett, Corporal
John Muth, Bugler
Augustus H. Willoughby, Fifer

PRIVATES:
1. Bennett, George H.
2. Benson, Samuel
3. Berringer, Leonard
4. Bettis, Harry
5. Blythe, Joseph
6. Boone, Frank (wounded at Glorieta)
7. Bradford, James (promoted to lieutenant; wounded at Glorieta)
8. Cornet, Theodore C.
9. Don, David
10. Doyle, John
11. Eichenscher, Louis
12. Eichhorn, John C.
13. Fidler, Samuel G.
14. Fisher, James
15. Graffrath, Jacob
16. Green, William
17. Harmon, John
18. Head, Richard M.
19. Hermann, Adolph (wounded at Glorieta)
20. Hicks, John
21. Kemper, Ephraim
22. Lowenstein, Herman (seriously wounded at Valverde)
23. Madison, William
24. Mann, John W.
25. Marbach, Sebastian
26. McCall, James
27. McDermott, James
28. McFarland, Bartholomew
29. McGuire, Thomas
30. McHugh, John
31. McKenna, Patrick
32. Messersmith, Adolph
33. Miller, Lares (?)
34. Miller, Louis
35. Murphy, Patrick
36. Phelan, James
37. Ridgen, Frank
38. Rogers, William T.

39. Schofield, Charles
40. Sharpe, William
41. Street, Henry K.
42. Sturdevant, Orville
43. Valentine, John
44. Wheat, Solomon
45. White, Arthur W. (wounded at Glorieta)
46. Wilmot, Richard

Casualties Not on Muster Roll:
Nicholas Mitchell, Sergeant (severely wounded at Valverde)
(?) Carter, Corporal (wounded at Glorieta)

PRIVATES:
1. Burris, (?) (killed at Glorieta)
2. Doued, (?) (wounded at Glorieta)
3. Logan, James (seriously wounded at Valverde)
4. Maloney, John (seriously wounded at Valverde)
5. Nettles, (?) (wounded at Glorieta)
6. Nurom, (wounded at Glorieta)
7. Page, Joseph (killed at Valverde)
8. Phillips, (?) (wounded at Glorieta)
9. Roff, (?) (wounded at Glorieta)
10. Ryman, Atticus H. (killed at Valverde)

SAN ELIZARIO SPY COMPANY
(As of July 11, 1861)**
This muster roll does not list the ages of the soldiers.
Mustered in El Paso County

Bethel Coopwood, Captain
J. R. Parsons, First Lieutenant
Jesse H. Holden, Second Lieutenant
Levi Southerland, Second Lieutenant
James H. Coulter, First Sergeant
H. B. Pendleton, Second Sergeant (probably transferred to Hunter's company)
Samuel Warren, Third Sergeant
J. Quinn, Fourth Sergeant (probably transferred to Hunter's company)
William Helminck (?), First Corporal

Silas Merchant, Second Corporal (severely wounded at Valverde)
Dennis Dunne, Third Corporal
Henry B. de Hamel, Fourth Corporal

PRIVATES:
1. Ball, J.
2. Banks, Charles
3. Burgess, Charles
4. Cleveland, S. C.
5. Cramer, Peter (transferred to Hunter's company)
6. Crompton, D. (probably transferred to Hunter's company; listed as Dewitt Crampton on Hunter's roll)
7. Davis, F. E.
8. Despain, J. W.
9. Dobson, J. A.
10. Hall, James M.
11. Hamby, E. G.
12. Hicks, J. W.
13. Holden, A. O.
14. Kappis, William
15. Keller, W. H.
16. Kepler (or Kessler), Frederick A.
17. McClintock, S. W.
18. McDonald, John
19. Nicholson, Lemuel (promoted to lieutenant)
20. Patterson, W. J.
21. Rivera, M.
22. Tardy, J. A.
23. Thompson, James
24. Tryer, W.

Names of Additional Personnel Derived from the Mesilla Times *of October 3, 1861:*
1. Brown, Frank
2. Childress, John
3. Coopwood, David
4. Cramer, Charles
5. Dougherty, James
6. Gilbert, T. (probably transferred to Hunter's company; listed as Thomas J. Gilbert on Hunter's roll)
7. Haire, T. S.

8. Holly, J. F.
9. Lamb, W. S. E.
10. Layman, N.
11. Loomis, W. W. (transferred to Hunter's company with the rank of corporal)
12. Lyon, Robert W. (mortally wounded at skirmish below Alamosa, September 26, 1861)
13. Maby, J. S. (probably transferred to Hunter's company; listed as John Mabry on Hunter's roll)
14. Maine, L. M.
15. Mattison, George
16. McClung, A. G.
17. McCormick, John F.
18. Moyer, Benjamin
19. Murray, W. H.
20. Norton, G. C.
21. Rea, J. W.
22. Tinney, W. S.
23. Wallard, Robert
24. Wilson, W. H.
25. Wright, Dr. W. C. (killed at skirmish below Alamosa, September 26, 1861)

ARIZONA RANGERS

(As of August 1, 1861)**
This muster roll does not list the ages of the soldiers.
Mustered in the Mesilla Valley

George M. Frazer, Captain
Sherod Hunter, First Lieutenant (resigned to form his own company)
Frank Bushick, Second Lieutenant
William Simmons, Second Lieutenant
Adolphe S— — (illegible), First Sergeant
Almond (?) Sapp, Second Sergeant
William Wright, Third Sergeant
Henry Elam, Fourth Sergeant
Edward Ferguson, First Corporal
Robert Buttler, Second Corporal
John Lamar, Third Corporal
Alfred Van Patten, Fourth Corporal
Eugene Van Patten, Musician

PRIVATES:

1. Benton, William
2. Bryant, William
3. Eauar (?), Gregoria
4. Estell, William
5. Fitch, James
6. Frazer, Edward
7. Hagan, George
8. Hamerick, William
9. Hampton, Thomas
10. Horan, James
11. Jones, John
12. Kirkes, Robert
13. Lauar, Massy
14. McGuire, Michael
15. McGuire, Pat
16. McLane, William
17. Morrison, Robert
18. Ramsy, William
19. Rodríquez, José
20. Roe, John
21. Rubles, John
22. St. Verin, Eric
23. Van Sickles, Isac
24. Warris, B— — (illegible)

ARIZONA GUARDS

(As of August 8, 1861)
Mustered in Pinos Altos

Thomas J. Mastin, Captain, 33 (mortally wounded by Indians)
Jack W. Swilling, First Lieutenant, 31
Thomas Helm, Second Lieutenant, 27 (promoted to captain on death of Mastin)
John A. Ring, Second Lieutenant, 25
G. W. Linn, First Sergeant, —
G. S. Carter, Second Sergeant, 40
John M. Smith, Third Sergeant, 23
Henry ("Hank") Smith, Fourth Sergeant, 37
Henry Holmes, First Corporal, 36 (transferred to Hunter's company; captured at the skirmish of Picacho, April 15, 1862)
L. S. Riggs, Second Corporal, 28
J. J. Jackson, Third Corporal, 30

Thomas (?) Buchanan, Fourth
Corporal, 27

PRIVATES:
1. Boyle, William, 26
2. Bowers, Joseph, 21
3. Bryan, John, 32
4. Burnell (?), Martin, 35
5. Crow, James,—
6. Crow, William, 45
7. E——(illegible), 40
8. Eaton, Edward, 25
9. Graham, A., 25
10. Hopson, William, 30
11. Houston, J. W., 29
12. Kidd, Thomas, 25
13. Pidcock, M., 28
14. Porter, (?). M., 39
15. Roy, William, 25
16. Scott, William, 25
17. Spriggs, John, 37
18. Starks, Conssand (?), 23
19. Wisdom, David, 22

**HUNTER'S COMPANY OF
ARIZONA VOLUNTEERS**
(As of November 1, 1862)**
This muster roll does not list the ages
of the soldiers.
Mustered in the Mesilla Valley

Sherod Hunter, Captain (formerly first
  lieutenant of the Arizona Rangers)
Robert S. Swope, First Lieutenant
James H. Tevis, Second Lieutenant
O. D. Price, Second Lieutenant
William H. Pettit, First Sergeant
  (probably transferred from
  Company E, Second Regiment)
Dewitt Crampton, Second Sergeant
  (probably D. Crompton from the
  San Elizario Spy Company)
Alex H. Layman, Third Sergeant
Henry Holmes, Fourth Sergeant
  (captured at skirmish of Picacho,
  April 15, 1862)
John Hill, Fifth Sergeant
Wellington W. Loomis, First Corporal
  (transferred from the San Elizario
  Spy Company)

Robert Shaw, Second Corporal
William Cockburn, Third Corporal
  (transferred from Company E,
  Second Regiment)
William Brown, Fourth Corporal
  (probably transferred from
  Company B, Second Regiment)
John Day, Bugler
William Barcley, Farrier

PRIVATES:
1. Baker, John C. (left sick at Fort
   Bliss on leaving for San Antonio)
2. Beacom, Robert
3. Berry, C. A.
4. (Illegible)
5. Byler, A. J.
6. Caloway, James
7. Campbell, John
8. Campbell, W. J.
9. Childs, Thomas
10. Clark, William A.
11. Coffer, William H.
12. Cramer, Peter (transferred from
    the San Elizario Spy Company)
13. Dean, Jesse A. (transferred from
    Company B, Second Regiment)
14. Denton, John
15. Dobson, James
16. Dwyer, William (transferred from
    Company E, Second Regiment;
    captured at skirmish of Picacho,
    April 15, 1862)
17. Embree, William
18. Fagan, A. T.
19. Fallan, Michael
20. Farrell, Thomas
21. Finley, William H.
22. Freed, John C.
23. Gilbert, Jasper
24. Gilbert, Newton
25. Gilbert, Thomas J. (probably T.
    Gilbert from the San Elizario Spy
    Company)
26. Gill, Patrick (transferred from
    Company E, Second Regiment)
27. Ham, John
28. Hampton, Thomas

29. Henry, George (transferred from Company E, Second Regiment)
30. Hill, John W. (captured at skirmish of Picacho, April 15, 1862)
31. Hudson, Amos (transferred from Company B, Second Regiment)
32. Insalman, John
33. Keegan, John
34. Keiff, John C. (transferred from Company E, Second Regiment)
35. King, James
36. Lemons, James
37. Mabry, John (probably J. S. Maby from the San Elizario Spy Company)
38. Mayers, J. C.
39. McAlpine, Thomas
40. McCarty, James (transferred from Company E, Second Regiment)
41. McClelland, Joseph P. (transferred from Company B, Second Regiment)
42. McClendall, Henry
43. McDougal, Henry (transferred from Company E, Second Regiment)
44. McLeod, John
45. McNamee, Henry
46. Morgan, Samuel
47. Myers, John
48. O'Neil, James (transferred from Company B, Second Regiment)
49. Parks, J. C.
50. Pater, John F.
51. Pendleton, H. D. (probably Sgt. H. B. Pendleton from the San Elizario Spy Company)
52. Quinn, John (probably Sgt. J. Quinn from the San Elizario Spy Company)
53. Rader, Jerry (probably Jeremiah D. Rader from Company E, Second Regiment)
54. Smith, John
55. Summit, Fred
56. Wesdem (?), David
57. Woods, George
58. Wybel, Peter
59. Young, Henry

Notes

Chapter 1

1. Houston *Tri-Weekly Telegraph*, May 12, 1862.

2. W. W. H. Davis, *El Gringo; or, New Mexico and Her People*, pp. 429–430.

3. *Ibid.*, p. 430.

4. Loomis M. Ganaway, *New Mexico and the Sectional Controversy, 1846–1861*, pp. 3–5, 12–13.

5. *Ibid.*, pp. 60–62.

6. A specimen issue of this paper first appeared on June 9, 1860, as the Mesilla *Miner*. With the beginning of full-time publication on October 18, 1860, the name was changed to Mesilla *Times*.

7. The American town of El Paso was also known as Franklin. This dualism prevailed until 1873, when the town was incorporated as El Paso. William J. Glasgow, "On the Confusion Caused by the Name of El Paso," *Pass-Word*, I (May, 1956), 65–67.

8. Colonel Thomas T. Fauntleroy of Virginia was in command of the department during the early part of 1861. He was succeeded in March, 1861, by Colonel William W. Loring of North Carolina.

9. Jackson to Orlando Davis, February 17, 1861. John T. Pickett Papers, Box 108A.

10. *Ibid.*

11. Ernest W. Winkler (ed.), *Journal of the Secession Convention of Texas 1861*, pp. 45, 67.

12. Mesilla *Times,* March 30, 1861.

13. The area encompassed in the Territory of New Mexico was designated as the Ninth Military District. In late 1861 this was changed to the Department of New Mexico.

14. The fact that New Mexico had no market for her surplus products other than that afforded by the Federal government (it was estimated that about 80 per cent of the money in circulation in the territory was contributed by the Federal civil and military departments) suggests that perhaps the legislature may have had more in mind than just protection against the Indians. A. B. Bender, "Military Posts in the Southwest, 1848–1860," *New Mexico Historical Review*, XVI (April, 1941), 142.

15. Lydia S. Lane, *I Married a Soldier, or Old Days in the Old Army*, p. 96.

16. George P. Hammond (ed.), *Campaigns in the West, 1856–1861: The Journal and Letters of Colonel John Van Deusen Du Bois*, pp. 110–111.

17. Sibley to Loring, June 12, 1861, *War of the Rebellion: A Compilation of the Official Records of the Union and Confederate Armies*, Series I, IV, 56. Hereafter cited as *O.R.A.* Unless otherwise noted, all citations are to Series I.

18. Canby to Isaac Lynde, June 30, 1861, *ibid.*, p. 57.

19. W. W. Mills to John S. Watts, June 23, 1861, *ibid.*, p. 56.

20. Mesilla *Times,* July 27, 1861.

21. Lynde to Acting Assistant Adjutant General, August 7, 1861, *O.R.A.,* IV, 6.

22. One of these three (Company I) had set out from Fort Craig to escort a beef herd to Fort Fillmore. On learning that the Texans held Mesilla, the company detoured to San Agustín Springs, joining Lynde's command shortly before the surrender.

23. On November 25, 1861, Major Lynde was dropped from the rolls of the United States Army. After the war he was restored to the retired list.

24. On February 14, 1862, President Davis issued a proclamation (which had been authorized by Congress on January 21) affirming Baylor's actions in establishing the Territory of Arizona.

Chapter 2

1. Sibley to W. W. Loring, June 12, 1861, *O.R.A.,* IV, 55.

2. *Ibid.,* pp. 55–56.

3. They were Henry C. McNeill, E. N. Covey, Thomas P. Ochiltree, and William H. Harrison.

4. Samuel Cooper to Sibley, July 8, 1861, *O.R.A.,* IV, 93.

5. San Antonio *Daily Ledger and Texan,* August 13, 1861.

6. Theo. Noel, *A Campaign from Santa Fe to the Mississippi; Being a History of the Old Sibley Brigade from Its First Organization to the Present Time; Its Campaigns in New Mexico, Arizona, Texas, Louisiana and Arkansas, in the Years 1861–2–3–4,* p. 8.

7. *Ibid.,* p. 7.

8. New Orleans *Daily Picayune,* October 20, 1861 (quoted from the Houston *Tri-Weekly Telegraph,* n.d.).

9. Mesilla *Times,* January 15, 1862

(Microfilm, courtesy of the New York Historical Society, New York City).

10. Noel, *A Campaign from Santa Fe to the Mississippi,* p. 9.

11. Austin *State Gazette,* November 2, 1861 (quoted from the San Antonio *Herald,* n.d.).

12. Noel, *A Campaign from Santa Fe to the Mississippi,* p. 9.

13. R. H. Williams, *With the Border Ruffians, Memories of the Far West, 1852–1868,* p. 201.

14. In addition to the numerous wagons carrying quartermaster, ordnance, and commissary supplies, each company was allotted three wagons—two for the enlisted men's equipment and one for the officers'.

15. Baylor to Sibley, October 25, 1861, *O.R.A.,* IV, 133.

16. Walter A. Faulkner (contrib.), "With Sibley in New Mexico; the Journal of William Henry Smith," *West Texas Historical Association Year Book,* XXVII (October, 1951), 115. Punctuation marks added.

17. *Ibid.*

18. W. W. Heartsill, *Fourteen Hundred and 91 Days in the Confederate Army,* p. 49.

19. Proclamation, December 20, 1861, *O.R.A.,* IV, 90.

20. Faulkner (contrib.), "With Sibley in New Mexico," *West Texas Historical Association Year Book,* XXVII (October, 1951), 117.

21. San Antonio *Herald,* December 14, 1861.

22. W. R. Howell, "Journal of a Soldier of the Confederate States Army."

23. It is not clear whether the new trail led all the way to the Río Grande, or ended at Eagle Springs. If the latter was the case, the men followed the regular stage road from Eagle Springs to the Río Grande and Fort Quitman.

24. Mesilla *Times,* January 15, 1862.

25. New Orleans *Daily Picayune,* March 27, 1862.

26. Faulkner (contrib.), "With Sibley in New Mexico," *West Texas Historical Association Year Book,* XXVII (October, 1951), 128.

27. Sutton's five companies (A, B, F, H, I) set out from Camp Pickett for Arizona on November 28. While Company K remained in San Antonio to escort the brigade paymaster and chief quartermaster, the other four, commanded by Colonel Steele and Major Bagby, left San Antonio around the middle of December. While Company E was en route, measles broke out among the men, necessitating the leaving of that unit at Fort Clark.

28. T. T. Teel, "Sibley's New Mexican Campaign. Its Objects and the Causes of its Failure," *Battles and Leaders of the Civil War,* II, 700.

29. Noel, *A Campaign from Santa Fe to the Mississippi,* p. 12.

30. When Sibley arrived at Fort Bliss Crosby joined his staff as acting chief quartermaster (Captain William H. Harrison, the regular chief quartermaster, was still in San Antonio), while James Magoffin joined his staff as a volunteer aide.

31. When within one day's march of Fort Bliss, Colonel Reily wrote, "We have made a halt here, on account of the rumors of small pox. Three hundred men have been vaccinated and we will have every soldier, teamster, servant, etc., attended to, having sent surgeon Southworth forward to obtain the vaccine matter." Austin *State Gazette,* January 18,1862.

32. H. C. Wright, "Reminiscences of H. C. Wright of Austin," p. 7.

33. Austin *State Gazette,* February 15, 1862.

34. New Orleans *Daily Picayune,* March 27, 1862.

35. *Ibid.*

Chapter 3

1. Shortly after Lynde's surrender, Fort Stanton was abandoned and the troops were marched to Albuquerque.

2. Canby to Assistant Adjutant General, August 16, 1861, *O.R.A.,* IV, 65.

3. W. R. Shoemaker to Canby, August 15, 1861, *ibid.,* p. 66.

4. E. D. Townsend to Canby, August 13, 1861, *ibid.,* p. 63.

5. Canby to Assistant Adjutant General, September 8, 1861, *ibid.,* p. 69.

6. Canby to Adjutant General, December 8, 1861, *ibid.,* p. 78.

7. The Confederates had no intention, of course, of invading New Mexico by way of the Pecos. It will be recalled that in following the road to Fort Bliss, Sibley's forces followed the course of the Pecos River for two days before turning westward to Escondido Springs and Fort Stockton. Canby's informants had apparently observed this movement up the Pecos and assumed that the Confederates planned to follow the river into New Mexico.

8. Canby to Adjutant General, January 11, 1862, *O.R.A.,* IV, 84.

9. Canby to Henry Connelly, January 21, 1862, *ibid.,* p. 87.

10. Ganaway, *New Mexico and the Sectional Controversy 1846–1861,* pp. 98–99.

11. *Ibid.,* pp. 88–90, 98.

12. *Ibid.,* pp. 95–98.

13. Connelly to William H. Seward, February 6, 1862, *O.R.A.,* IX, 644.

14. Collins to William P. Dole, February 11, 1862, Records of the Bureau of Indian Affairs, Selected Documents Concerning the Administration of Indian Affairs in Texas and New Mexico, 1861–1862.

15. On February 14 Canby issued an order concerning the arrangement of his columns for field operations.

The number of regulars involved was 1,079. On the assumption that others were to remain at the post in the various administrative and supporting positions, the total number of regulars was probably near 1,200, although some estimates run as high as 1,500.

16. William Clark Whitford, *Colorado Volunteers in the Civil War, The New Mexico Campaign in 1862,* p. 43.

17. Faulkner (contrib.), "With Sibley in New Mexico," *West Texas Historical Association Year Book,* XXVII (October, 1951), 129.

18. *Ibid.,* p. 133.

19. *Ibid.,* p. 134.

20. Ebenezer Hanna, "Journal of Ebenezer Hanna, February 10 to March 27, 1862," p. 1.

21. Captain Jerome B. Cown stated in a letter published in the Bellville *Countryman* of June 7, 1862, that Colonel Steele held the Mesilla Valley with a force of two hundred fifty men from his own Seventh Regiment. It seems likely that this contingent was augmented by volunteer companies from Baylor's command, as well as by convalescents from the hospital established at Doña Ana.

22. Houston *Tri-Weekly Telegraph,* June 18, 1862; *ibid.,* June 2, 1862 (quoted from the San Antonio *Herald,* n.d.); New Orleans *Daily Picayune,* March 9, 1862.

23. Canby reported that, based on captured muster rolls, Sibley had an aggregate of nearly three thousand men. The Colonel believed, however, that by the time the Confederates appeared before Fort Craig this number had been reduced by disease and the posting of detachments to about twenty-six hundred. Canby to Adjutant General, March 1, 1862, *O.R.A.,* IX, 488.

24. That Green commanded the army when it challenged Canby is an assumption. It is possible that Sibley, though ill, may still have been in charge. Major Willis L. Robards stated in a letter published in the Austin *State Gazette* of April 5, 1862, that the general had been sick since February 11. Sibley notes in his official report (Sibley to Samuel Cooper, May 4, 1862, *O.R.A.,* IX, 507) that, at least as far as the subsequent operations after the challenge were concerned, Green was definitely in charge. His statement is not clear, and he may have meant that Green was in command at the time of the challenge as well. Adding credence to this assumption is the fact that Green called the council of war after the failure to entice the Federals to battle.

25. F. Stanley, *Fort Union,* p. 158. Reproduced in this volume is a primary reminiscence written in 1882, "Notes on the Affair at Valverde and Glorieta in the Late War of the Rebellion," which points out that many soldiers believed that a major reason for Canby's reluctance to fight was the fact that Sibley was his brother-in-law. Several secondary sources also state that the two commanders were related through marriage (Mrs. Canby was Sibley's sister), but I have found no valid evidence to support the contention that they were brothers-in-law.

26. George H. Pettis, "The Confederate Invasion of New Mexico and Arizona," *Battles and Leaders of the Civil War,* II, 105–106.

Chapter 4

1. Sibley to Samuel Cooper, February 22, 1862, *O.R.A.,* IX, 506.

2. Sometime during the action one of Hall's twenty-four–pounders was put out of action when its tail was broken. Whether this occurred before or after crossing the river is not clear. A. W.

Evans, "Canby at Valverde," *Battles and Leaders of the Civil War*, II, 699.

3. Theo. F. Rodenbough (comp.), *From Everglade to Cañon with the Second Dragoons*, p. 240.

4. Green in his official report stated that Raguet's force was about 250 men. Raguet, however, reported it to be "less than 200." Raguet to Alexander M. Jackson, February 23, 1862, *O.R.A.*, IX, 518.

5. James L. Collins to William P. Dole, March 1, 1862, Records of the Bureau of Indian Affairs.

6. Evidence indicates that most of the regulars supporting the battery were just as panic-stricken as the volunteers, and fled from the scene accordingly. Canby toned down this aspect, and placed full blame upon the volunteers. Canby to Adjutant General, March 1, 1862, *O.R.A.*, IX, 490–491.

7. Green to Alexander M. Jackson, February 22, 1862, *ibid.*, p. 520.

8. Howell, "Journal of a Soldier."

9. Sibley to Samuel Cooper, February 22, 1862, *O.R.A.*, IX, 506.

10. Green to Alexander M. Jackson, February 22, 1862, *ibid.*, p. 521. Green reported that since the compilation of this list two privates of the Fifth, two of Teel's artillery, and Lieutenant Colonel Sutton had died of wounds. The San Antonio *Herald* of May 3, 1862, published an official casualty list which stated that of those hospitalized for wounds about thirty-eight had later died.

11. Howell, "Journal of a Soldier."

12. Sibley to Samuel Cooper, February 22, 1862, *O.R.A.*, IX, 506.

13. Canby to Adjutant General, March 1, 1862, *ibid.*, p. 493. Three officers were among the killed, viz., Captains Alexander McRae and George N. Bascom and Lieutenant Lyman Mishler. Captain William H. Rossell, of the Tenth Infantry, was a prisoner. Seventeen of the wounded later died.

Basil Norris to E. I. Baily, March 5, 1862, *ibid.*, p. 647.

14. Houston *Tri-Weekly Telegraph*, March 29, 1862.

15. See James L. Collins to William P. Dole, March 1, 1862, Records of the Bureau of Indian Affairs; Connelly to Secretary of State, March 1, 1862, *O.R.A.*, IX, 638.

16. Canby to Adjutant General, February 22, 1862, *O.R.A.*, IX, 487.

17. San Antonio *Herald*, March 22, 1862 (quoted from the Mesilla *Times*, March 1, 1862).

Chapter 5

1. Howell, "Journal of a Soldier."

2. Noel, *A Campaign from Santa Fe to the Mississippi*, p. 20.

3. Green to Alexander M. Jackson, February 22, 1862, *O.R.A.*, IX, 522.

4. A staff officer, Major Willis L. Robards, on the other hand, had nothing but praise for Sibley. "In the morning of the battle (21st) Gen. Sibley assumed command, and ordered the distribution of the forces, but having been sick for ten days, the fatigue was too great for him, and he was forced to turn the entire command over to Col. Green. He is entitled to great foresight and sagacity, however, in protecting the long train of transportation, and properly disposing of the forces in the face of the enemy, expecting an attack in front, flank and rear. Every one desired his presence, and greatly regretted his indisposition." Austin *State Gazette*, April 5, 1862.

5. Austin *State Gazette*, April 5, 1862.

6. Canby to Adjutant General, February 23, 1862, *O.R.A.*, IX, 633.

7. Wesche to General, May 5, 1862, *ibid.*, p. 605.

8. Hanna, "Journal," p. 5.

9. *Ibid.,* p. 6.

10. Faulkner (contrib.), "With Sibley in New Mexico," *West Texas Historical Association Year Book,* XXVII (October, 1951), 136.

11. Enos was in command of twelve regulars. Also present were several companies of unreliable militia and volunteers.

12. Among the buildings destroyed were twelve houses and seven corrals belonging to the children of James H. Carleton—commanding officer of what was to become known as the California Column—who had leased them to the War Department. Total damage to this property was assessed at $7,600.

13. Promoted from lieutenant to replace Powhatan Jordan, who had been elevated to major after the death of Lieutenant Colonel John S. Sutton at Valverde.

14. Baird, an outspoken Southerner, was an attorney who had come to New Mexico as the representative of Texas when that state claimed New Mexico to the Río Grande. After the boundary settlement in 1850 he decided to settle in the territory.

15. Santa Fé *Gazette,* April 26, 1862.

16. Sibley to Samuel Cooper, May 4, 1862, *O.R.A.,* IX, 511.

17. Ford's company, eventually to become Company B, Second Regiment Colorado Volunteers, received orders on February 4 at Fort Garland to proceed as rapidly as possible to Santa Fé. After a harrowing adventure of twenty-eight days, the greater part of which involved "breaking the track" through the snow-covered mountain passes, the company reached Santa Fé just in time to leave with Donaldson for Fort Union.

18. Ellen Williams, *Three Years and a Half in the Army; or History of the Second Colorados,* pp. 14–17.

19. The facts relating to this incident are derived entirely from Ellen Williams' book (p. 19). She refers to the Confederates who first entered Santa Fé as "stragglers." Whether she is describing the actions of the eleven scouts, or those of Pyron's command who arrived a few days later, is not clear. She does, however, note that the officer in charge was a Captain (perhaps she meant Lieutenant) Battles. A check of the existing muster rolls of the various Arizona companies lists no officer by that name. However, the muster roll for Captain John Phillips' "Brigands," has been lost. It is possible that Battles and his group of scouts were from that unit.

20. Santa Fé *Gazette,* April 26, 1862.

21. Faulkner (contrib.), "With Sibley in New Mexico," *West Texas Historical Association Year Book,* XXVII (October, 1951), p. 137.

22. Hanna, "Journal," p. 8.

23. Company A of the Seventh, under Captain Thurmond, was still at Cubero as late as March 19. Consequently that unit did not take part in this movement.

Chapter 6

1. Canby to Donaldson, March 7, 1862, *O.R.A.,* IX, 647.

2. Whitford, *Colorado Volunteers,* p. 75. The First Regiment had been organized during the latter part of August, 1861, for the twofold purpose of suppressing secessionist sentiment in Colorado and protecting the territory's supply line to the east.

3. Lewis Weld to Canby, February 14, 1862, *O.R.A.,* IX, 632.

4. These officers believed that heavy snows in the mountains over which the regiment would have to march to get

to New Mexico would delay them. It was their belief that troops from the area of Kansas could reach the territory much more quickly.

5. Paul to Adjutant General, March 11, 1862, *O.R.A.,* IX, 646.

6. Woefully Paul wrote the adjutant general that he had been deprived of a command which he had taken "so much pains to organize and with which ... [he] expected to reap laurels." Pointing out the injustice of a situation in which an inexperienced officer of only six month's service took precedence over him who had many years' service, including battle, Paul "modestly" asked the War Department to bestow upon him the rank of brigadier general of volunteers. *Ibid.*

7. When Canby learned that Slough had assumed command, he sent essentially the same instructions to that officer.

8. Paul to Adjutant General, March 24, 1862, *O.R.A.,* IX, 652.

9. Connelly to William H. Seward, March 23, 1862, *ibid.,* p. 651.

10. On February 27 Canby had sent Captains R. S. C. Lord and George W. Howland, each with fifty cavalrymen, from Fort Craig to the northern district. Their purpose was twofold: to observe the movements of the enemy and to bolster the northern defenses.

11. One company of the Fourth Regiment New Mexico Volunteers also may have comprised part of Slough's column.

12. According to a letter written by Captain Jerome B. McCown, published in the Bellville *Countryman* of June 7, 1862, Pyron and Shropshire, finding forage inadequate in the capital, set out down the Santa Fé Trail *solely* for the purpose of grazing their horses. The facts of what took place during the ensuing skirmish are derived almost exclusively from Union sources. General Sibley stated in his official report (Sibley to Samuel Cooper, May 4, 1862, *O.R.A.,* IX, 509) that Pyron wrote a report of the engagement. This apparently was lost, for it is not in the *O.R.A.,* nor in the War Department collection of Confederate records in the National Archives. On Pages 166–170 of Ovando J. Hollister, *History of the First Regiment of Colorado Volunteers,* reprinted as *Boldly They Rode,* there is reproduced a letter purportedly written by a Confederate who took part in the skirmish of Apache Canyon. A close scrutiny of some details, as well as the "propaganda" tone of the material, leads me to believe that perhaps part, if not all, of it may be a forgery.

13. Hollister, *History of the First Regiment,* p. 59.

14. *Ibid.,* p. 61.

15. John M. Chivington, "The Prospective," p. 27.

16. Hollister, *History of the First Regiment,* p. 62.

17. *Ibid.*

18. *Ibid.,* p. 63.

19. Cook was also hit in the foot, but as the charge swept down the canyon, he was able to limp to one side and escape further injury.

20. Hollister, *History of the First Regiment,* p. 64.

21. *Ibid.*

22. *Ibid.,* p. 169.

23. Hollister relates that just as Chivington's command arrived at Pigeon's Ranch, a reinforcement of five hundred men, including Claflin's howitzer battery, came in from Bernal Springs, "and the woods rang for half an hour with their cheering." *Ibid.,* p. 66. Neither Chivington nor Slough in their official reports mention this reinforcement.

24. Chivington listed the Confederate losses as thirty-two killed, forty-three wounded, and seventy-one prisoners. Hollister, however, noted that "As near as we could learn, the Texan loss yesterday [March 26] was 16 killed, 30 to 40 wounded, and 75 prisoners, including 7 commissioned officers." Hollister, *History of the First Regiment*, p. 67.

25. *Ibid.*

26. *Ibid.*

Chapter 7

1. Company A remained in Albuquerque to help guard the depot and hospital.

2. Lansing B. Bloom (ed.), "Confederate Reminiscences of 1862," *New Mexico Historical Review*, V (July, 1930), 316–317.

3. Slough to Adjutant General, March 30, 1862, *O.R.A.*, IX, 533.

4. Company I was composed of Germans. Though Maile was the captain, Lieutenant Charles Kerber commanded the unit during the battle.

5. Whitford, *Colorado Volunteers*, p. 107.

6. Before Shropshire's assault Tappan reported that a group of men dressed in uniforms of Colorado volunteers approached his line requesting that he not fire, since they were his own men. Thinking they might be from Chivington's command, Tappan allowed them to come closer. When they could not give satisfactory answers to questions about their commanders, Tappan recognized them to be Texans. Immediately he ordered his men to open fire, and the enemy fled, leaving several dead and wounded. If Tappan is correct, it is a mystery where the Confederates could have obtained Colorado uniforms. Perhaps some of the Texans, as a result of confiscations, had appropriated some uniforms of the New Mexican volunteers. These were similar to those worn by the Coloradoans.

7. Hollister, *History of the First Regiment*, p. 71.

8. Scurry to Alexander M. Jackson, March 31, 1862, *O.R.A.*, IX, 544.

9. A. A. Hayes, Jr., *New Colorado and the Santa Fe Trail*, p. 169.

10. Bloom (ed.), "Confederate Reminiscences of 1862," *New Mexico Historical Review*, V (July, 1930), 318.

11. *Ibid.*

12. Scurry to Alexander M. Jackson, March 31, 1862, *O.R.A.*, IX, 545.

13. *Ibid.*

14. *Ibid.*

15. Santa Fé *Gazette*, April 26, 1862.

16. Hollister, *History of the First Regiment*, p. 72.

17. Although Slough lists Chivington's force as about 430, the Major's figures total only 357. In listing the units involved, Chivington was seemingly careless regarding the numbers in the first battalion. He apparently did not list the number in Ford's company. Chivington to General, March 28, 1862, *O.R.A.*, IX, 538.

18. A. A. Hayes, "The New Mexican Campaign of 1862," *Magazine of American History*, XV (February, 1886), 180.

19. The Santa Fé *Gazette* of April 26, 1862, maintained that it took the subordinate officers two hours to convince Chivington he should attack.

20. Hayes, "The New Mexican Campaign of 1862," *Magazine of American History*, XV (February, 1886), 180.

21. Whitford, *Colorado Volunteers*, p. 119. There were two companies of Germans in the Sibley Brigade: Company G, Fourth Regiment, and Company B, Seventh Regiment.

22. There was a difference of opinion as to the number of wagons in the train. Chivington listed the number as eighty, while Slough wrote there were only sixty.

23. Although Chivington makes no mention of it in his official report, in his manuscript "The First Colorado Regiment" (written in 1884), he asserts that his men bayoneted 1,100 mules which had pulled the Confederate train. Scurry makes no mention of this in his report. H. C. Wright, a participant, denies it emphatically in his memoirs.

24. Scurry to Alexander M. Jackson, March 31, 1862, *O.R.A.,* IX, 544.

25. Hollister, *History of the First Regiment,* p. 72.

26. Slough maintained in his report to Canby that he had received notice of Chivington's successful raid, and so decided to abandon the field of Glorieta. This appears doubtful. Undoubtedly Slough wrote this in an effort to smooth over the fact that he had engaged the Texans in force—an action contrary to Canby's orders.

Many New Mexicans believed that Chivington unjustly received the credit for the burning of Scurry's supply train. In 1864 the Territorial Legislature petitioned the President to confer the rank of major on Captains William H. Lewis and Asa B. Carey for their services in attacking the Rebels' rear guard. No mention was made of Chivington.

The *Río Abajo Press* of March 8, 1864, denounced Chivington for his "strutting about in plumage stolen from Captain William H. Lewis." The editor pointed out that it took two hours to convince Chivington to attack, and then he remained safely behind on the hill while Captain Lewis carried out the attack.

Chapter 8

1. Hollister, *History of the First Regiment,* p. 73.

2. *Ibid.,* p. 74.

3. Governor Henry Connelly had nothing but praise for Slough: "We are greatly indebted to the command under Colonel Slough, from Denver City, for this favorable result [stopping the Confederate advance at Glorieta] in our struggle with the Texas invaders. Their defeat and utter annihilation is now sure, and I think it will be the last attempt upon the Territory from that quarter." Connelly to William H. Seward, April 11, 1862, *O.R.A.,* IX, 662.

4. Sante Fé *Gazette,* April 26, 1862.

5. Williams, *Three Years and a Half in the Army,* p. 20.

6. Bloom (ed.), "Confederate Reminiscences of 1862," *New Mexico Historical Review,* V (July, 1930), 320.

7. Santa Fé *Gazette,* May 31, 1862.

8. It is not entirely clear whether Green had already set out for Santa Fé, or whether he was still in Albuquerque when the news of Glorieta arrived. There are some indications that he had started for Santa Fé around March 25, but after a day or so on the road had been ordered to return to Albuquerque to protect the town against the supposed advance of Canby from Fort Craig. If this was so, the story of Canby's advance, apparently, was afterward considered to be false. Otherwise Green would never have set out from Albuquerque.

9. Sibley's report to the adjutant general informing him of the battle of Glorieta was written in Albuquerque on March 31. Apparently Sibley left for Santa Fé either on March 31 or the following day.

10. A Confederate correspondent reported that the army at this time

consisted of about 1,700 men. Whether he was referring only to those fit for duty, or including the sick and wounded is not clear. Houston *Tri-Weekly Telegraph*, May 28, 1862.

11. Canby reported that Colonel Steele with a force of five hundred men had unsuccessfully attempted to reinforce Sibley about March 20. Canby to Adjutant General, May 18, 1862, *O.R.A.*, IX, 673.

12. Santa Fé *Gazette*, April 26, 1862. A Federal Indian agent at Maxwell's Ranch reported on March 19, 1862, that the Texans set up a territorial government with William Pelham as governor. Pelham supposedly had appointed Indian agents and a super-intendent of Indian affairs. The Federal agent also asserted that he had heard that Pelham had issued a proclamation requiring New Mexicans to swear allegiance to the Confederate States under penalty of the confiscation of their property. W. F. M. Arny to General, March 19, 1862, Records of the Bureau of Indian Affairs. The Santa Fé *Gazette* of April 26, 1862, however, emphatically denies that the Confederates installed a governor.

13. Sibley to Samuel Cooper, May 4, 1862, *O.R.A.*, IX, 510.

14. In 1889 these howitzers were dug up in a garden that, in 1862, had been a corral just a little north of the town plaza. Captain Trevanion T. Teel, under whose direction the guns had originally been buried, was visiting in Albuquerque and he pointed out their exact location. After their recovery four of the weapons were retained by the city of Albuquerque, while the state of Colorado received the others.

15. Canby to Adjutant General, March 31, 1862, *O.R.A.*, IX, 658.

16. William J. L. Nicodemus to Carson, March 31, 1862, *ibid.*, p. 659.

17. Stanley, *Fort Union*, p. 176.

18. *Ibid.*, p. 177.

19. Estimates by contemporaries run from as low as 130 to as high as 250.

20. Hollister, *History of the First Regiment*, p. 79.

21. The exact number is not known. On the assumption that it was about the same size as Slough's, less the casualties from Glorieta and the units which remained to garrison Fort Union, twelve hundred appears to be a reasonable estimate.

22. Hollister, *History of the First Regiment*, p. 81.

23. *Ibid.*, pp. 82–83.

24. *Ibid.*, p. 83.

25. *Ibid.*, p. 85.

26. *Ibid.*

27. *Ibid.*, p. 86.

28. Slough's military career was not over. He went to Washington where, in the spring of 1863, he was commissioned a brigadier general and placed in command of the Military District of Alexandria, Virginia.

29. Hollister, *History of the First Regiment*, p. 89.

30. *Ibid.*

31. Connelly to William H. Seward, April 20, 1862, *O.R.A.*, IX, 665.

Chapter 9

1. Hollister, History of the First Regiment, p. 92.

2. Noel, who was not at Peralta, maintained in his account (A Campaign from Santa Fe to the Mississippi, p. 26) that when the heavy wagons did not get in Green sent back some empty ones to lighten the load and ordered all to come into camp. The wagon master had already turned his mules out to graze, and believing there was no

danger, disobeyed the order and stayed where he was.

3. Judge Baird and his family were not alone. When the Confederates began to evacuate Rafael and Manuel Armijo also abandoned "luxurious homes and well-filled storehouses" to join their fate to the Confederacy. Sibley to Samuel Cooper, May 4, 1862, O.R.A., IX, 511.

4. There is a discrepancy between the figures of Hollister (cited above) and those found in Canby's official report. Canby states that there were thirty-one men in the escort, six of whom were killed, three wounded, and twenty-two captured. Since Hollister was a participant and his figures are corroborated by a story appearing in the Houston Tri-Weekly Telegraph of July 4, 1862, I presume his are the more nearly accurate.

5. Hollister, History of the First Regiment, p. 94. Hollister asserted that one of the Confederate gunners had been captured at Apache Canyon and, though released on parole, was now "paying his respects." There is no evidence to substantiate this claim.

6. According to the Santa Fé Gazette of April 26, 1862, a captured Confederate surgeon stated that about 250 Texans refused to follow Scurry into action, openly threatening his life if he forced them to do so. No mention of this is made in any Confederate accounts, official or private.

7. Hollister, History of the First Regiment, p. 95.

8. Captain Jerome B. McCown, Company G, Fifth Regiment, acknowledged that he left nine men in the hospital at Peralta. It is not known how many from other companies were left. Bellville Countryman, June 7, 1862.

9. Hollister, History of the First Regiment, pp. 94–96.

10. Ibid., p. 102.

11. Ibid., p. 98.

12. Houston Tri-Weekly Telegraph, June 6, 1862.

13. Hollister, History of the First Regiment, p. 99.

14. Houston Tri-Weekly Telegraph, June 6, 1862 (quoted from the Victoria Advocate, n.d.). A Confederate correspondent implied that Sibley himself made the proposition to surrender. There is no evidence to substantiate this claim.

15. Hollister, History of the First Regiment, p. 101.

16. Ibid., p. 103.

17. Ibid., p. 104.

18. General Orders, No. 41, May 4,1862, O.R.A., LI, 523–524.

19. Connelly to William H. Seward, May 17, 1862, ibid., IX, 673.

20. Contemporary accounts refer to this as either "Amilla or Arnilla" Creek. A close check of current maps indicates that this must have been what is called today the Alamosa River.

21. Noel, A Campaign from Santa Fe to the Mississippi, p. 30.

22. Ibid., p. 31.

23. Pettis, "The Confederate Invasion of New Mexico," Battles and Leaders of the Civil War, II, 111.

24. James D. Richardson (comp.), Messages and Papers of the Confederacy Including the Diplomatic Correspondence, 1861–1865, I, 231.

25. Howell, "Journal of a Soldier."

26. Noel (A Campaign from Santa Fe to the Mississippi, p. 33) reported that Captain Alfred S. Thurmond's Company A, Seventh Regiment, set out to reconnoiter at San Agustín Springs and beyond. Before returning the men were forced "to eat snakes and insects to keep soul and body together."

27. The account of this raid comes exclusively from Union sources. Tilford

was not at all certain that the Confederate commander's name was Bowman. According to Confederate muster rolls there was a Lieutenant Isaac G. Bowman in Company K, Seventh Regiment.

28. According to Confederate muster rolls there was a Lieutenant John W. Taylor in Company I, Seventh Regiment. It was this Taylor who had taken charge of Scurry's wagon train when that officer marched directly through the mountains to Pyron's camp at Johnson's Ranch.

29. On May 25 Canby reported from Santa Fé that a superior force of the enemy had attacked an outpost eight miles below Fort Craig on May 23. He stated that there were no Union casualties, but the Confederates had lost four men. Since Paraje is eight miles below Fort Craig, Canby was undoubtedly referring to Tilford's affair of May 21. Tilford's report, written on May 30, made no mention of casualties, and definitely stated that there were no further hostilities. It is safe to assume that Canby had received unreliable information concerning this incident. Canby to Adjutant General, May 25, 1862, O.R.A., IX, 608–609; Tilford to A. L. Anderson, May 30, 1862, ibid., p. 608.

Chapter 10

1. A merchant of El Paso del Norte, Mexico, reported that Sibley's army on its return to the Mesilla Valley consisted of only 1,250 men. Canby to Adjutant General, June 21, 1862, O.R.A., IX, 678. This seems to be an exaggeration, but if Sibley's effective invasion force consisted originally of only 2,000 men, as the Houston *Tri-Weekly Telegraph* of May 1, 1862, states,

then the merchant may have been correct. A correspondent in the June 2, 1862, issue of the *Telegraph* asserted that of the 924 men originally mustered into the Fifth Regiment, only 429 were fit for duty after the return from New Mexico. Of course, some members of the Fifth had died before setting out on the campaign, others who were sick in the hospital would later return to duty, and those who had been captured and paroled in New Mexico would be eligible for duty once they were exchanged.

2. Sibley to Samuel Cooper, May 4, 1862, O.R.A., IX, 511–512.

3. Because of the widespread depredations of the Apaches and the inability of the Confederate forces to extend adequate protection to the gold and silver mines of Arizona, little, if any, bullion was extracted during Confederate tenure. Had the mines been in operation, Sibley's monetary problems would have been solved.

4. Bellville *Countryman*, June 7, 1862.

5. Noel, *A Campaign from Santa Fe to the Mississippi*, pp. 38–39.

6. Formerly captain of Company A. As a result of casualties, many officers and enlisted men had been promoted during the course of the campaign. Shortly after the army had emerged on the Río Grande after the retreat through the mountains, Colonel Scurry left his regiment for San Antonio. Apparently he was sent by Sibley to inform his superiors of the latest developments and/or to make preparations for the return of the brigade.

7. According to the Houston *Tri-Weekly Telegraph* of June 27, 1862, Steele was to be augmented by a battalion of men raised locally by Colonel Philemon T. Herbert, and by Teel's battery.

8. San Antonio *Herald*, July 5, 1862.

9. The men were following the

regular stage route, rather than the new cutoff they had used on the way out, which had passed by Sibley Springs and Brigade Springs.

10. San Antonio *Herald*, July 5, 1862.

11. Howell, "Journal of a Soldier."

12. Noel, *A Campaign from Santa Fe to the Mississippi*, p. 36.

13. San Antonio *Herald*, July 5, 1862.

14. Lieutenant Joseph D. Sayers, because of distinguished gallantry and bravery on the field of battle, was appointed to organize a new battery to be composed of the pieces captured at Valverde. This was accomplished while the army was recuperating in the Mesilla Valley prior to the evacuation.

15. Houston *Tri-Weekly Telegraph*, May 28, 1862.

16. *Ibid.*, June 6, 1862.

17. Austin *State Gazette*, June 7, 1862.

18. Houston *Tri-Weekly Telegraph*, June 18, 1862.

19. New Orleans *Daily Picayune*, April 24, 1862 (quoted from the Houston *Telegraph*, n.d.).

20. On May 7 Canby issued a conditional pardon for deserters from the New Mexican volunteers. The General reported on June 21 that about half of the deserters—521—had taken advantage of the pardon. The remainder were still at large, "giving much trouble to the frontier settlements." Canby to Adjutant General, June 21, 1862, *O.R.A., IX*, 677.

21. Canby to Chivington, June 20, 1862, *ibid.*, p. 678.

22. After the posting of detachments in western Arizona, Carleton expected to reach Mesilla with fourteen hundred men. Carleton to Canby, August 2, 1862, *ibid.*, p. 559.

23. Steele to Commanding Officer United States Forces, July 5, 1862, *ibid.*, p. 687.

24. Charles S. Walker, Jr., "Confederate Government in Doña Ana County as Shown in the Records of the Probate Court, 1861–62," *New Mexico Historical Review*, VI (July, 1931), 302.

25. *San Antonio Herald*, August 16, 1862. Later when President Davis learned of Baylor's "extermination" policy toward hostile Indians, he removed him from office.

26. When Carleton's forces occupied El Paso in August, 1862, they found a surgeon and twenty-five sick and disabled Confederate soldiers in the hospital. Twelve wagon-loads of hospital and quartermaster supplies were located in storerooms connected with the custom house in El Paso del Norte, Mexico. Carleton managed to recover these supplies and the remaining Confederates were made prisoners of war. Carleton to Richard C. Drum, September 20, 1862, *O.R.A., L, i*, 101.

27. Sibley's failure to conquer New Mexico did not completely dispel, however, the hopes of the Southern "manifest destiny" school. Until the closing days of the war various schemes were advanced from time to time to secure Arizona and New Mexico. None of these, however, got beyond the planning stage, and the Far West remained securely in the hands of the Union.

Bibliography

BOOKS AND PAMPHLETS:

Bancroft, Hubert H., *History of Arizona and New Mexico, 1530–1888.* The History Company, San Francisco, 1889.

———, *History of California, 1860–1890.* The History Company, San Francisco, 1890.

———, *History of the Life of William Gilpin.* The History Company, San Francisco, 1889.

———, *History of Nevada, Colorado, and Wyoming, 1540–1888.* The History Company, San Francisco, 1890.

———, *History of Utah, 1540–1886.* The History Company, San Francisco, 1889.

Barber, John W., and Henry Howe, *All the Western States and Territories.* Howe's Subscription Book Concern, Cincinnati, 1867.

Barnes, Charles M., *Combats and Conquests of Immortal Heroes.* Guessaz & Ferlet Company, San Antonio, 1910.

Bartlett, John R., *Personal Narratives of Explorations and Incidents in Texas, New Mexico, California, Sonora, and Chihuahua.* D. Appleton and Company, New York, 1856.

Bender, Averam B., *The March of Empire, Frontier Defense in the Southwest, 1848–1860.* University of Kansas Press, Lawrence, 1952.

Browne, J. Ross, *Adventures in the Apache Country: A Tour through Arizona and Sonora, with Notes on the Silver Regions of Nevada.* Harper & Brothers, New York, 1869.

Callahan, James M., *The Diplomatic History of the Southern Confederacy.* Johns Hopkins Press, Baltimore, 1901.

Coan, Charles F., *A History of New Mexico.* 3 vols. The American Historical Society, Inc., Chicago and New York, 1925.

Conkling, Roscoe P., and Margaret B., *The Butterfield Overland Mail.* 3 vols. The Arthur H. Clarke Co., Glendale, California, 1947.

Cozzens, Samuel W., *The Marvellous Country, or Three Years in Arizona and New Mexico.* Lee and Shepard, Boston, 1876.

Davis, William H., *Seventy-Five Years in California.* J. Howell, San Francisco, 1929.

Davis, W. W. H., *El Gringo; or, New Mexico and Her People.* Harper & Brothers, New York, 1857.

Drumm, Stella M. (ed.), *Down the Santa Fe Trail and into New Mexico, The Diary of Susan Shelby Magoffin, 1846–1847.* Yale University Press, New Haven, 1926.

Evans, Clement A. (ed.), *Confederate Military History.* 12 vols. Confederate Publishing Company, Atlanta, 1899.

Farber, James, *Texas*, C.S.A. The Jackson Company, New York, 1947.

Farish, Thomas Edwin, *History of Arizona*. 8 vols. Filmer Brothers Electrotype Company, San Francisco, 1915–1918.

Fritz, Percy S., *Colorado, The Centennial State*. Prentice-Hall, Inc., New York, 1941.

Ganaway, Loomis M., *New Mexico and the Sectional Controversy, 1846–1861*. University of New Mexico Press, Albuquerque, 1944.

Griggs, George, *History of Mesilla Valley, or the Gadsden Purchase*. Bronson Printing Company, Las Cruces, New Mexico, 1930.

Hafen, LeRoy, and Carl Coke Rister, *Western America*. Prentice-Hall, Inc., New York, 1941.

Hall, Frank, *History of the State of Colorado*. 4 vols. The Blakely Printing Company, Chicago, 1889–1895.

Hamersly, T. H. S. (comp. and ed.), *Complete Regular Army Register of the United States: For One Hundred Years (1779 to 1879)*. T. H. S. Hamersly, Washington, 1880.

Hamilton, Patrick, *The Resources of Arizona*. A. L. Bancroft & Company, San Francisco, 1884.

Hammond, George P. (ed.), *Campaigns in the West, 1856–1861: The Journal and Letters of Colonel John Van Deusen Du Bois*. Arizona Pioneers Historical Society, Tucson, 1949.

Hardee, W. J., *Rifle and Light Infantry Tactics, for the Exercise and Manoeuvres of Troops When Acting as Light Infantry or Riflemen*. 2 vols. Lippincott, Grambo, and Company, Philadelphia, 1855.

Harris, Gertrude, *A Tale of Men Who Knew Not Fear*. Alamo Printing Company, San Antonio, 1935.

Harwell, Richard B. (ed.), *The Confederate Reader*. Longmans, Green and Co., New York, 1957.

———(ed.), *The Union Reader*. Longmans, Green and Co., New York, 1958.

Hayes, A. A., Jr., *New Colorado and the Santa Fe Trail*. Harper & Brothers, New York, 1880.

Heartsill, W. W., *Fourteen Hundred and 91 Days in the Confederate Army*. W. W. Heartsill, Marshall, Texas, 1876.

Henderson, Harry M., *Texas in the Confederacy*. The Naylor Company, San Antonio, 1955.

Hinton, Richard J., *The Handbook to Arizona*. Payot, Upham & Company, San Francisco, 1878.

Hollister, Ovando J., *History of the First Regiment of Colorado Volunteers*. Thos. Gibson & Co., Denver, 1863. Reprinted as *Boldly They Rode*. The Golden Press, Lakewood, Colorado, 1949.

Horgan, Paul, *Great River; the Rio Grande in North American History*. 2 vols. Rinehart & Company, New York, 1954.

Howard, Percy, *The Barbarities of the Rebels*. Printed for the Author, Providence, 1863.

Hunt, Aurora, *The Army of the Pacific*. The Arthur H. Clarke Co., Glendale, California, 1951.

Inman, Henry, *The Old Santa Fe Trail; The Story of a Great Highway*. Crane & Company. Topeka, 1899.

Johnson, Allen, and Dumas Malone (eds.), *Dictionary of American Biography*. 20 vols. Charles Scribner's Sons, New York, 1928–1936.

Johnson, Robert U., and Clarence C. Buel (eds.), *Battles and Leaders of the Civil War*. 4 vols. The Century Company, New York, 1884–1888.

Johnson, Sid S., *Texans Who Wore the Gray*. Tyler, Texas, c. 1907.

Johnston, William P., *The Life of General Albert Sidney Johnston*. D. Appleton and Company, New York, 1878.

Keleher, William A., *Turmoil in New Mexico, 1846–1868.* The Rydal Press, Santa Fe, 1952.

Kendall, George W., *Narrative of the Texan Santa Fe Expedition.* 2 vols. Harper & Brothers, New York, 1844.

Kennedy, Elijah R., *The Contest for California in 1861.* Houghton Mifflin Company. New York, 1912.

Lane, Lydia S., *I Married a Soldier, or Old Days in the Old Army.* J. B. Lippincott Company, Philadelphia, 1893.

Lockwood, Frank C., *Arizona Characters.* The Times-Mirror Press, Los Angeles, 1928.

————, *Pioneer Days in Arizona, from the Spanish Occupation to Statehood.* The Macmillan Company, New York, 1932.

————, and Donald W. Page, *Tucson— The Old Pueblo.* The Manufacturing Stationers, Inc., Phoenix, 1930.

Lossing, Benson J., *Pictorial History of the Civil War in the United States of America.* 3 vols. G. W. Childs, Philadelphia, 1866–1868.

McClintock, James H., *Arizona, Prehistoric, Aboriginal, Pioneer, Modern; The Nation's Youngest Commonwealth Within a Land of Ancient Culture.* 3 vols. The S. J. Clarke Publishing Company, Chicago, 1916.

McKee, James C., *Narrative of the Surrender of a Command of U.S. Forces, at Fort Fillmore, N. M. in July, A. D., 1861.* John A. Lowell and Company, Boston, 1886.

Miller, Francis T. (ed.), *The Photographic History of the Civil War in Ten Volumes.* 10 vols. Patriot Publishing Company, Springfield, Massachusetts, 1911.

Mills, Anson, *My Story.* Edited by C. H. Claudy. Press of Byron S. Adams, Washington, 1918.

Mills, W. W., *Forty Years at El Paso, 1858–1898.* W. B. Conkey Company, Chicago, 1901.

Moore, Frank (ed.), *The Rebellion Record: A Diary of American Events.* 12 vols. D. Van Nostrand Company, New York, 1862–1868.

Morris, Richard B. (ed.), *Encyclopedia of American History.* Harper & Brothers, New York, 1953.

Mowry, Sylvester, *The Geography and Resources of Arizona and Sonora.* H. Polkinhorn, Washington, 1859.

————, *Arizona and Sonora: The Geography, History, and Resources of the Silver Region of North America.* Harper & Brothers, New York, 1864.

Nankivell, John H., *History of the Military Organizations of the State of Colorado, 1860–1935.* W. H. Kistler Stationery Company, Denver, 1935.

Noel, Theo., *A Campaign from Santa Fe to the Mississippi; Being a History of the Old Sibley Brigade from Its First Organization to the Present Time; Its Campaigns in New Mexico, Arizona, Texas, Louisiana and Arkansas, in the Years 1861–2–3–4.* Shreveport News Printing Establishment, Shreveport, 1865.

————, *Autobiography and Reminiscences of Theophilus Noel.* Theo. Noel Company Print, Chicago, 1904.

O'Neil, James B., *They Die but Once; the Story of a Tejano.* Knight Publications, Inc., New York, 1935.

Orton, Richard H. (comp.), *Records of California Men in the War of the Rebellion, 1861 to 1867.* Adjutant General Office, Sacramento, 1890.

Pettis, George H., *The California Column. Its Campaigns and Services in New Mexico, Arizona and Texas.* New Mexico Historical Society, Santa Fe, 1908.

Poston, Charles D., *Apache-Land*. A. L. Bancroft & Company, San Francisco, 1878.

Pumpelly, Raphael, *Across America and Asia; Notes of a Five Years' Journey Around the World, and of Residence in Arizona, Japan, and China*. Leypoldt & Holt, New York, 1870.

Richardson, Albert D., *Beyond the Mississippi: From the Great River to the Great Ocean*. American Publishing Company, New York, 1867.

Richardson, Rupert Norval, *Texas, The Lone Star State*. Prentice-Hall, Inc., New York, 1943.

———, and Carl C. Rister, *The Greater Southwest*. The Arthur H. Clarke Co., Glendale, California, 1934.

Rippy, J. Fred, *The United States and Mexico*. F. S. Crofts & Company, New York, 1931.

Rodenbough, Theo. F. (comp.), *From Everglade to Cañon with the Second Dragoons*. D. Van Nostrand, New York, 1875.

Rowland, Dunbar (ed.), *Jefferson Davis, Constitutionalist, His Letters, Papers and Speeches*. 10 vols. Mississippi Department of Archives and History, 1923.

Sabin, Edwin L., *Kit Carson Days, 1809–1868*. 2 vols. The Press of the Pioneers, Inc., New York, 1935.

Scott, Winfield, *Infantry-Tactics; or Rules for the Exercise and Manoevres of the United States Infantry*. Harper & Brothers, New York, 1854.

Smiley, Jerome C., *History of Denver*. The Times-Sun Publishing Company, Denver, 1901.

Smithwick, Noah, *The Evolution of a State, or Recollections of Old Texas Days*. Gammel Book Company, Austin, 1900.

Stanley, F., *Fort Union*. The World Press, Canadian (?), Texas, 1953.

Taylor, Richard, *Destruction and Reconstruction: Personal Experiences of the Late War*. D. Appleton and Company, New York, 1879.

Tevis, James H., *Arizona in the '50's*. University of New Mexico Press. Albuquerque, 1954.

Twitchell, Ralph Emerson, *The Leading Facts of New Mexican History*. 5 vols. The Torch Press, Cedar Rapids, 1911–1917.

Webb, Walter P., and H. Bailey Carroll (eds.), *The Handbook of Texas*. 2 vols. The Texas State Historical Association, Austin, 1952.

Wellman, Paul I., *Glory, God and Gold*. Doubleday & Company, Inc., Garden City, 1954.

Whitford, William Clark, *Colorado Volunteers in the Civil War, The New Mexico Campaign in 1862*. The State Historical and Natural History Society, Denver, 1906.

Williams, Ellen, *Three Years and a Half in the Army; or History of the Second Colorados*. Fowler & Wells Company, New York, 1885.

Williams, R. H., *With the Border Ruffians, Memories of the Far West, 1852–1868*. Edited by E. W. Williams. The Musson Book Company, Toronto, 1919.

Wilson, James G., and John Fiske (eds.), *Appleton's Cyclopaedia of American Biography*. 7 vols. D. Appleton and Company, New York, 1888–1901.

Wooten, Dudley G., *A Comprehensive History of Texas*. William G. Scarff, Dallas, 1898.

Wyllys, Rufus K., *Arizona, the History of a Frontier State*. Hobson & Herr, Phoenix, 1950.

ARTICLES:

Anderson, Hattie M. (contrib.), "Mining and Indian Fighting in Arizona and New Mexico, 1858–1861—Memoirs of Hank Smith," *Panhandle-Plains Historical Review*, I (1928), 67–115.

————, "With the Confederates in New Mexico—Memoirs of Hank Smith," *Panhandle-Plains Historical Review*, II (1929), 65–97.

Anderson, Latham, "Canby's Services in the New Mexican Campaign," *Battles and Leaders of the Civil War*, II, 697–699.

Bender, A. B., "Frontier Defense in the Territory of New Mexico, 1853–1861," *New Mexico Historical Review*, IX (October, 1934), 345–373.

————, "Military Posts in the Southwest, 1848–1860." *New Mexico Historical Review*, XVI (April, 1941), 125–147.

Bloom, Lansing B. (ed.), "Confederate Reminiscences of 1862," *New Mexico Historical Review*, V (July, 1930), 315–324.

Boyd, Le Roy, "Thunder on the Rio Grande, the Great Adventure of Sibley's Confederates for the Conquest of New Mexico and Colorado." *Colorado Magazine*, XXIV (July, 1947), 131–140.

Clendenen, Clarence C., "General James Henry Carleton," *New Mexico Historical Review*, XXX (January, 1955), 23–43.

Cooney, Percival J., "Southern California in Civil War Days," *Annual Publication of the Historical Society of Southern California*, XIII (1924), Part 1, 54–68.

Crimmins, M. L. (contrib.), "The Battle of Val Verde," *New Mexico Historical Review*, VII (October, 1932), 348–352.

————, "Fort Fillmore." *New Mexico Historical Review*, VI (October, 1931), 327–333.

Darrow, Caroline B., "Recollections of the Twiggs Surrender," *Battles and Leaders of the Civil War*, I, 33–39.

Dodson, S. H. (comp.), "Diary and Correspondence of Salmon P. Chase," *Annual Report of the American Historical Association for the Year 1902*. Part II, 11–527.

Donnell, F. S., "The Confederate Territory of Arizona, from Official Sources," *New Mexico Historical Review*, XVII (April, 1942), 148–163.

————, "When Las Vegas Was the Capital of New Mexico," *New Mexico Historical Review*, VIII (October, 1933), 265–272.

Earlie, John J., "The Sentiment of the People of California with Respect to the Civil War," *Annual Report of the American Historical Association for the Year 1907*. Part I, 123–135.

Eaton, W. Clement, "Frontier Life in Southern Arizona, 1858–1861," *Southwestern Historical Quarterly*, XXXVI (January, 1933), 173–192.

Evans, A. W., "Canby at Valverde," *Battles and Leaders of the Civil War*, II, 699–700.

Faulkner, Walter A. (contrib.), "With Sibley in New Mexico; the Journal of William Henry Smith," *West Texas Historical Association Year Book*, XXVII (October, 1951), 111–142.

Gilbert, Benjamin F., "The Confederate Minority in California," *California Historical Society Quarterly*, XX (June, 1941), 154–170.

Glasgow, William J., "On the Confusion Caused by the Name of El Paso," *Password*, I (May, 1956), 65–67.

Hayes, A. A., "The New Mexican Campaign of 1862," *Magazine of American History*, XV (February, 1886), 171–184.

Holden, W. C., "Frontier Defense in Texas During the Civil War," *West Texas Historical Association Year Book*, IV (June, 1928), 16–31.

Hunsaker, William J., "Lansford W. Hastings' Project for the Invasion and Conquest of Arizona and New Mexico for the Southern Confederacy," *Arizona Historical Review*, IV (July, 1931), 5–12.

Lockwood, Frank C., "Arizona and Its Heritage," *University of Arizona Bulletin*, VII (April, 1936), 134–148.

McCoy, Raymond, "The Battle of Glorieta Pass," *United Daughters of the Confederacy Magazine*, XV (February, 1952), 12–13, 23.

———, "Confederate Cannon," *New Mexico Magazine*, XXXI (September, 1953), 18, 49.

Pettis, George H., "The Confederate Invasion of New Mexico and Arizona," *Battles and Leaders of the Civil War*, II, 103–111.

Rippy, J. Fred, "Mexican Projects of the Confederates," *Southwestern Historical Quarterly*, XXII (April, 1919), 291–317.

Rodgers, Robert L., "The Confederate States Organized Arizona in 1862," *Southern Historical Society Papers*, XXVIII (1900), 222–227.

Santee, J. F., "The Battle of La Glorieta Pass," *New Mexico Historical Review*, VI (January, 1931), 66–75.

Scammell, J. M., "Military Units in Southern California, 1853–1862," *California Historical Society Quarterly*, XXIX (September, 1950), 229–249.

Smith, C. C., "Some Unpublished History of the Southwest," *Arizona Historical Review*, IV (July, 1931), 13–38.

Teel, T. T., "Sibley's New Mexican Campaign. Its Objects and the Causes of its Failure," *Battles and Leaders of the Civil War*, II, 700.

Tittmann, Edward D., "Confederate Courts in New Mexico," *New Mexico Historical Review*, III (October, 1928), 347–356.

———, The Exploitation of Treason," *New Mexico Historical Review*, IV (April, 1929), 128–145.

Walker, Charles S., Jr., "Causes of the Confederate Invasion of New Mexico," *New Mexico Historical Review*, VIII (April, 1933), 76–97.

———, "Confederate Government in Doña Ana County as Shown in the Records of the Probate Court, 1861–62," *New Mexico Historical Review*, VI (July, 1931), 252–302.

Wallace, R. B., "My Experiences in the First Colorado Regiment." *Colorado Magazine*, I (November, 1924), 307–312.

Waller, J. L., "The Civil War in the El Paso Area," *West Texas Historical Association Year Book*, XXII (October, 1946), 3–14.

Watford. W. H., "Confederate Western Ambitions," *Southwestern Historical Quarterly*, XLIV (October, 1940), 161–187.

———, "The Far-Western Wing of the Rebellion," *California Historical Society Quarterly*, XXXIV (June, 1955), 125–148.

NEWSPAPERS:

Albuquerque *Río Abajo Press*
Austin *State Gazette*
Bellville *Countryman*
Denver *Rocky Mountain News*
Houston *Chronicle*
Houston *Tri-Weekly Telegraph*
Las Vegas *Gazette*
Mesilla *Miner*
Mesilla *Times*
New Orleans *Daily Picayune*
Sacramento *Daily Union*
San Antonio *Herald*
San Antonio *Daily Ledger and Texan*
San Francisco *Daily Herald and Mirror*
Santa Fé *Gazette*
Santa Fé *New Mexican*
Tucson and Tubac *Weekly Arizonian*
Victoria *Advocate*

UNPUBLISHED PRIMARY SOURCES:

Chivington, John M., "The First Colorado Regiment." MS, Bancroft Library, University of California.

———, "The Prospective." MS, Brancroft Library, University of California.

Hanna, Ebenezer, "Journal of Ebenezer Hanna, February 10 to March 27, 1862." MS, Texas State Library, Archives Division, Austin.

Howell, W. R., "Journal of a Soldier of the Confederate States Army." MS, University of Texas Library.

McCleave, William A., "Recollections of a California Volunteer." MS, Bancroft Library, University of California.

Wright, H. C., "Reminiscences of H. C. Wright of Austin." MS, University of Texas Library.

UNPUBLISHED THESES AND DISSERTATIONS:

Bewley, Mary, "The Indians of New Mexico in the Civil War." M.A. Thesis, University of New Mexico, 1938.

Connor, Daniel A., "Military Operations in the Southwest, 1861–1865: Battles and Movements of the Union and Confederate Forces and Campaigns against the Indians in Northwest Texas, New Mexico and Arizona During the Civil War Period." M.A. Thesis, Texas Western College, 1949.

Felgar, Robert P., "Texas in the War for Southern Independence, 1861–1865." Ph.D. Dissertation, University of Texas, 1935.

Hall, Martin H., "Confederate Military Operations in Arizona and New Mexico." M.A. Thesis, University of Alabama, 1951.

Hammons, Nancy Lee. "A History of El Paso County, Texas, to 1900." M.A. Thesis, Texas Western College, 1942.

Ivey, Rosalie, "A History of Fort Bliss." M.A. Thesis, University of Texas, 1942.

Killin, Hugh E., "The Texans and the California Column." M.A. Thesis, Texas Technological College, 1931.

Kroh, Robert F., "Tom Green: Shield and Buckler." M.A. Thesis, University of Texas, 1951.

O'Malley, Catherine B., "A History of El Paso Since 1860." M.S. Thesis, University of Southern California, 1939.

Reid, Robert L., "The Early History of Fort Bliss." M.A. Thesis, Baylor University, 1947.

Taylor, Albion, Jr., "Military Operations in Texas During the Civil War." M.A. Thesis, Baylor University, 1931.

Waldrip, William I., "New Mexico During the Civil War." M.A. Thesis, University of New Mexico, 1950.

Whitworth, Bonnye R., "The Role of Texas in the Confederacy." M.A. Thesis, North Texas State College, 1951.

GOVERNMENT DOCUMENTS:

Confederate States:

Journal of the Congress of the Confederate States of America, 1861–1865. 7 vols. *Senate Documents*, 58th Congress, 2nd Session. Government Printing Office, Washington, 1904–1905.

Official Reports of Battles, as Published by the Order of the Confederate Congress at Richmond. Charles B. Richardson, New York, 1863.

Pickett (John T.) Papers. Domestic Correspondence of the Confederacy. Office of the Secretary of

State, Library of Congress, Washington.

Richardson, James D. (comp.), *A Compilation of the Messages and Papers of the Confederacy Including the Diplomatic Correspondence, 1861–1865.* 2 vols. United States Publishing Company, Nashville, 1905–1906.

Selected Confederate Muster Rolls, 1861. War Department Collection of Confederate Records. National Archives, Washington.

New Mexico:

House Executive Document No. 1, 37th Congress, 3rd Session, Volume V. Government Printing Office, Washington, 1862 (Serial 1160).

Laws of the Territory of New Mexico. Passed by the Legislative Assembly, Sessions of 1856–1857, 1859–1860.

Records of the Bureau of Indian Affairs, Selected Documents Concerning the Administration of Indian Affairs in Texas and New Mexico, 1861–1862. New Mexico: Letters Received. Record Group 75, National Archives, Washington.

Reports of Committees of the Senate of the United States for the Third Session of the Thirty-Seventh Congress. 4 vols. Government Printing Office, Washington, 1863 (Serials 1151–1154).

Russell, John T. (comp.), *Official Register N. M. Volunteers Called into Service of the United States, under the President's Proclamation of May 3, 1861.* Gazette Office, Santa Fé, 1862.

Texas:

Confederate Military Affairs, 1861–1865. Papers pertaining to military affairs in Texas during the Civil War. Texas State Library, Archives Division.

Executive Record Book: Governor Edward Clark, 1861, III, 39. Texas State Library, Archives Division.

Letters Received: Governor Edward Clark. Texas State Library, Archives Division.

Letters Received: Governor Francis R. Lubbock. Texas State Library, Archives Division.

Winkler, Ernest W. (ed.), *Journal of the Secession Convention of Texas 1861.* Austin Printing Company, Austin, 1912.

General:

Annual Report of the American Historical Association for the Year 1902. 2 vols. Government Printing Office, Washington, 1903.

Atlas to Accompany the Official Records of the Union and Confederate Armies. Government Printing Office, Washington, 1891–1895.

Heitman, Francis B., *Historical Register and Dictionary of the United States Army, from Its Organization, September 29, 1789, to March 2, 1903.* 2 vols. Government Printing Office, Washington, 1903.

Kennedy, Joseph C. G. (comp.), *Population of the United States in 1860; Compiled from the Original Returns of the Eighth Census, under the Direction of the Secretary of the Interior.* Government Printing Office, Washington, 1864.

Malloy, William M. (comp.), *Treaties, Conventions, International Acts, Protocols and Agreements Between the United States of America and Other Powers, 1776–1909.* 2 vols. Government Printing Office, Washington, 1910.

War of the Rebellion: A Compilation of the Official Records of the Union and Confederate Armies. 128 vols. Government Printing Office, Washington, 1880–1901. Referred to in footnotes as O.R.A.

Index

abandoning, 156; Federal army abandoning, 17
Fort Craig, 17; Canby at, 47, 135–36; capitulation demanded, 73; destruction contemplated, 132; movement against, 37; reinforced, 48; strengthened, 43
Fort Davis, 30
Fort Fillmore, 7, 14, 16–17, 18–19, 139, 151
Fort Garland, 16
Fort Leavenworth, Kansas, 16
Fort Quitman, 30
forts built, 12–13
Fort Stanton, 17
Fort Stockton, 34
Fort Thorn, 37–38, 154
Fort Union: after Confederate retreat, 155; Colorado volunteers, 88–89; Donaldson withdraws to, 82; moved, 43; revolt among militia, 49; Sibley advance, 84
Fort Yuma, 157
Fourth Regiment , Texas Cavalry, 26, 27, 28, 29, 34, 35, 37, 84; Albuquerque skirmish, 120; Battle of Glorieta, 99, 101, 110, 111; Battle of Valverde, 53, 59, 60, 61, 66, 77–78; companies listed, 101; evacuation, 118, 133, 138, 139, 146–48; Fort Craig, 53–54
Fourth Regiment New Mexico Volunteers, 52, 119
Frazer, George M. (Captain), 32, 57, 59, 76
Fremont, John C. (General), 44

Gadsden Purchase, 6
Galisteo, 99, 123
Gardenhier, George, 80
Gardner, James W., 101
Giesecke, Julius, 101
Gillespie, Richmond, 79, 80
Gilpin, William (Governor), 16, 44, 47
Graydon, James "Paddy" (Captain), 52, 57–58, 120, 128, 131, 134, 135, 136
Grayson, John B., (Lieutenant Colonel), 13–14
Green, Thomas Jefferson, xiii
Green, Thomas ("Tom" or "Daddy"), xiii, 54, 118; background, 26; Battle of Valverde, 63, 64, 66, 69, 70, 71,

73; evacuation, 133, 146; Fort Craig, 55, 56; Peralta, 128; retreat, 130, 139, 149, 151; Santa Fé, 116, 117; strict routine, 37; strong guard, 53
Gregg, Alexander, 29

Hall, Captain, 92
Hall, Martin Hardwick, xii–xiii
Hall, Robert H. (Lieutenant), 52, 60, 61, 64, 66, 67
Halleck, Henry W. (Major General), 88
Hampton, George J. (Major), 101, 146
Hardeman, William P., xiv, 26, 30, 64, 69, 73, 120, 146, 151
Harrison, William H. (Captain), 142
Hart, Simeon, xii, 7, 8, 11–12, 14, 38, 39
Hébert, P.O. (General), 24
Helms, Thomas (Captain), 32
Herbert, Philemon T., 11, 12
Hoffman, Gustav (Captain), 26, 101
Holland, James B. (Lieutenant), 101
Holmes, Henry (Lieutenant), 243
Hoppin, Charles A., 155
horses and mules, 15–16, 77–78
Howland, George W. (Captain), 90, 91, 93, 94, 103, 123, 124, 154; Battle of Valverde, 61
Hubbell, Santiago (Captain), 60, 64, 72
Hunter, David (Major General), 87
Hunter, Sherod (Captain), 32, 38, 54–55, 142–43

Independent Spy Company, 52, 58, 60, 120, 128, 131, 134
Indians: raids, 45–46; slavery, 6, 40
Ingraham, Charles H. (Captain), 60, 64, 66

Jackson, Alexander M., 10, 123
Johnson's Ranch, 91, 96, 100, 102
Jones, L.H. (Reverend), 110
Jordan, Powhatan (Captain), 26, 77, 84, 101

Kavenaugh, F.E. (Doctor), 79, 80
Kelly, Private, 104
Killough, Ira G. (Captain), 31
Kozlowski's Ranch, 92, 97, 102, 113, 122

La Joyita, 77
lancers unit, 26, 64, 77
Lang, Willis L. (Captain), 28, 64, 71

Lee, Robert E., 143
Lemitar, 77
Lesueur, Charles M., xvi, 101
Lewis, William H. (Captain), 90, 109, 110, 115, 136
Lincoln, Abraham, 10
Lindsay, Andrew J. (Captain), 14
Lockridge, Samuel A. (Major), 32, 53, 55, 63, 64, 66, 69, 71
Longstreet, James (Major), 14
Lord, R.S.C. (Captain), 66, 68, 91, 94, 97, 122
Loring, William W. (Colonel), 14–15
Los Lunas, 79, 130, 132
Lynde, Isaac (Major), 17, 18–19, 43

McCown, Jerome B. (Captain), 28, 77
McGuinness, Joseph H., 62, 63
McIntire, Lieutenant, 92
McNeill, Henry C. (Lieutenant Colonel), 24, 63, 71, 74, 123; advance, 76–77
McRae, Alexander (Captain), 52, 60, 61, 64, 65–66, 67, 68, 69, 70, 72
Magoffin, James W., xii, 7–8, 14
Maile, Charles (Captain), 103
manifest destiny notion, 3, 151
Manzano, New Mexico, 117
Marshall, William F. (Lieutenant), 95, 97
martial law, 32
Maury, Dabney H. (Captain), 14
Mesilla, 7, 17, 18, 155
Mesilla Valley, 6–7, 8, 12, 39–40, 139, 144; flooding, 154
Mexicans. see Native/Hispanic New Mexicans (author calls "Mexicans")
Mexico: annexation plans, 23; Confederate scrip, 39; Federal army landing, 30; New Mexico as key, 4; Reily mission, 35–36; supplies, 144, 148, 153; taxation, 10
militia, 48, 51–52, 65
Mills, Charles H. (Lieutenant), 108
miners, 10
Mishler, Lyman (Captain), 68
Missouri, 11
morale, 41, 74
Mormons, 85
Morris, Captain, 131
Mortimore, William (Captain), 60, 64, 72
Mowry, Sylvester, 9

Native/Hispanic New Mexicans (author calls "Mexicans"): after Sibley's

departure, 152; foraging operations, 39–40, 152, 155; hatred of U.S., 49, 50; southern New Mexico, 7
Nelson, George (Lieutenant), 92, 95
New Mexican volunteers: Canby critiquing, 47, 87, 153; captured, 54; choice of officers, 50; in Donaldson force, 82; pay problems, 49; reported demoralized, 40
New Mexico: Anglo settlement, 5; importance to Confederacy, 3–4; pro–Texan sentiments, 76; slave code, 3, 10–11
New Mexico campaign: assessed, 149–51; California as real objective, ix; reasons for failure, x; significance, ix
New Orleans, 22
Nicodemus, William (Captain), 123

Oakes, Pleasant J. (Lieutenant), 101
Ochiltree, Thomas P. (Captain), 71, 143–44
Odell, James M., 101
Ortiz, Padre, 111
Otero, Miguel A.: changed views, 50–51; pro–Southern viewpoint, 5, 9, 40, 80
Owings, Lewis S., 9, 12

Paraje skirmish, 140
Paul, Gabriel R. (Colonel), 88, 89–90, 122, 123, 124, 129, 131
pay problems, New Mexican volunteers, 49
Pecos–Canadian plan, 47–48
Pelham, William, 117, 134
peonage, 6
Peralta, 80, 118, 125; skirmish of, 128–30
Phillips, John (Captain), 32, 61
Picacho, skirmish of, 143
Pierce, George W. (Private), 106
Pigeon's Ranch, 92, 96, 97; described, 102
Pike's Peakers, 10–11
pillage, 39–40, 152
Pino, Miguel E. (Colonel), 52, 56–57, 60, 63, 65, 66, 70, 72
Pino, Nicolás (Colonel), 76–77
Pinos Altos, 12, 153
Plympton, P.W.L. (Captain), 58, 62, 66
Polvadera, 134
proclamation at Albuquerque, 81, 83
proclamation of December 20, 32–33
Pyron, Charles L. (Major), 53, 54, 83;

Albuquerque stores, 78, 79; Apache Canyon skirmish, 93–96, 100; Battle of Glorieta, 101, 106; Battle of Valverde, 59, 61, 62, 63, 71; command, 32, 38; evacuation, 146; Santa Fé, 83, 84, 91

Ragsdale, Daniel H., 101
Raguet, Henry (Major), 59–60, 62, 63, 64, 66–67, 69, 70, 104, 104–5, 108
railroads, 3
Real de Dolores, 99
recruiting volunteers: Colorado, 16, 44; Federal army, 43–44, 45; Texan, 26–27
Reeve, I.V.D. (Lieutenant Colonel), 14
Reily, James (Colonel), 26, 29, 30, 54–55, 61, 62, 66, 116, 120, 139, 148; mission to Mexico, 35–36
Reily, John (Lieutenant), 28, 54
Rencher, Governor, 16
revolt among militia, 49
Reynolds, R.B. (Major), 14
Ritter, John F. (Captain), 90, 103, 104, 106
Robbins, Samuel M. (Captain), 103
Roberts, Benjamin S. (Lieutenant Colonel), 48, 57, 60, 61, 62–63, 64, 65, 69, 131

Sabinal revolt, 49
St. Vrain, Ceran (Colonel), 44, 45, 52
San Antonio, New Mexico, 122
San Antonio, Texas: Camp Sibley, 26; Ladies Southern Aid Society, 28; returning to, 142–43, 156; Sibley arrival, 24; training, 27
San Elizario Spy Company, 32, 54
San Felipe Springs, 31–32
San Mateo Mountains, 137–38
Santa Fé, 4–5, 13, 82, 114–17, 131
Sayers, Joseph D., xvi
Scarborough, Andrew J. (Captain), 26, 35, 63
Scott, John J. (Lieutenant), 101
Scurry, Colonel William R. "Dirty Shirt," 30, 54, 84; Battle of Glorieta, 99, 101, 102–4, 107–8, 111, 113, 114; Battle of Valverde, 59–60, 61, 62, 63, 64, 70, 71, 73, 74; evacuation, 133; Peralta skirmish, 129; promotion, xiv; secession, 11; war hero, xiv

secession issue, 11–12, 51
Second Dragoons, 21
Second Regiment, Federal army, 45
Second Regiment Colorado Volunteers, 53
Second Regiment New Mexico Volunteers, 52, 55, 70, 72, 119
Second Regiment Texas Mounted Rifles, 18, 32, 54, 101, 146
Selden, Henry R. (Captain), 62, 63, 64, 66, 69, 70
Seventh Infantry (Federal), 52, 55, 60, 62, 66; Fort Fillmore, 16
Seventh Regiment, Texas Cavalry, 26, 27, 37, 54, 80, 120; after Sibley's departure, 151–52; Battle of Glorieta, 99, 101, 111; Battle of Valverde, 59; evacuation, 118, 139–40, 149
Shannon, Denman W. (Captain), 73, 74, 101, 106
Shropshire, John S. (Captain), 26, 84, 91, 101, 105–6, 108
Sibley, Henry Hopkins (Brigadier General): Albuquerque proclamation, 81, 83; ambitions, 23, 85; assessed, 150; background, 21; Battle of Valverde, 59, 62, 63, 71; brigade review, 28, 29; California ambitions, 23, 85, 156–57; commission, 23; Davis interview, 22–23; Davis's congratulations, 144; evacuation of forces, 132–33; Fort Bliss command, 32; Fort Union, 84–85; heavy drinking, 38, 74; ill health, 31, 38, 55, 63; imploring Loring to stay, 14; logistics, 38; Peralta, 129; report of campaign, 141–42; resigning from Federal army, 14; in Santa Fé, 116; surrender proposal, 133; truce, 73; valedictory proclamation, 145; weaknesses as general and strategist, 38
Sibley Brigade, described, 27
slavery issue, 3–4, 5–6, 11–12; Indian, 6, 40; New Mexico antislavery views, 51
Slough, John P. (Colonel), 88–91, 96, 101–2, 103, 105, 107, 111, 113–14, 124
Socorro, 74, 119–20, 135
Sopris, Richard (Captain), 103